25

A [illegible] WAY

By the same author in PAN Books

THE LONELY SEA AND THE SKY

GIPSY MOTH CIRCLES THE WORLD

ALONG THE CLIPPER WAY

FRANCIS CHICHESTER

with extracts from Francis Drake, Shackleton, Slocum and Smeeton, Dana and Ann Davison, Bardiaux and Basil Lubbock, Bullen, Bombard and Conor O'Brien, Anson, Dumas and Alan Villiers, John Masefield and Joseph Conrad

UNABRIDGED

PAN BOOKS LTD : LONDON

First published 1966 by Hodder & Stoughton Ltd
This edition published 1967 by Pan Books Ltd,
33 Tothill Street, London, S.W.1

ISBN 0 330 30040 7

2nd Printing 1974

PRINTED AND BOUND IN ENGLAND BY
HAZELL WATSON AND VINEY LTD
AYLESBURY, BUCKS

Contents

Foreword

FOR YEARS I pondered the matter of sailing round the world by way of Cape Horn, but I told myself that anyone who tried to round it in a small yacht must be crazy. Of eight yachts I knew to have attempted it, six had been capsized or somersaulted before, during or after the passage. Yet it had a fearsome fascination and it certainly offered one of the greatest challenges left in the world. I started reading up every interesting account I could find and from nearly every success or failure there was something to be learned. Finally I began to cheer up; most of the yachts were, I considered, unsuitable for the task, yet only two had been lost with their crews. I thought that with a suitable craft and suitable tactics I could make the voyage. Four years ago I made up my mind to try it, and before the 1964 Singlehanded Trans-Atlantic Race I was already thrashing out the design for a boat. The second solo race across the Atlantic in 1964 chiefly interested me as a testing ground for my ideas for my Cape Horn special. In that race there were fourteen starters and I came second in my *Gipsy Moth III*, losing the race to the French naval officer, Lieutenant Eric Tabarly, who had the first yacht to be specially built for the race. My losing to him was a lucky thing for me because my sporting and generous cousin, Tony Dulverton, said that he would build a suitable boat for me to compete on equal terms with the Frenchman in the next race. I told him of my Cape Horn ambition and he agreed to build the boat as I wanted it.

I am not sure of the exact date when I decided to race against the average passage times of the clipper ships out to Sydney and on home to England. I estimated that the average time to Sydney for the gold, wool and grain clippers was 100 days for a sailing distance of 13,750 miles; and from Sydney to Plymouth, a sailing distance of 14,750 miles, another 100 days. I did not dare to enquire too thoroughly into the clipper records for fear that my project would be found out. However, the *Cutty Sark*'s fastest passage to Sydney was 72 days, and from Sydney to England, 84 days. But I think the *Cutty Sark* holds the world's record for the fastest six days' run of any sailing ship – 2,180 miles in 6 days – and I could hardly hope to compete with her times singlehanded in a yacht, but I could compete with the sixteen grain clippers which raced home from Australia in 1927 and averaged 132 days over the passage.

All parts of the clipper way to Australia have been sailed over by a few yachts, either with a crew or singlehanded. None of the crewed-up yachts made fast passages or particularly long ones. I think the Argentinian, Vito Dumas, sailing alone, made the longest passage of all – 7,400 miles from Cape Town to Wellington, New Zealand. His average speed was 71 miles per day. I think that Nance in 1965 has made the fastest long solo passage so far achieved – 6,500 miles from Auckland to Buenos Aires at 121 miles per day. During this voyage he made the fastest six day run that has been achieved by a singlehander – more than 925 miles in 6 days. This beat a singlehanded speed record which has stood for 70 years, made in 1896 by the great Joshua Slocum when he sailed 900 miles in 6 days during a W to E passage across the North Atlantic.

I read and studied so many logs or accounts of sailing along this clipper way that I felt I knew the route better than I knew the North Atlantic. I came across some lovely stories which were a joy to read and presently found that, in discussing them, I had written enough to fill a third of a book. So I decided to wrap up the lot in the form of this book, *Along the Clipper Way*. In the end the book seemed to me like the story of one great and continuous voyage round the world.

I am sorry that Sheila, my wife, did not sail with me along the clipper way. She has twice sailed home from America in *Gipsy Moth III* with me after I had raced across alone; but sailing past the three most notorious capes of the world, Good Hope, Leeuwin and the Horn, entails some very rough going; while racing against time in a comparatively small boat makes it rougher still.

If it had not been for Tony Dulverton I should not have had *Gipsy Moth IV* specially built, with all my ideas for safety and fast passage-making, without disclosing my project years before I could set out. Therefore it is with great gratitude and affection that I dedicate this book to him.

June, 1967

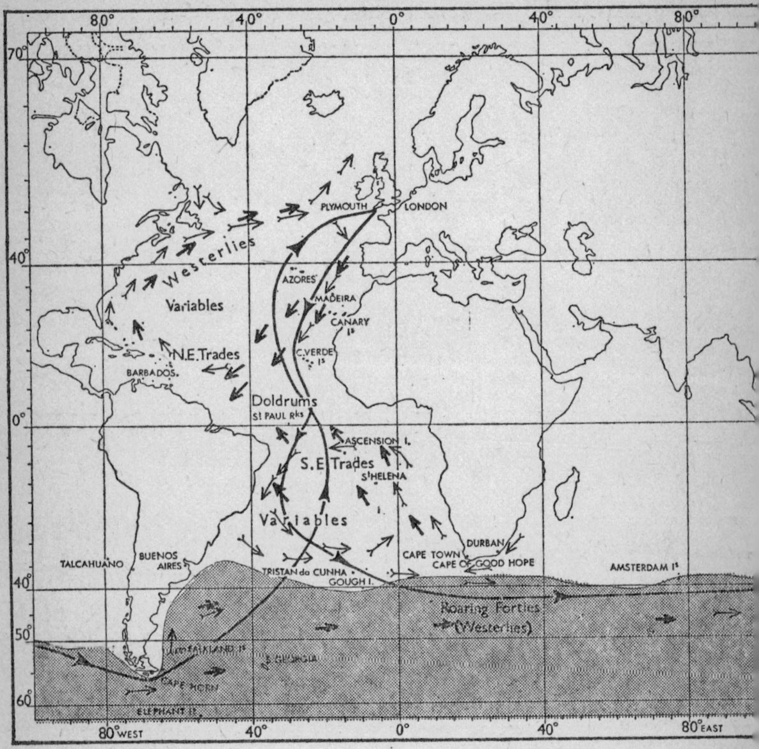

80°
40°
0°
40°
80°
70°
40°
0°
40°
50°
60°
PLYMOUTH
LONDON
Westerlies
AZORES
Variables
MADEIRA
CANARY Is
N.E.Trades
C.VERDE Is
BARBADOS
Doldrums
St PAUL Rks
ASCENSION I.
S.E Trades
St HELENA
Variables
DURBAN
CAPE TOWN
CAPE OF GOOD HOPE
TALCAHUANO
BUENOS AIRES
TRISTAN da CUNHA
GOUGH I.
AMSTERDAM Is
Roaring Forties
(Westerlies)
FALKLAND Is
S.GEORGIA
CAPE HORN
ELEPHANT Is
80° WEST
40°
0°
40°
80° EAST

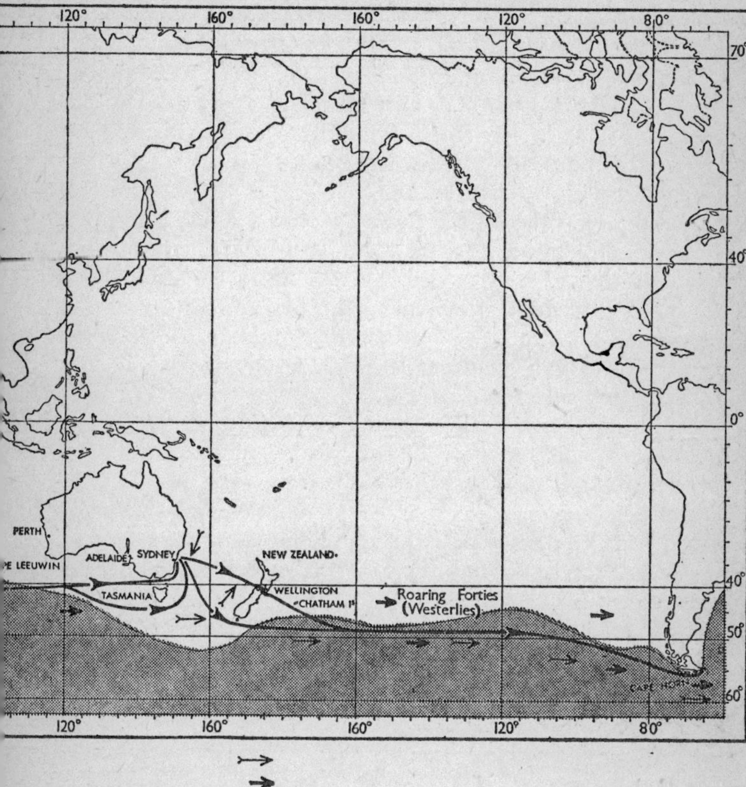

120°
160°
160°
120°
80°
70°
40°
0°
40°
50°
60°
PERTH
PE LEEUWIN
ADELAIDE
SYDNEY
TASMANIA
NEW ZEALAND
WELLINGTON
CHATHAM Is
Roaring Forties
(Westerlies)
CAPE HORN

The small-scale map on the previous two pages shows the great clipper way – Sydney-Plymouth. A circumnavigation of the world was completed when the homeward-bound track crossed the outward-bound track at Latitude 30° South. The circumnavigation was a sailing distance of 17,500 nautical miles, and the distance from Plymouth to 30° South and back was 11,000 nautical miles, making a total distance for the voyage of 28,500 nautical miles.

Distances are deceptive on a small map. For instance, the run from Greenwich Meridian at 40° South (which is about 1,000 miles WSW of Cape Town) to Bass Strait is 7,000 nautical miles straight along the Roaring Forties and the run from Sydney to the Horn is 6,500 nautical miles. 7,000 nautical miles equal 8,060½ statute miles. Incidentally, for people used to measuring speed in miles per hour, 13 knots equal 15 mph.

The heavy arrows showing the prevailing winds for the month of September indicate how the clipper navigators planned their route where they could expect the most favourable winds. The average wind in September could be expected to blow in the direction of the arrow but some years it may blow from the opposite or some other direction throughout the month.

The currents, as shown by the light arrows, roughly follow the winds, but not everywhere. The tinted area shows the maximum limit of the iceberg area for the month of September.

To
Tony

Acknowledgements

The author would like to thank the following for their permission to use passages from the named copyright works:

Messrs Adlard Coles Ltd for *Four Winds of Adventure* by Marcel Bardiaux, *Alone Through the Roaring Forties* by Vito Dumas, *Trekka Round the World* by John Guzzwell and *Once is Enough* by Miles Smeeton

Messrs Arthur Barker Ltd for *Seagoing Gaucho* by Ernesto Uriburu

Messrs Curtis Brown Ltd for *Falmouth for Orders* by Alan Villiers, published by Geoffrey Bles Ltd

Messrs Brown, Son and Ferguson Ltd for *Colonial Clippers* by Basil Lubbock

Messrs J. M. Dent and Sons Ltd and the Trustees of the Joseph Conrad Estate for *The Mirror of the Sea* by Joseph Conrad

Messrs André Deutsch Ltd for *The Bombard Story* by Alain Bombard

Messrs A. M. Heath Ltd and the author for *My Ship is so Small* by Ann Davison

Messrs William Heinemann Ltd for *South* by Sir Ernest Shackleton

Messrs Hutchinson and Co Ltd for *Kingdom of the Octopus* by Frank Lane

The Society of Authors and the late Dr John Masefield, OM, for *Bird of Dawning*, published by William Heinemann Ltd

Mrs Elinor Wiltshire for *Across Three Oceans* by Conor O'Brien

I

The Clipper Way

MY OBJECT IN this book is to take the reader stage by stage along the great clipper way followed by the gold, wool and grain clippers from Britain round the Cape (of Good Hope) to Australia and then on round Cape Horn back to Britain. Every mile of this 28,500-mile-long route round the world has given pleasure, pain or drama to thousands of sailors. I have collected what I think are the best accounts by seamen and the most artistic descriptive passages of famous authors who have written about one section or another of the route.

This great clipper way was like a broad path curving down through the North Atlantic and the South Atlantic, passing between 300 and 800 miles south of Cape Town and then running down the Easting for 6,600 miles to Bass Strait either keeping within the Roaring Forties or south of them. The clipper ships sailed to different ports in Australia, Tasmania or New Zealand but the route I have selected is the one to Sydney. After leaving Sydney, the clippers either passed between, or south of, the New Zealand islands, then again they ran their Easting down in the Forties or the Fifties. The next landmark was Cape Horn, 5,000 miles on from New Zealand, and once they had doubled the Horn the sailors reckoned they were as good as home, though in fact they had another 8,000 miles to sail through both Atlantics.

This is the most romantic sea route of the world and the stories chosen cover many different aspects of it. They are about crewed-up yachts and singlehand yachts as well as big sailing ships; they are about some of the finest sailing in the world as well as sailing through storms of wind, sleet and snow; they include racing, shipwreck and total disappearance; record speeds, adventures with icebergs and ice; whales, giant squid and even the dreaded scurvy. There are narratives from the only three solo yachtsmen to have survived doubling the Horn; and from the man who twice tried to round the Horn but was capsized and dismasted each time.

I have read and thought so much about the clipper way that I feel I know the route, all twenty-eight thousand miles of it, better than I know the North Atlantic after sailing across it six times.

And the route has become more simple, the more I have learned of it; it now seems to be principally a fascinating voyage southward through both Atlantics, eastward through the Roaring Forties for 11,000 miles and then northward 8,000 miles through the two Atlantics again.

2

Halcyon Sailing

THE FIRST quarter of the clipper way round the world seldom varied from a traditional path. After leaving the English Channel which the clipper captains, who navigated their ships themselves, referred to as 'Channel', the route by-passed Madeira, the Canary Islands and St Pauls Rocks near the Equator, passing through the prevailing westerlies in the North Atlantic, and through the Variables into the north-east trade winds. Out of the trade-wind belt it passed into the Doldrums near the Equator. A fast passage to Australia often depended on how long the ship was becalmed in the Doldrums. So far it was wonderful sailing, with warm winds, warm seas, steady fresh breezes in the trade-wind zone with flying fish lying on the deck for breakfast each morning. It is true that a ship might be becalmed and wallowing on the oily-looking surface for up to three weeks in the Doldrums, but was this too great a price to pay for 6,000 miles of the best sailing in the world?

Most sailors in full-rigged ships paid no attention to good sailing, or, if they did, they have not told us about it; they have only left us stories of drama or disaster except when they were sailing at a record speed.

Conor O'Brien, in his yacht *Saoirse*, sailed along the clipper way in 1923 and in his inimitable style he has painted a delightful picture of the start of the voyage:

*

It was a fine night, the sea smooth, and at noon next day we took our departure from the Tuskar, and settled into sea routine.

We were lucky in getting gentle NNW breezes after clearing the land, freshening by degrees, but not so much as to prevent our making all the westing we wanted. The third night out indeed it seemed to me to be distinctly fresh, with a pretty rough beam sea, but in those early days I used to be scared of every puff of wind. . . . I really took things ridiculously seriously; even after two years I connect my passage down the Atlantic with nothing else but anxious readings of the barometer and thermometer, and speculations about wind and weather; I cannot get away from the navigational problems and play with situations as I did on the homeward voyage.

That was the final kick of the miserably cold and stormy early summer from which we had suffered in Dublin; the next day we ran into real summer. In lat. 49°N. and long. 10°W. we got the Portuguese Trades and knew we should have a fair wind for the next 2,500 miles; with indeed a chance of a day or two of calm in the middle of that distance, but with the knowledge that the breeze would be constant in direction and for the most part just the strength we wanted it. It certainly began very light, but the sea had become glassy smooth and the ship was gliding along at 5 knots right before the wind. We sent up the foreyard and set the foresail, lashed the wheel, fed the kitten, of whose life we had despaired, on sardines, as she would not touch condensed milk, and disposed ourselves to sleep on the shadier parts of the deck. It is not always that the yacht will steer herself with both square and fore-and-aft canvas set; for when she starts rolling she shakes the wind out of the mainsail, and the foresail, being less affected, pulls her head round. But at that time, with her original mast, she would generally look after herself for a considerable time; it was considered a great hardship if we could not all sit down to dinner together. This afternoon it was my wheel, a fact which I recognized suitably by going to sleep; but not in the shade, whereby I burned most of the skin off my back. It is necessary, however, to lose a skin or two in order to become sun-proof, a very convenient quality when one can only wash one's clothes after a heavy shower of rain. It was interesting to observe that whereas the mate and I never wore hats, or indeed anything else except for the sake of warmth, and the third hand never went on deck without a red flannel shirt and a green umbrella, he was the only one on board who complained of the heat. Strange that one should babble about Trade Winds and green umbrellas here, three days out from Dublin and 1,500 miles from the Tropic of Cancer! It shows how small the world is, and how readily anyone that has a boat can exchange the cold grey of our coast for the sapphires and diamonds of the south.

The good north-east wind held steady, freshening day by day; the blue seas rolled up astern, each day steeper and with a heavier crest of white; the foam lapped over in the waist and hissed along the rail to the bows; and our wake showed green farther and farther astern. That foam that lapped over the waist found one of our weaknesses; just there was the galley skylight, and just abaft the skylight was the mainsheet; and on occasions of injudicious gybing bights of the mainsheet had more than once got round that skylight and had lifted it off its coamings. And what looked like foam on deck proved to be green water in the galley. Now I had designed that galley with great consideration for light and air, and with a head wind and sea, which at home is the time one gets wettest, it is the driest part of the ship. But we were going to run with the wind aft for weeks at a time, and I had put that galley in the wettest part of a running ship; and just now I was running her. With little effort she did 160 and then 170 miles in the day, the mate sitting on the taffrail playing the mandolin and steering with one foot, the third hand foolishly trailing a line over the stern in quest of fish. I say foolishly, because I find that he trailed that line for about 6,700 miles and caught four fish on it; that is one to every 1,675 miles, or less frequently than once a fortnight. I told him there was more than a possibility of an accidental gybe, as the ship was rolling badly and the wind was unsteady; and sure enough, while it was my wheel, the gybe came, and the mizzen-sheet caught my unfortunate fisherman and gave him concussion of the brain. Four months later I thought: 'It was my wheel; I tried to kill him but failed'; but at the time I was not convinced of the justification for murder, and set to reducing canvas so that the mate and I could both bear a hand to get him below. And this meant first of all taking in the foresail, which I proceeded to do, while the mate steered. In those days there was no gear on the foresail, which travelled on hoops on the yard, except the inhauls and outhauls; consequently when one had hauled in the head one had to get the whole contraption down on deck, keeping the inhauls taut and muzzling the sail with one hand while one lowered away on the halliards with the other. In ten minutes I thought out half-a-dozen better ways of doing the job. Without the foresail two of us could do anything with the ship; the wind and sea went down, the patient improved, and we got on with our voyage towards Madeira.

Next day the wind fell very light, and the mate and I were busy shifting sails. There had been a possibility of heavy weather on the coast, so we had left home with the new suit bent; besides it looked better, for the old sails were very patched and parti-coloured. There was nothing else to do this day, and we did not want to leave the work to be done at Madeira, where we were going to amuse ourselves. Those sails were not only very patched but they were very old. The jib was made by Ratsey, but some twenty years ago; the mainsail, a much better setting sail than the new one, only twelve, but one of them was spent covering a hayrick. The rest were good enough for a steady following breeze, but would probably blow away in the South-East Trades. While we were bending them our patient sat up and took an interest in turtle, which we could not catch, but which were a pleasant reminder that we were approaching tropical seas. This was the only time we saw them, and in those days we kept a good look-out for birds and beasts. These seas, however, did not seem a very good hunting ground for the naturalist; beyond shoals of leaping squid and a number of birds which looked like skuas and were apparently after the squid, there was nothing conspicuous. But there were some very beautiful small jelly-fishes, marked with a cross-pattern of iridescent scales; and a small fleet of Portuguese men-of-war.

Meanwhile we had lost the Portuguese Trades and did not get the genuine article for two days, and when it came, on the 2nd of July, it was very light. But it was enough to give us flying-fish for breakfast. . . .

The sea was full of flying-fish, and as it was so smooth one could observe them with some facility from the lee bow, or from an even better point of vantage, the bob-stay, and thus get them against the sky where they are far more visible than against the water, the tone of which they imitate closely. I am prepared to swear that they can and do fly, all the statements of the anatomists notwithstanding. At least I say that by vibrating their wings they can increase their height and their speed and make abrupt turns in circumstances which preclude the hypothesis of an ascending puff of wind under them. But they cannot rise from the deck, and they are very good eating. This last opinion is shared by the dolphin, the *coryphæna,* that is, the dolphin of the seaman, who was hot in their pursuit but curiously enough turned aside to investigate a piece of white rag with a hook in it. He was even better eating. It is no fable about the changing colours of the dying dolphin; the colours indeed are more beautiful when he is alive, but they are more permanent.

The past couple of days the flying-jib had been set and not before it was time, for, being a cotton sail, it was a mass of mildew; but very much to the annoyance of the cat and to our anxiety. She fortunately could not climb the rigging – which is the foolish habit of ships' cats, for they cannot get down again – for my shrouds were not served over and her claws got no grip on the bare wire; but she used to promenade along the jib-boom. This was all right when she had the flying-jib sheets and downhaul to hold on to on the way out, and the soft canvas of the sail to turn round on; on the morning of the 24th of July she was not to be found, and it is supposed that she slipped off the naked varnished spar. This sad accident left a great gap in the community; and yet I don't know why I should feel the loss of a cat, for she was an undeniable nuisance. But cats would be the best kind of sea-going stock if it were not for their inconvenient love of exploration; they are so cosy in repose, and in action so independent and unconscious of the movement of the ship.

On the next day we lost the Trade Wind, in lat. 10° 20′N, and were left anxiously wondering what would come next.

*

The Admiralty Pilot says that the north-east trade wind extends from about 15°N to 35°N in July and August at the time of Conor O'Brien's passage, so the reader may wonder why O'Brien writes that he sailed into the north-east trade wind soon after leaving Ireland, at 50°N. Presumably that year the easterly which usually blows in the Channel approaches in the spring of the year, and blows steadily and regularly enough then to be called a trade wind, had not given place to westerlies in the middle of May as usual, but had lasted into July.

3

Singlehanders

BEFORE LEAVING the north-east trades I want to introduce you to the only woman who has sailed across an ocean alone, Ann Davison. In 1952 she made a passage from Plymouth to Antigua in the West Indies. This is not properly along the clipper way, because for the first half of her voyage – although she was following the general direction of the route down to the Canary Isles – she made short hops; and her next stage, the passage from the Canaries to the West Indies, cut across the clipper way instead of continuing along it.

What a comparison – the thoughts and feelings of a young woman sailing across an ocean alone and those of the big crews of the big clippers! Ann Davison and her husband had previously set off to cross the Atlantic in a converted old fishing ketch of 70 feet overall. This ship was untried and unready, and the difficulties they immediately got into, combined with fatigue, were more than Davison could stand. His mind could not bear the strain. Eventually they were wrecked on Portland Bill, escaped in a liferaft but were swept into the Portland race. The raft capsized time after time and finally Ann found that her husband was dead. Fourteen hours after leaving the wreck, the raft was swept ashore.

She climbed the cliffs to start life again, alone. She bought a 23-foot sloop built by Mashford Brothers in Plymouth. It was 19 feet on the waterline with a beam of 7½ feet and a draught of 4½ feet. Total sail area was 237 square feet. It was called *Felicity Ann.* In this she set off alone to cross the Atlantic.

Here she is writing about the passage from Casablanca to the Canary Isles. *Felicity Ann* took 29 days for the passage of about 530 miles – an average of 18¼ miles per day.

*

It was an extraordinarily pleasant voyage, certainly the nicest so far, and I enjoyed the sort of lazy-hazy lotus-eating sea life one dreams of walled up in a city.

Conditions had a delicious dreamy Southern feel about them, calm and unhurried. There were lovely soft pearl-grey nights of a peculiar luminosity and soothing restfulness that were the physical manifestation of contentment. There were sunrises of such crystalline clarity and pristine glory that one could forgive any amount of travail for the joy of beholding those few golden moments when the world was born anew. There were sunsets so lurid, when an orange sun crept down a black and blood-red sky into a smooth lead-coloured sea, that one was convinced there was nothing less than a hurricane in the offing. I would shorten sail and batten down and prepare for the worst, only to discover that all the fuss in the heavens was for a few drops of rain. The weather eye I had acquired through years of flying and farming in England was sadly out in the lower latitudes, where the familiar signs and portents meant nothing at all. The weather could, and did, change with extraordinary rapidity, and the minutest rise or fall in barometric pressure might mean a severe blow, or nothing. As John said in Casablanca, if the glass fell the way it does in England, it would mean the end of the world. Moreover the alteration in pressure seemed to take place as conditions actually changed. The sky would throw a few clouds together and the wind, sea, and pressure rise at the same time to conjure a squall out of a flat calm with the apparent intention of working up into something big, but in a couple of hours it would all peter out and leave a subsiding sea babbling and gossiping like a football crowd dispersing after a close game. I soon gave up trying to forecast and took the weather as it came. After all, there is very little else you can do in the ocean, with no convenient ports to run to for shelter there, so I gave up reefing until it was necessary, and it was hardly ever necessary on this trip, as most of the time there was either a glass calm or a very light breeze, and our average day's progress was twenty miles.

The snail-like advance was a straight incitation to barnacles to grow on the log line, and they were surprisingly tenacious and difficult to remove. The water was so still and clear that sometimes it was almost as if you could see straight down to the bottom of the sea. Fascinating little striped fish, black and bright blue, swam about in the shade of the ship. A few flying fish skittered across the surface like flat stones thrown on a pond. They were very small flying fish, no bigger than minnows. There were times when rubbish thrown over the side in the morning would still be alongside at nightfall. Then the air was breathless and there would not be the smallest sound from the ship, not even a creak, and the silence was primeval. One might have been alone on the planet where even a cloud spelt companionship.

Most of the time, however, there was a huge swell in which *FA* rolled abominably and flung her boom from side to side with a viciousness that threatened to wrench it clean out of its fastenings. She rattled her blocks and everything not immovably fast below with an aggravating irregularity so that I was driven to a frenzy of restowing and rigging preventers in an effort to restore peace. An intermittent blop – rattle – crash on a small boat at sea is the nautical version of the Chinese water torture. . . .

For the first nine days out of Casablanca there was not a ship to be seen, and I missed them, grizzling quietly to myself at the loneliness; then we joined the north- and south-bound shipping lane and two steamers appeared on the horizon at the same time, whereon, embarrassed by riches perhaps, I perversely resented their presence. 'What are you doing on my ocean?'

Being in the shipping lane again meant the resumption of restless, sleepless nights. I figured out it took twenty minutes for a ship invisible over the horizon to reach us, and as a big ship was extremely unlikely to see me I had to see her, so any rest below was broken every twenty minutes throughout the hours of darkness. Enough practice since leaving England had endowed me with a personal alarm system which rang me out of a comatose condition at the appropriate intervals. Occasionally it let me oversleep, and once I awoke to find a south-bound steamer twenty-five yards astern of us. She was deep in Aldis conversation with another vessel, northward bound to west-ward of her, and utterly oblivious of our existence. A miss is as good as a mile maybe, but twenty-five yards is a narrow enough margin in the ocean, and it gave the required jolt to the personal alarm clock. On these ship-watching nights I used to get two hours of genuine sleep at dawn, when it could be assumed that *FA* was reasonably visible, and I couldn't care less by then anyway, but the overall lack of sleep did not improve the general physical condition, already much lowered by dysentery. The thought processes, never on Einstein levels, were reduced to a positively moronic grasp, and I had some rare hassels with navigational problems. However, the balance of nature was somewhat restored in that I was eating better on this trip than on any of the previous ones – the voyage from Douarnenez to Vigo was made almost exclusively on oranges – and there are several references to cooked meals in the log book.

I may say that anything mentioned in the log book at this stage outside of navigation notes was a sure indication of an *Occasion*, though they were simple enough meals in all conscience, consisting mainly of scrambled eggs, or an omelette and coffee, or weird mixtures of cheese and onions. One reads of explorers and other isolated people dreaming up extravagant concoctions they are going to eat on returning to civilisation, but quails in aspic were not for me. I had an uncomplicated yearning for plain boiled potatoes and cabbage. As these do not represent a normal taste on my part, I concluded it was a deficiency desire, and stepped up the daily dose of vitamin tablets: a strict necessity for ocean voyagers, as I discovered on the nineteen-day Vigo to Gibraltar run, when I tried to do without them and broke out into reluctant-to-heal sores. The only canned goods whose vitamin content survives the canning process are tomatoes, which probably explains why canned foods lost all appeal for me as soon as I went to sea. Very practically I was learning what stores would be required for the long passage.

One supper was especially memorable, though not for the menu. At 1750 hours, Sunday, 5 October to be exact, I was fixing some cheese nonsense on the stove, for it was a flat calm and I was in an experimental mood, and whilst stirring the goo in the pan I happened to glance through the porthole over the galley and spied a steamer way over on the horizon, the merest speck to eastward of us, going south. A few minutes later I looked out again and to my surprise saw she had altered course and was making towards us. Coming out of her way specially to look at a little ship. Thrilled to the quick, I abandoned supper, brushed my hair, and made up my face, noting with detached amazement that my hands were trembling and my heart was beating, and I was as excited as if I was preparing for a longed-for assignation.

She was a tall, white-grey Italian liner, the *Genale* of Rome, and she swept round astern of us, the officers on her bridge inspecting *FA* keenly through their binoculars. As she had so kindly come many miles out of her way, I had no wish to delay her needlessly, for minutes are valuable to a ship on schedule, so I made no signals, but waved, and the whole ship seemed to come alive with upraised arms waving in reply. She went on her way satisfied that all was well with her midget counterpart, and the night was a little less lonely from the knowledge of her consideration.

*

Not many women like navigating. Here are Ann Davison's views on this important item of seamanship.

*

The lazy weather gave ample opportunity to practise celestial navigation, and I spent hours taking sights and worrying out little sums and drawing fantastic position lines on the chart, for the results of my workings were invariably crazy. But not quite crazy enough to convince me they were wrong. They had a tendency to put us near the Salvage Islands, an uninhabited group of rocks with all sorts of outlying horrors north of the Canaries, where I least desired to be, and there was a bad twenty-four hours spent wondering if after all the workings could be right. When you have only yourself with whom to discuss a situation, you can argue from ten different viewpoints and sell yourself on any one of them. Dead reckoning, on the other hand, put us on our course over the Conception Bank, which seemed reasonable as the seas had the shorter, shallower appearance of water over a bank, yet there was this doubt milling about in the back of my mind, so I kept alert and anxious until the evening of 15 October, when a peak of land appeared in the clear light of the westering sun. It was only a shadow, and looked like a dark cloud on the horizon, but the outlines were harder, more definite than those of a cloud and it did not alter shape. I reckoned it must be at least sixty miles distant and felt sure it was the peak of Tenerife. All would have been well except that the following morning we met a Spanish fishing boat whose crew volunteered the information that 'Palma' lay in the direction we were going. After they were hull down on the horizon the thought occurred to me, did they mean Las Palmas or the Island of Palma? It makes quite a difference, I pointed out to *FA* as she curtseyed along in a freshening breeze. It was not impossible for us to be further to the southwest of our course than we believed, and for the land to be nearer and to be the peak of some other island – Palma, say – and the more I thought about it the more I was confused. A long wrestle with the sextant revealed nothing useful. The positions obtained were all wildly divergent, and after eliminating all the other errors, I concluded my timing was at fault, and that it was impracticable to work single-handed without a stopwatch. Counting seconds ('one-and-two-and-three') from the moment the sun bounced on the horizon until I reached the chronometer, gimballed in its case and screwed down right forrard in the cabin, was altogether too inaccurate, a hit-and-miss method not assisted in any way by the concern of holding the sextant protectively meanwhile. For it is impossible to lay anything down haphazardly aboard a small ship; it must be held until it is safely stowed, otherwise it is apt to find its way overboard or to be shattered to pieces. Lurching through the companion hatch, clutching the sextant, I would murmur, 'One and two and oops and three, no four, and oh-oh, and six, where was I? and – oh damn,' and climb out again to take another sight. Resolving to buy a stopwatch at the first opportunity, I sailed on towards the island, now rendered invisible by the day haze, to find out what it was when we got there. But two days later, the winds being slight and fitful, more land showed up in the sunset, which eventually turned out to be Fuertaventura, volcanic and forbidding, but welcome because it was where it should be. Confidently, at last, we continued on our way to Las Palmas, arriving there on October 24th, to be greeted with the unrestrained enthusiasm usually reserved for the prodigal son, or one given up as lost.

*

Here are her views on the passage across the ocean from Las Palmas to Antigua which now faced her.

*

Preparing for this voyage had been in a way unlike preparing for any of the others, although naturally it was a projection and development of them all, and the preparations were more in the nature of a mental strengthening of the skipper than a material provisioning of the ship, a feature with which I was now pretty well acquainted. It was to be a much longer passage than any of the others, and it would be much lonelier; there would not be the comforting knowledge of vast continents only a hundred miles or so to the eastward, and I could not expect to see any ships en route. Once the busiest sea lanes, the trade wind belts are now the most deserted, for steamships have no need of following winds, but sail great circle courses direct to where they want to be. And there could be no turning back on this voyage. No change of plan. This sort of certainty was sobering. When there is no way back, no way out, you must be very, very sure of what you are doing. I did not know how I would react to absolute solitude. It is an experience few of us are ever called upon to undergo and one which few of us would voluntarily choose. It is almost unimaginable, because solitude is something that normally can be broken at will. Even being on one's own in undeveloped country, popularly supposed to epitomise loneliness, is not true solitude, for one is surrounded by trees and bush and grass and animals, all part of the substance of one's own living. But the sea is an alien element; one cannot live in it or on it for long, and one survives that little time by one's own wit and judgment and the Grace of God. When a man says he loves the sea, he loves the illusion of mastery, the pride of skill, the life attendant on sea-faring, but not the sea itself. One may be moved by its beauty or its grandeur, or terrified by its immensity and power of destruction, but one cannot love it any more than one can love the atmosphere or the stars in outer space.

*

This crossing of the Atlantic with following winds and a strong favourable current, a constant fresh sailing breeze, sparkling warm waters, warm air and a great abundance of entrancing fish life is the most desired and longed-for voyage of all deep-sea sailors. Naturally it seemed an awesome, tremendous, frightening project for Ann Davison. She found, however, that there were too many calms, too much of light airs and too many squalls. Five and a half weeks out she wrote, 'The sun glides down in golden splendour and another day of light wind and still cloud comes to an end. The sea has been strangely silent all day and in spite of increasing anxiety I am still capable of appreciation and find something hauntingly beautiful about all this . . .' Next day she wrote:

*

Throughout today we have advanced at the rate of one knot and at sundown we approached a dirty big bunch of rain clouds, the kind associated with those villainous squalls, but as one knot is one knot only, I did not reef but left *FA* sailing herself closehauled with all sail, and I came below to make supper, having acquired an appetite from somewhere. Made a queer batter from one spoonful of gofio and two spoonfuls of dried egg and ate the result with margarine and brown sugar and liked it very much indeed. *FA* meantime slid between two black and trailing clouds.

The following day:

06.00. Surface reluctantly after wretched night, and the morning does not promise to be much better. Although not in the least hungry am preparing breakfast as it is doing something positive which is the only protection against apathy and despair.

15.00. First opportunity to take a sight. Almost an impossibility in this sea. Will work it out tonight.

17.00. Heave to, absolutely beat. Today touched an all-time low.

1 January, 1953:

Regret not being able to use this wind tonight but am too exhausted to go on. If this is the Trade Wind it will be here tomorrow, and maybe in better shape, both it and me, to allow the twins up. And if it is not the Trade Wind then I won't have used my depleted store of energy for nothing. Feel sick and dizzy tonight.

*

This sounds to me as if vitamin deficiency is beginning to take effect, if not the dreaded scurvy itself. It appears from her story that she used plenty of vitamin pills, but if she had neglected to take these, or for some reason they had proved ineffective then the diet, a sort of bachelor diet of which she gives samples, is what I would expect to result in the symptoms just described and such as she records in the next entry of her log.

*

Friday, January 2nd. 06.00. Still calm with just a slight breeze from the north-east. Had a long night's sleep but still feel tired and bereft of energy. Dreamt in nightmares all night long and the horror of them still lingers . . . although I cannot remember what they were about. . . .

I don't know what to do about this nervousness. I feel dizzy most of the time and am completely at the mercy of uncontrollable emotional impulses. The least little thing can delight or distress beyond measure. Mostly it is distress and I have wept more in these last few days than I have ever done in my whole life and for such trivial reasons as failing to light the stove with one match.

January 10th:

16.15. Feeling rather lousy this evening – too long sea voyage is telling physically as well as mentally. Have painful sty on eye, and sea boils are manifest in spite of vitamin tablets.

On Sunday, January 18th, she makes a landfall, Barbados. She writes in the log:

We round Harrison Point, well off shore, towards the end of the afternoon and I am fascinated by the occasional glimpse of a red roof and a stone wall. The island looks peculiarly English from the little I can see . . . None of this is true . . . We make south towards Carlisle Bay, Bridgetown, and HAVEN.

We cannot make it before dark, though, and I have hove-to on the starboard tack, about 8 miles off shore, so I can fill the lamps, tidy the ship and myself, get supper as have neither fed nor drunk today and feel pretty whacko. . . . Then we can go in in the morning all fresh . . .

And, anyway, *we have crossed the ruddy ocean.*

*

While Ann Davison was making her crossing in 1952, Dr Bombard was following the clipper way from the Canaries to near the Cape Verde Islands and then on to the West Indies in a rubber dinghy. Its maximum length was 15 feet and its overall width 6 feet 2 inches. It was a horseshoe-shaped tube with a wooden transom a few feet from the extreme stern end and it had a short mast with about 30 square feet of sail.

Bombard was a man with an idea and it is men with ideas who accomplish great things. He had found out that 200,000 people lost their lives every year through shipwreck or accidents to boats. Of these, 50,000 reached lifeboats, etc., but, having survived disaster, died quickly, sometimes within a few hours. They died, he reckoned, because they thought they were going to die, and were attacked by panic or despair. In fact, a castaway, as he called a shipwrecked person, could survive indefinitely on the open ocean without having any water or food in the boat when wrecked. He set out to prove that he was right. The only way to do this was to cross the North Atlantic alone in a rubber dinghy without taking any fresh water or any food.

He started from the Canary Islands exactly one month before Ann Davison and he arrived at Barbados exactly one month before she reached Dominica – that is to say he made the 2,750 mile passage in 65 days at an average speed of 42 miles per day. Quite apart from having no food or water this was a remarkable feat, since he was a poor seaman and an even poorer navigator. At that time it was assumed that no one could exist for more than two or three days, with only sea-water to drink and fresh fish to eat. Many officials and others tried to prevent Bombard from starting because they thought it was pure suicide. People must have attacked his wife – with the best of intentions, of course – saying that she ought to stop her husband. Often a great feat of this kind owes its success indirectly to a woman behind the man. Bombard himself writes:

*

Nothing could shake the courage and faithful self-abnegation of my wife. She was confident, had seen me at work, knew that what I was attempting was possible and understood my purpose: to save lives, thousands of lives. Not that she was happy to see me leave, but she saw the necessity for it and knew that I must complete my voyage to prove my case. She made no attempt to restrain me.

*

He set out from Las Palmas of the Canary Isles on 19 October, 1953. It was not the smooth passage that he might have expected in the halcyon trade-wind belt but waves are sure to seem bigger from a rubber dinghy than from a ship. Four days after starting:

*

The trade wind sprang up again. Soon it approached gale strength. Carrying me first on their crests and then in their troughs, the waves either protected me from or exposed me to its blast. Their tops were breaking all round me. I wondered what would happen if *L'Hérétique* came just under one of these on-rushing waterfalls.

Unable to do anything about it, but confident in the dinghy's stability, I dropped off to sleep, expecting an untroubled night. It became a nightmare. Suddenly, half in a dream, I seemed to be surrounded by water. Confused and panic-stricken, I tried to gather my thoughts. Was there still a boat under me? Was I in it or in the water? I started swimming, and then struck out desperately. Half dead with fright

I woke right up. *L'Hérétique* was completely submerged. I realised that a wave must have broken right on top of me. I must start baling at once. Only the inflated floats showed above the water. Everything else had become part of the sea, but *L'Hérétique* continued imperturbably on its course, like a wreck. Once I had woken up there was no time to be frightened. Almost instinctively I started scooping out water with my two hands and then with my hat, a ludicrous utensil for what seemed a superhuman task. I had to bale furiously between each big wave so that *L'Hérétique* would survive the next. But even with a proper baler I would have needed to display a degree of energy which would soon have exhausted me. Each big wave hit the stern-board with a thud, and the water flowed in anew, making the work of the previous ten minutes or quarter of an hour useless, pointless and hopeless. It is still beyond my comprehension how, numbed with cold, I managed to keep this up for 2 hours. That was the time it took to get the dinghy properly afloat again. I can only say to my fellow castaways: be more obstinate than the sea and you will win.

I was safe, but everything in the dinghy was completely soaked, and when the sun started to dry things out, they would all be covered with a film of salt, which was going to absorb the humidity every time night fell. The whole craft had become a sort of salt marsh. Most of the equipment was in watertight containers, and fortunately the radio had not been affected. The matches, on the other hand, were absolutely soaked. In due course, I spread them out in the boat to dry in the sun, with very little hope of their ever being any use again, but at least I had to try. Fortunately I had about a hundred boxes with me, but I would be lucky to find one in each box that would light. The one great satisfaction was that *L'Hérétique* was at least never going to capsize. The dinghy had behaved exactly as I hoped, like an aquaplane or floating platform, sliding over the crests of the waves without offering any resistance. There was a reasonable hope that she would reach the other side in one piece.

*

I do not think that Bombard could have been even a small boat sailor before he started, but he was unusually intelligent and learned to adapt himself quickly. Two days later he writes:

*

There is no entry in my log for Thursday, the 23rd, because I was too busy all day with needle and thread. The wind had blown up fresh and strong from the right direction; the faithful trade wind from the north-east which was to carry me to my destination. But fate has its own ironies; hardly had I trimmed the sail to the wind, when it tore right across at its broadest part. It had brought me all the way from Monaco to the Canaries. When I started off again, I had made up my mind to use it as long as possible, and then replace it with the new sail I had in reserve, but I had not expected I would need to change them so soon. I threw out my sea anchor, lowered the sail and rigged the new one to the yard. Half an hour later a sudden violent gust wrenched it away and sent it flying away like a kite. I saw it splash into the sea a little way off. What was worse, it had carried away not only the rigging, but also the main sheet and halyards.

I had no alternative but to rely on my old, torn sail, so I started laboriously to sew it together again. All I had was a reel of ordinary black thread and a few darning needles. I had to work on it inch by inch, as the lack of space prevented me from laying the sail out. I had to mend the rent little by little. By the time evening came I had just about finished.

*

Stories about voyages normally highlight the dangers and disaster even if for most of the time it is fascinating and wonderful sailing. Occasionally a paragraph gives us a glimpse of the good sailing such as when Bombard writes: 'The wind had now become predictable and regular. I left my sail set night and day, and with no land obstacles to avoid I was able to run before it without worry, watching the slightly faster swell roll past me. Just as speed assures a cyclist's balance, so it gave me additional security.'

Now he has been at sea for 9 days and all this time he

has been subsisting on up to 1½ pints of seawater a day with the liquid squeezed from fish which he caught each day. The seawater, he said, could satisfy thirst safely provided a person did not wait until dehydrated before starting to drink it. He must start drinking seawater from the moment he was cast away. Dr Bombard goes into detail about the salts and vitamins needed to sustain life and he describes – in too much detail for some people – the effects of his diet and experiment on his body and its functions throughout the voyage. Each day he caught 2 coffee spoons or so of plankton which he needed to keep scurvy at bay. This was done by towing a net of straining cloth or fine silk.

Nine days out from the Canaries:

*

I am not dreaming about food; a good sign. Indeed, it was the best proof that I was not hungry, because hunger is above all an obsession. I had no cravings of any sort.

Ten days out:

*

I was suddenly overwhelmed by the thought of the grave situation I was in. Apart from its length, this part of my voyage had an inexorable quality absent from the previous laps. It was impossible for me to stop or turn round, there was not the slightest possibility of any help. I was just a drop in the ocean, part of a world not to be measured in human terms. I often had cold shivers down my spine and I had not sighted a ship for some time. The previous day I had seen my first shark since leaving the Canaries, but it passed quickly by. The dolphins (dorades), on the other hand, had become familiar acquaintances. I even talked to them at times, as the only friends in sight. When I woke up during the night I was always struck by the beauty of these creatures, swimming parallel to me, and leaving phosphorescent wakes like some shooting star.

From sheer curiosity I thought I would see what effect the gleam of an electric torch would have. As soon as I switched it on, all the fish concentrated in its circle of light. I was still lost in admiration of their intricate evolutions, which I could direct more or less at will, when a sudden buffet forced me to clutch the side of the boat. It was a large shark, the upper part of its tail much longer than the lower. It had turned over on its back to swim towards me. All its teeth flashed in the light of the torch, and its underside gleamed pure white. It butted its snout repeatedly on the side of the dinghy. Whether it was trying to take a good bite I do not know, but I had always heard that sharks turned on their back to seize their prey. I snapped out the light in the hope that it would go away. For a moment or two its tail continued to beat around me like the cracks of a whip, splashing me with sea-water from head to foot. Its white stomach appeared from time to time amidst the phosphorescence, but then, presumably bored by my inactivity, it made off. It is more than likely that the attack was serious, but I comforted myself with the thought of how difficult it must be to bite a football.

12 days out:

The solitude must have been starting to affect me. I had begun to understand the difference between solitude and isolation. Moments of isolation in ordinary life can soon be ended; it is just a question of going out of the door into the street or dialling a number on the telephone to hear the voice of a friend. Isolation is merely a matter of isolating oneself, but solitude is an oppressive thing and slowly wears down its lonely victim. It seemed sometimes as if the immense and absolute solitude of the ocean's expanse was concentrated right on top of me, as if my beating heart was the centre of gravity of a mass which was at the same time nothingness. The day I dropped the tow off Las Palmas I thought that solitude was something I would be able to master, once I had become accustomed to its presence on board. I had been too presumptuous. It was not something I had carried with me, something that could be measured by the confines of myself or the boat. It was a vast presence which engulfed me. Its spell could not be broken, any more than the horizon could be brought nearer. And if from time to time I talked aloud in order to hear my own voice, I only felt more alone, a hostage to silence. To add to the turmoil in my head, I became very superstitious about small things, the inevitable accompaniment of solitude. If I could not find my pipe the moment I looked for it, I considered it a bad omen. The little doll mascot, which my friends had given me on the Canaries, began to acquire a tangible personality. I used to look at her and start a conversation, first of all in monosyllables, then whole sentences, describing exactly the next thing I was going to do. I did not wait for a reply, it was not yet a dialogue, although that would come; for the time being I just needed to assert myself.

Two weeks out he was in a panic.

Sunday, 2nd November, will remain in my memory because I did a very stupid thing. For some days my health had not been too good. The change of food and the constant humidity had caused a general skin eruption of painful little spots. I hoped to prevent them forming scabs by resting my weight on a little pneumatic cushion, the only one I had. Some clumsy movement must have knocked it overboard, a fact I only realised when I saw it floating a couple of hundred yards or so astern. I lowered the sail, put out the sea anchor and dived in to fetch it. I am a strong swimmer and reached the cushion in a few minutes. Imagine my horror, when I turned round, to see the dinghy sailing off without me, too fast for me to be able to catch it. The sea anchor, normally shaped like a parachute, had fouled itself and was no longer arresting the drift. It was quite clear I would become exhausted long before I could overhaul it. At that moment *L'Hérétique* very nearly continued the voyage without me.

When I was training to swim the English Channel in 1951, in top physical condition, I once swam for twenty-one hours. Weakened as I was by privation and lack of exercise, I could not possibly have equalled the feat. I abandoned the cushion to its fate and concentrated on the fastest haul of my life. I managed to cut down the distance a little but then had difficulty in even maintaining it. Suddenly I saw *L'Hérétique* slow down. I caught it up and just managed to hoist myself on board. By a miracle, the cords of the sea anchor had disentangled themselves in the nick of time. I was physically and morally exhausted and swore it was the last dip I would take on the journey.

*

Lots of fish swam along with him. They like the shade of a boat and also, I believe, the barnacles and weed on the bottom. Incidentally, I wonder if Bombard sampled the weed on the bottom of his dinghy. I have always understood that Poon Lim, the greatest raft survivor of all time, who lived alone on a raft for 120 days after being torpedoed in the war, ate the weed growing on the bottom of the raft. This must have acted as an anti-scorbutic. All the dorades and sea perch swarming round Bombard's raft attracted bigger fish.

He goes on:

*

During the night of Thursday, 6th November, I was again attacked by a shark. He seemed to be a particularly tough customer and I could not keep him off – he must have acquired a taste for human flesh. I fixed my knife at the end of an oar while he butted away at the floats. I got ready to defend myself and the next time he turned on his back to attack at an angle I stuck the knife in him and slit him from throat to tail. The sea burned a blackish colour round him and I saw his entrails spilling out. My dolphins pounced on them. They always seemed hungry. For once, anyway, the hunter had become the hunted.

On November 11th he had another big visitor. First he says that he had the pleasure of a visit from

. . . a new sort of bird, an attractive creature called, in English, I believe, a white-tailed tropic bird, and which the French call a Paillecul. It looks like a white dove with a black beak and has a long quill in its tail, which, with an impertinent air, it uses as an elevator. As it could only come from the American continent, being completely unknown in the Old World, it was a good sign. For the first time, I had met a bird which came, without a shadow of doubt, from my destination.

This pleasant interlude was succeeded at about 2 o'clock in the afternoon by twelve hours of terror, which lasted until two the next morning. Just as I was peacefully reading a little Aeschylus, there was a violent blow on the rudder: 'That's another shark,' I thought, and looked up. What I saw was a large swordfish of undeniably menacing aspect. He was following the dinghy at a distance of about 20 feet, seemingly in a rage, his dorsal fin raised like hackles. In one of his feints round the boat he had collided with my rudder oar. I found I had a determined enemy. If I only succeeded in wounding him, he would surely attack again, and that would be the end of *L'Hérétique.* What was worse, as I was hurriedly getting my harpoon ready, a clumsy movement knocked it into the sea. It was my last one. Now I was disarmed. I fixed my pocket knife on to my underwater gun as a makeshift bayonet, determined to sell my life dearly if he attacked in earnest.

This intolerable anxiety lasted twelve long hours. As night fell I could follow the swordfish's movements by his luminous wake and the noise his dorsal fin made cutting the water. Several times his back bumped the underside of the dinghy, but he still seemed a little afraid of me. He never approached from ahead, and every time he came at me he changed course at the last moment before striking the floats. I came to believe that he was frightened, probably as frightened as I was. Every living creature possesses some means of defence, but it must perturb an attacker not to know what it is. In the early hours of the morning his wake disappeared, but I spent a sleepless night...

On that same day it rained for the first time.

For three weeks I had not had a drop of fresh water, only the liquid I pressed from my fish, but my reactions were perfectly normal, just the marvellous sensation of swallowing a real drink at last. I had proved conclusively that a castaway could live for three weeks (and even longer, because I could have continued perfectly well) without fresh water. It is true that providence was to spare me the ordeal of having to rely again on the flat insipid fish juice. From that day on I always had enough rain water to slake my thirst. It sometimes seemed as if my stock was about to run out but a shower always came in time.

*

On November 23rd, 35 days out, the wind dropped and he was becalmed for the first time. It seems to me a wonderful sailing breeze, 35 days of constant wind, but the good doctor complained bitterly of the calm spells which afflicted him from now on. Ann Davison on this day had been 3 days at sea from the Canaries and she too had complained about the calms. The doctor is outspoken about all the textbooks, such as the Admiralty Pilots, which state that the north-east trade wind blows steadily in November and December.

*

The same applies [that the author is dishonest in making statements he knows to be false, or if he has not confirmed them then he should leave them out] to those who make assertions about the trade wind. It is perfectly clear that they have never had to make the journey themselves, or else they were in a ship with an engine. In the area of the West Indies, in November and December, there are two days of wind for every ten days of flat calm.

I am exhausted. If I fail it will be because everything has turned against me; no wind and a scorching sun. Yesterday it rained all round the horizon but not a drop fell into the boat, it really is too much. My sail is flapping from left to right, so much for the trade wind. Definition of the trade wind area: a region where there is practically never any wind. I cannot even explain it by saying that I am in the Doldrums. At this time of year they lie about latitude 5° north.

*

The dinghy was in latitude 12°N. The Admiralty Pilot Book (West Indies, volume 2, lines 9-14) states: 'The Trade wind is at its strongest and most regular from December to March or April. It is at that time at its furthest north and blows from ENE to NE, strength about 4 on the Beaufort Scale.' The doctor was much more angry about the Frigate Birds than about the trade winds. On November 23 he wrote:

Just as the storm reached me, a frigate bird flew over. Another encouraging note in the handbook [he is referring to Gatty's *Raft Book*]: 'The Frigate Bird never spends the night at sea and is seldom found more than a hundred miles from land. In one exceptional instance one was sighted three hundred miles from the nearest coast.'

*

After he had sailed another 100 miles or so and continued to see Frigate Birds but no land, the doctor began to get very annoyed with Gatty's *Raft Book for Castaways* etc. On the 5th December he wrote:

Am completely baffled, have no idea where I am. If the dinghy is thrown up with me as a corpse, I have only one request, and that is that someone goes and boxes the ears of the author of this Castaways' Handbook. It only serves to demoralise anyone who has been unfortunate enough to buy it. It states in black and white: 'A considerable number of frigate birds means that land is about a hundred miles away.' I have seen quite a number during the last week and have covered about three hundred miles. The only moral is that the author is dishonest to make statements he knows to be false, or if he has not confirmed them then he should leave them out.

*

Poor Harold Gatty! He has been a friend of mine since 1936 when he advised me to set up as a navigation specialist, and he was once himself a great practical and theoretical navigator. He navigated one-eyed Wiley Post in his flight round the world. He wrote the *Raft Book* as a navigational guide to survival in the 1939 war. He published it himself and sold, he told me, 400,000 copies. It was a fine book which gave hope to many thousands of people who were on the ocean in small boats after being torpedoed or shot down, and he gave heart to many more who had to face the possibility of such a predicament. But he did make one or two mistakes like this one about the Frigate Birds. When Bombard saw his first Frigate Bird I estimate he was 1,200 miles from the West Indies and 850 miles from the Cape Verde Islands – certainly more than 300 miles from land. The next time I met Harold after the doctor's book had been published, I told him about the Frigate Bird episode so that he could correct it in another edition, but he was not too pleased. Evidently it seemed much more amusing to me than it did to him. As for Bombard, the more debilitated he became, the more embittered he was about this affair:

*

Still nothing in sight and the wind has fallen again. I can hardly believe that people like the author of this Castaways' Handbook could be asked to write something for the official use of the American navy and fill it with nothing but misstatements. It says that a frigate bird has never been seen more than three hundred miles from the coast.

Later that day something took his mind off Frigate Birds:

It was during this period of uneventful calm that I had the most dangerous encounter of all. Sitting in the stern of *L'Hérétique*, watching the feeble wake, I saw appear, still some way off, a flat, black, undulating mass in the water. As it came nearer, I saw it had white patches which caught the sun. When it was about 50 feet away I realised that it was a giant ray. Contrary to all logic I somehow felt reassured and took out the cine-camera to film it, without stopping to think that it probably regarded me as a good meal. It followed me for about two hours, keeping its distance all the time. Then it suddenly disappeared as if sucked down to the depths. It was only after my return that a fisherman from Dakar told me: 'That was probably your moment of greatest danger; the ray could have capsized you with a single flip of a fin or could have leapt clean out of the water on top of you.'

*

The doctor had been expecting to sight land for many days when, 53 days out, he had the shock of seeing a ship. He flashed his heliograph at the bridge, the ship slowed down and gave him his position accurately. The doctor had never done any navigating before this voyage; he had a weird method for finding his longitude and instead of being close to land, as he thought he was, his longitude was 600 miles in error. He recorded:

I felt as if someone had hit me over the head with a hammer. It was more than I could stand. Seizing the scull, I made for the boat, muttering feverishly to myself: 'This is it, 53 days, I give up.' The captain hailed me again. 'Will you come aboard?'

'I will get the dinghy hoisted in, the experiment is over,' I thought. 'After all, 53 days must prove something.'

*

After 53 days alone in the dinghy existing on liquid and flesh from raw fish, the temptation to accept the offer of a lift for the rest of the passage was almost insuperable. Judging by his own past experience, however, he felt sure that people would say his experiment had failed if he did so. His will was strong enough for him to return to his dinghy and continue his voyage.

Unfortunately the captain of the ship first persuaded him to accept a meal, a simple hot meal – a fried egg, a little piece of liver, a spoonful of cabbage and some fruit. Later this nearly killed him. He wrote that his stomach had got used to the other fare, but after this little meal it refused to go back to the raw fish diet. His stomach, he says, became prey to a sort of despair. He lost more weight during the next 12 days before reaching land than in the 53 days before meeting the ship. However, the captain of the ship had helped him with his navigation, and given him details of the magnetic variation along the rest of the route, also a copy of the *British Admiralty Sailing Instructions* which he had abused so roundly over the description of trade winds.

Eventually the doctor made his landfall where he had

intended, at Barbados, on December 24th. His was an achievement valuable to humanity. His fantastic voyage had forced the idea into many reluctant minds that it was possible for an ordinary person to survive in the Poon Lim manner. Maybe, as his critics claimed, his survival had been under the most favourable conditions of warm sea, warm air, following winds and strong favourable current abundant with many kinds of palatable fish.

It is interesting to compare Bombard's carefully theorised scientific experiment with Poon Lim's survival feat. Poon Lim used common sense and what must have been the coolest thinking possible, in addition to a tenacious hold on life. He gnawed a nail out of the raft wood to make a fish hook, ate the weed under the raft for his greens and, I believe, steeped himself in salt water to allay his thirst. I think he was kept supplied with rain for drinking water as was Bombard for 44 of his 65 days of passage. I do not think he knew that he could drink sea water or that he could extract fresh water from the flesh of fish. Presumably he got enough by eating the flesh.

The doctor lost 55 pounds in weight during the passage.

4

The Doldrums and the Line

ANN DAVISON and Doctor Bombard left the clipper way near the Cape Verde Islands but I continued their voyages across the Atlantic because a sailing voyage is nearly always a drama of the classic form – if it has a quiet start, it should be allowed to build up to a natural climax, the end of the voyage. The clipper captains would have been horrified both at the diversion to the West Indies from their usual route and at the slow pace of the singlehanders; a good passage in a clipper was only 21 days for the 3,275 miles from Plymouth to the Equator – 'The Line.'

However, before reaching the Line the clipper route passed

from the NE trade-wind zone to the Doldrums. If lucky, a ship sailed right through the Doldrums; if unlucky, she might be held up there for three weeks. For Dr Bombard and Ann Davison at the end of their passages the Doldrum belt appears to have reached further north than usual and touched them both.

I am going to call on Joshua Slocum to speak of his passage through the Doldrums. I say 'speak' because in his famous book, *Sailing Alone Around the World*, the style is so strong and direct that one can imagine he is in the room telling his tale in person. He was the first man to sail alone around the world. Although he circumnavigated west-about instead of east-about as did the clippers, he followed the clipper route down to the south side of the Doldrums. He was a Canadian, born in Nova Scotia, who became a naturalised American. He was a wonderful seaman, a great navigator and a great character. His circumnavigation was started in April 1895 and finished in June 1898. His boat, the *Spray*, was 35 feet overall. He had rebuilt her himself from the remains of an old hull which had been lying in a field for many years. In 1909, at the age of 65, he was posted missing without trace on a solo voyage in the Atlantic. I wonder if a whale or giant squid got him?

*

The sloop was now rapidly drawing towards the region of doldrums, and the force of the trade-winds was lessening. I could see by the ripples that a counter-current had set in. This I estimated to be about 16 miles a day. In the heart of the counter-stream the rate was more than that setting eastward.

September 14th [1895] a lofty three-masted ship, heading north, was seen from the masthead. Neither this ship nor the one seen yesterday was within signal distance, yet it was good even to see them. On the following day heavy rain-clouds rose in the south, obscuring the sun; this was ominous of doldrums. On the 16th the *Spray* entered this gloomy region, to battle with squalls and to be harassed by fitful calms; for this is the state of the elements between the northeast and the southeast trades, where each wind, struggling in turn for mastery, expends its force whirling about in all directions. Making this still more trying to one's nerve and patience, the sea was tossed into confused cross lumps and fretted by eddying currents. As if something more was needed to complete a sailor's discomfort in this state, the rain poured down in torrents day and night. The *Spray* struggled and tossed for ten days, making only three hundred miles on her course in all that time. I didn't say anything!

On September 23 the fine schooner *Nantasket* of Boston, from Bear River, for the river Plate, lumber-laden, and just through the doldrums, came up with the *Spray*, and her captain passing a few words, she sailed on. Being much fouled on the bottom by shell-fish, she drew along with her fishes which had been following the *Spray*, which was less provided with that sort of food. Fishes will always follow a foul ship. A barnacle-grown log adrift has the same attraction for deep-sea fishes. One of this little school of deserters was a dolphin that had followed the *Spray* about a thousand miles, and had been content to eat scraps of food thrown overboard from my table; for, having been wounded, it could not dart through the sea to prey on other fishes. I had become accustomed to seeing the dolphin which I knew by its scars, and missed it whenever it took occasional excursions away from the sloop. One day, after it had been off for some hours, it returned in company with three yellowtails, a sort of cousin to the dolphin. This little school kept together, except when in danger and when foraging about the sea. Their lives were often threatened by hungry sharks that came around the vessel, and more than once they had narrow escapes. Their mode of escape interested me greatly and I passed hours watching them. They would dart away, each in a different direction, so that the wolf of the sea, the shark, pursuing one, would be led away from the others; then after a while they would all return and rendezvous under one side or the other of the sloop. Twice their pursuers were diverted by a tin pan, which I towed astern of the sloop, and which was mistaken for a bright fish; and while turning, in the peculiar way that sharks have when about to devour their prey, I shot them through the head.

Their precarious life seemed to concern the yellowtails very little, if at all. All living beings without doubt are afraid of death. Nevertheless, some of the species I saw huddled together as though they knew they were created for the larger fishes, and wished to give the least possible trouble to their captors. I have seen, on the other hand, whales swimming in a circle around a school of herrings, and with mighty exertion 'bunching' them together in a whirlpool set in motion by their flukes, and when the small fry were all whirled nicely together, one or the other of the leviathans, lunging through the centre with open jaws, took in a boat-load or so at a single mouthful. Off the Cape of Good Hope I saw schools of sardines or other small fish being treated in this way by great numbers of cavally-fish. There was not the slightest chance of escape for the sardines, while the cavally circled round and round, feeding from the edge of the mass. It was interesting to note how rapidly the small fry disappeared; and though it was repeated before my eyes over and over, I could hardly perceive the capture of a single sardine, so dexterously was it done.

Along the equatorial limit of the south-east trade winds the air was heavily charged with electricity and there was much thunder and lightning. It was hereabout I remembered that, a few years before, the American ship *Alert* was destroyed by lightning.

*

Near the Line at the southern edge of the Doldrums the clipper way approached St Paul Rocks, of nearly 30° W. longitude. Frank Bullen writes about catching bonito here in his book, *The Cruise of the Cachalot.* The *Cachalot* was an American whaler on her way round the world and Frank Bullen, an Englishman, was one of the crew. For this stage of her voyage the *Cachalot* was following the clipper way. Bullen writes:

*

For the first and only time in my experience, we sighted St Paul Rocks, a tiny group of jagged peaks protruding from the Atlantic nearly on the Equator. Stupendous mountains they must be, rising almost sheer for about four and a half miles from the ocean bed. Although they appear quite insignificant specks on the vast expanse of water, one could not help thinking how sublime their appearance would be were they visible from the plateau whence they spring. Their chief interest to us at the time arose from the fact that, when within about three miles of them, we were suddenly surrounded by a vast school of bonito. These fish, so named by the Spaniards from their handsome appearance, are a species of mackerel, a branch of the Scombridae family, and attain a size of about two feet long and forty pounds weight, though their average dimensions are somewhat less than half that. They feed entirely upon flying fish and the small leaping squid or cuttle-fish, but love to follow a ship, playing around her, if her pace be not too great, for days together. Their flesh resembles beef in appearance, and they are warm-blooded; but, from their habitat being mid-ocean, nothing is known with any certainty of their habits of breeding.

The orthodox method of catching them on board ship is to cover a suitable hook with a piece of white rag a couple of inches long and attach it to a stout line. The fisherman then takes his seat upon the jib-boom end, having first, if he is prudent, secured a sack to the jibstay in such a manner that its mouth gapes wide. Then he unrolls his line, and as the ship forges ahead the line, blowing out, describes a curve, at the end of which the bait, dipping to the water occasionally, roughly represents a flying fish. Of course, the faster the ship is going, the better the chance of deceiving the fish, since they have less time to study the appearance of the bait. It is really an exaggerated and clumsy form of fly-fishing, and, as with that elegant pastime, much is due to the skill of the fisherman.

As the bait leaps from crest to crest of the wavelets thrust aside by the advancing ship, a fish more adventurous or hungrier than the rest will leap at it, and in an instant there is a dead, dangling weight of from ten to forty pounds hanging on at the end of your line thirty feet below. You haul frantically, or he may be poorly hooked, and you cannot play him. In a minute or two, if all goes well, he is plunged in the sack, and safe. But woe unto you if you have allowed the jeers of your shipmates to dissuade you from taking a sack out with you.

The struggles of these fish are marvellous, and a man runs great risk of being shaken off the boom, unless his legs are firmly locked in between the guys. Such is the tremendous vibration that a twenty-pound bonito makes in a man's grip, that it can be felt in the cabin at the other end of the ship; and I have often come in triumphantly with one, having lost all feeling in my arms and a goodly portion of skin off my breast and side where I have embraced the prize in a grim determination to hold him at all hazards, besides being literally drenched with his blood.

We were now fairly in the 'horse latitudes', and, much to our relief, the rain came down in occasional deluges, permitting us to wash well and often. The nearest I can get to it is the idea of an ocean suspended overhead, out of which the bottom occasionally falls. Nothing is visible or audible but the glare and roar of falling water, and the ship's deck, despite the many outlets, is full enough to swim about in in a very few minutes. At such times the whole celestial machinery of rain-making may be seen in full working order. Five or six mighty water-spouts in various stages of development were often within easy distance of us; once, indeed, we watched the birth, growth, and death of one less than a mile away. First, a big black cloud, even among that great assemblage of nimbi, began to belly downward, until the centre of it tapered into a stem, and the whole mass looked like a vast irregularly moulded funnel. Lower and lower it reached, as if feeling for soil in which to grow, until the sea beneath was agitated sympathetically, rising at last in a sort of pointed mound to meet the descending column. Our nearness enabled us to see that both descending and rising parts were whirling violently in obedience to some invisible force; and when they had joined each other, although the spiral motion did not appear to continue, the upward rush of the water through what was now a long elastic tube was very plainly to be seen. The cloud overhead grew blacker and bigger until its gloom was terrible. The pipe, or stem, got thinner gradually, until it became a mere thread; nor, although watching closely, could we determine when the connection between sea and sky ceased – one would not call it severed. The point rising from the sea settled almost immediately amidst a small commotion, as of a whirlpool. The tail depending from the cloud slowly shortened, and the mighty reservoir lost the vast bulge which had hung so threateningly above. Just before the final disappearance of the last portion of the tube, a fragment of cloud appeared to break off. It fell near enough to show by its thundering roar what a body of water it must have been, although it looked like a saturated piece of dirty rag in its descent.

For whole days and nights together we sometimes lay almost 'as idle as a painted ship upon a painted ocean,' when the deep blue dome above matched the deep blue plain below, and never a fleck of white appeared in sky or sea.

*

The food on this whaler was primitive and unsatisfying and Bullen, unlike Slocum, was always anxious to catch a fish. Here he describes fishing for dorade or dolphin:

*

While loitering in these smooth waters, waiting for the laggard wind, up came a shoal of dolphin, ready as at all times to attach themselves for a while to the ship. Nothing is more singular than the manner in which deep-sea fish will accompany a vessel that is not going too fast – sometimes for days at a time. Most convenient too, and providing hungry Jack with many a fresh mess he would otherwise have missed. Of all these friendly fish, none is better known than the 'dolphin' as from long usage sailors persist in calling them, and will doubtless do so until the end of the chapter. For the true dolphin (Delphinidae) is not a fish at all, but a mammal – a warm-blooded creature that suckles its young, and in its most familiar form is known to most people as the porpoise. The sailors' 'dolphin', on the other hand, is a veritable fish, with vertical tail fin instead of the horizontal one which distinguishes all the whale family, scales and gills.

It is well known to literature, under its sea-name, for its marvellous brilliancy of colour, and there are few objects more dazzling than a dolphin leaping out of a calm sea into the sunshine. The beauty of a dying dolphin, however, though sanctioned by many generations of writers, is a delusion, all the glory of the fish departing as soon as it is withdrawn from its native element.

To resume then: when this school of dolphin came alongside, a rush was made for the 'grains' – a sort of five pronged trident, if I may be allowed a baby bull. It was universally agreed among the fishermen that trying a hook and line was only a waste of time and provocative of profanity! Since every sailor knows that all the deep-water big fish require a living or apparently living bait. The fish, however, sheered off, and would not be tempted within reach of that deadly fork by any lure. Then did I cover myself with glory. For he who can fish cleverly and luckily may be sure of fairly good times in a whaler, although he may be no great things at any other work. I had a line of my own, and begging one of the small fish that had been hauled up in the gulf weed, I got permission to go aft and fish over the taffrail. The little fish was carefully secured on the hook, the point of which just protruded near its tail. Then I lowered him into the calm blue waters beneath, and payed out line very gently, until my bait was a silvery spot about a hundred feet astern. Only a very short time, and my hopes rose as I saw one bright gleam after another glide past the keel, heading aft. Then came a gentle drawing of the line, which I suffered to slip slowly through my fingers until I judged it time to try whether I was right or wrong. A long hard pull, and my heart beat fast as I felt the thrill along the line that fishermen love. None of your high art here, but haul in hand over hand, the line being strong enough to land a 250-pound fish. Up he came, the beauty, all silver and scarlet and blue, five feet long if an inch, and weighing 35 pounds. Well, such a lot of astonished men I never saw.

They could hardly believe their eyes. That such a daring innovation should be successful was hardly to be believed, even with the vigorous evidence before them. Even the grim captain came to look and turned upon me as I thought a less lowering brow than usual, while Mr Count, the mate, fairly chuckled again at the thought of how the little Britisher had wiped the eyes of these veteran fishermen.

Bullen also describes how he caught flying fish:

The calm still persisted, and, as usual, fish began to abound, especially flying-fish. At times, disturbed by some hungry bonito or dolphin, a shoal of them would rise – a great wave of silver – and skim through the air, rising and falling for perhaps a couple of hundred yards before they again took to the water; or a solitary one of larger size than usual would suddenly soar into the air, a heavy splash behind him showing by how few inches he had missed the jaws of his pursuer. Away he would go in a long, long curve, and meeting the ship in his flight, would rise in the air, turn off at right angles to his former direction, and spin away again, the whirr of his wing-fins distinctly visible as well as audible. At last he would incline to the water, but just as he was about to enter it there would be an eddy – the enemy was there waiting – and he would rise twenty, thirty feet, almost perpendicularly, and dart away fully a hundred yards on a fresh course before the drying of his wing membranes compelled him to drop.

The weather continued calm and clear, and as the flying fish were about in such immense numbers, I ventured to suggest to Goliath that we might have a try for some of them. I verily believe he thought I was mad. He stared at me for a minute, and then, with an indescribable intonation, said, 'How de ol' Satan yew think yew gwane ter get'm – hey? Ef yew spects ter fool dis chile wiv any dem lime-juice yarns 'bout lanters 'n boats at night-time, yew's 'way off.' I guessed he meant the fable current among English sailors, that if you hoist a sail on a calm night in a boat where flying fish abound, and hang a lantern in the middle of it, the fish will fly in shoals at the lantern, strike against the sail, and fall in heaps in the boat. It *may* be true, but I never spoke to anybody who has seen it done, nor is it the method practised in the only place in the world where flying-fishing is followed for a living. So I told Mr Jones that if we had some circular nets of small mesh made and stretched on wooden hoops, I was sure we should be able to catch some. He caught at the idea and mentioned it to the mate, who readily gave his permission to use a boat. A couple of 'Guineamen' (a very large kind of flying-fish, having four wings) flew on board that night, as if purposely to provide us with the necessary bait.

Next morning, about four bells, the sea being like a mirror, unruffled by a breath of wind, we lowered and paddled off from the ship about a mile. When far enough away, we commenced operations by squeezing in the water some pieces of fish that had been kept for the purpose until they were rather high-flavoured. The exuding oil from this fish spread a thin film of some distance around the boat, through which, as through a sheet of glass, we could see a long way down. Minute specks of the bait sank slowly through the limpid blue, but for at least an hour there was no sign of life. I was beginning to fear that I should be called to account for misleading all hands when, to my unbounded delight, an immense shoal of flying-fish came swimming round the boat, eagerly picking up the savoury morsels. We grasped our nets, and, leaning over the gunwale, placed them silently in the water, pressing them downward and in towards the boat at the same time. Our success was great and immediate. We lifted the wanderers by scores, while I whispered imploringly, 'Be careful not to scare them; don't make a sound.' All hands entered into the spirit of the thing with great eagerness. As for Mistah Jones, his delight was almost more than he could bear. Suddenly one of the men, in lifting his net, slipped on the smooth bottom of the boat, jolting one of the oars. There was a gleam of light below as the school turned — they had all disappeared instanter.

5

Trade Winds and Variables

AFTER CROSSING the Line the clipper way continues due south through the south-east trade-wind belt for 1,200 miles. At first the ship is in a west-flowing current and later in a south-west one which averages from 12 to 24 miles per day. The route passes out of the trade-wind belt near the islands of South Trinidad and Martin Vaz. After that it begins curving south-eastwards through the Variables, a belt of variable winds from 600 to 1,000 miles wide. Here the ocean current, after curving southwards between South Trinidad and South America, is now flowing north-eastwards across the clipper path. As the clipper way passes near the Tristan Da Cunha group of islands it enters the zone of the westerly winds blowing right round the earth in the Roaring Forties and further southward.

The clippers seem to have had unadventurous voyages until south of Trinidad Island but Conor O'Brien in his yacht was following the clipper way and has a little to say about the south-east trade-wind belt:

*

If we had a complaint it was that the wind was too light. This was a better sun that passed day by day over the sky which brought up only a few small tongues of crimson and orange flame against the sunset, and a bar or two of purple to divide the sunrise from the waning moon, but by day or night was cloudless.

While we were in these light Trades all hands slept all night, and all hands worked all day, P. most virtuously, overhauling and drying out the stores; H. and myself principally with our pens. However, for the sake of the ship I rigged an electric bell so that the helmsman could call the watch below without leaving the wheel, and I cut an opening from the chart-room to the galley so that he could get his cocoa more safely than by carrying it across the deck; while H. made a weathercloth for the poop rail. But we were mightily relieved when, on the evening of the 10th September, we saw a little group of clouds, differing slightly from the other clouds that drift across the Trade Wind area, hanging stationary above the horizon on our lee bow; for under them lay the island of Trinidada, and south of Trinidada we might expect a change, for better or for worse, in the weather.

Observe my procedure that night. I was steering for the Channel between Trinidada and Martin Vaz. Now at sunset I had only seen the land clouds over the former, being, as I judged, about forty miles away. The latter, being low, I had not seen at all. It was an abominably dark night, I could see no horizon, and I only imagined that I could see a blacker patch of darkness to leeward than elsewhere. At midnight the islands should be abeam, for I had been cracking on in a moderate breeze of wind the better to ensure that no unsuspected current should set me out of my course. Was I carrying too much canvas? Was I risking getting dismasted somewhere near a lee shore which I could not see? Or was I giving that shore an excessive berth, to pile up on the lower islets that lie on the windward side of the channel? At last I saw a little spot of blackness for an instant on the weather beam; that was Martin Vaz, and it might have been five miles away or it might have been one. I went through that channel like a scared cat, with all the deep-water man's panic upon me; and, note, that channel is twenty-six miles wide, and I was in a small and handy fore-and-after. Thus does the ocean make a coward of one.

At sunrise the fantastic peaks of Trinidada stood out for a few minutes, clear of their customary clouds, now far astern of us. There was a singular romance about these tiny outposts of earth pushed a thousand miles into the waters, barren masses of volcanic rock, once milestones on the long colonial passage (the clipper way) but now rarely seen by human eye: Penhedo de Sao Pedro (St Paul Rocks), Ilha da Santissima Trinidada, Tristan Da Cunha, Amsterdam (an uninhabited island between South Africa and Australia). We missed the first, here was the second, and our next objective was the third.

If another indication than Trinidada were wanting to show that we were approaching a fresh stage of our journey, we saw for the first time on the same day an albatross.

On the 12th September we lost the Trades in lat. 22°S, and very soon our surroundings began to change. The increase in bird life was most conspicuous. The avifauna of the tropics is very poor; a few Bosun birds and a solitary gannet who had probably strayed north on a fishing excursion from Trinidada were all I noticed; but now albatrosses were seen by twos and threes, and Cape pigeons by scores. We had seen the last of the flying-fish, but bonitos and dolphins were still with us, feeding, I suppose, on something else which I did not see and could not catch; their beat was shared by an occasional whale and innumerable porpoises; all in increasing numbers as we drew to the southward.

*

The character of the ocean changes as the clipper way curves south-eastward until the Roaring Forties are reached, when the ship heads nearly due east and begins running down its easting to Australia.

Being in a little ship, Conor O'Brien called at Cape Town and therefore headed east before reaching the Roaring Forties. However, he describes well the changing character of the ocean:

*

Dark mountain ranges, their lower slopes netted with the tracery of spindrift, reared snowy crests against the sky; from them jutted sharp-cut spurs, which, growing with incredible rapidity, exploded against the bulwarks and discharged a salvo of spray into the belly of the sails. The ship, her jib-boom sweeping the water already mottled by the fountain thrown by her cutwater, rose on the steep face of the advancing swell and drowned the lighter patter of the drops torn from its summits with the shrieking in the rigging of the now unimpeded wind; then with a great crash the sea spread out under her in a boiling sheet of white. On this, or, as it seemed, suspended over this, and uncontrolled by contact with the firm support of the waters, she flew for a long space, then gradually settled down on the streaked back of the roller; the singing of the wind in the stays dropped to a low murmur, and in an uncanny quiet she shook herself and prepared for the next onset. So hour after hour the rhythm goes on, a hissing, rattling, shrieking crash; and then the bubbling of foam; a hypnotic influence. H. said that I was asleep when he relieved me at the wheel, but I do not believe that was literally true.

I have very frequently been asked whether my sails, which on a day like this would be little more than twenty feet above the water level, were not becalmed between the seas. What I have described in the last paragraph certainly gave the illusion of being becalmed; but it was, I imagine, only an illusion, due to the fact that on the back of a wave one is undoubtedly moving slowly because one is sailing uphill, and that one is in smooth water after a very noisy and agitated few moments. It is physically impossible that the wind should be lighter on this, the windward, slope of the sea, where one might expect a calm would be close under the crest; but here, it seemed to me, probably because it was puffy, that it blew the hardest. In connexion with this I noticed one fact that surprised me very much, that there was always a smooth depression in the crest immediately astern of us (I was not using oil, it was just providence) and one might expect a strong wind to blow over that as it would over a mountain pass. But the fact that I lost no sails running in heavy weather proves that the puffs cannot have been very heavy or the soft spots very light.

We had now managed to get back to lat. 32°S, but in long. 4°W the wind left us again. Probably we should have been somewhere about the 40th parallel.

*

The clipper joins the Roaring Forties in the same longitude as Greenwich. The distance from Plymouth to this point is 6,500 miles. Conor O'Brien, calling at various ports along the route, took 108 days from Dublin to Cape Town, which is

950 miles to the ENE. For a clipper, it would have been reckoned a good passage from Plymouth to the Roaring Forties of 43 days. It is after this sort of period that scurvy will begin to take effect if it has not been guarded against.

6

The Dreaded Scurvy

SCURVY MAY be thought a disease which was cured and abolished 150–200 years ago; but this is not so. Many small-boat sailors develop mild scurvy without realising it.

Even that great ocean racer, Captain J. H. Illingworth, a naval officer who knew all about scurvy and its treatment in submarines, was caught out when sailing across the North Atlantic a few years ago. He had been living in the United States and then in Bermuda after racing there. A lot of the vegetables and food eaten there are tinned. As a naval officer he well knew about scurvy and was used to taking vitamin C and D pills to counteract it; but with only a short passage of a few weeks from Bermuda to Brixham facing him, and having plenty of fresh fruit on board for the first week, he thought there was no danger. A week out from Bermuda he recognised the symptoms of the dreaded scurvy – teeth becoming loose, boils and a very depressed state. Subsequently he lost a dozen of his teeth, so he was in a bad way. However, after reaching land, with his exceptionally tough physique he was off racing again to Spain after a week of the right food.

I think that Conor O'Brien had scurvy on board at the end of his voyage round the world. He himself could not see to read his sextant, and one of his crew thought himself about to die though he got well again as soon as he landed in Fayal. Also, whenever other members of his crew were damaged their wounds refused to heal or their swellings to go down, even after they had taken to their bunks.

Ann Davison was another ocean-crosser who, I think, had mild scurvy without realising it. She took vitamin pills but her diet seemed incredibly bad for a woman. In her story she mentions several scurvy symptoms.

I discussed scurvy with Doctor Gordon Latto, a dietic specialist and he emphatically states that raw food, such as raw carrots, apples, oranges, or any food such as that, are the best preventive. He mentioned that he had recently seen a baby suffering very badly from scurvy with bleeding from the mouth, bleeding under the skin, and swollen limbs; it had been fed on powdered milk and bottled orange juice. As soon as it was fed on raw juices, apple juice etc., in place of its previous diet, it recovered quickly.

The value of juice from raw food was demonstrated in a spectacular way in R. H. Dana's *Two Years Before the Mast.* Dana describes how, when the ship was 150 miles SSE of the Bermudas on the return voyage to New England, they were lucky to beg some potatoes and onions from a brigantine which they met.

*

It was just dinner-time when we filled away; and the steward, taking a few bunches of onions for the cabin, gave the rest to us with a bottle of vinegar. We carried them forward, stowed them away in the forecastle, refusing to have them cooked, and ate them raw, with our beef and bread. And a glorious treat they were. The freshness and crispness of the raw onion, with the earthy taste, gave it a great relish to one who has been a long time on salt provisions. We were perfectly ravenous after them. We ate them at every meal, by the dozen; and filled our pockets with them to eat in our watch on deck. The chief, however, of the fresh provisions was for the men with the scurvy. One of them was able to eat, and he soon brought himself to by gnawing upon raw potatoes; but the other, by this time, was hardly able to open his mouth; and the cook took the potatoes raw, pounded them in a mortar, and gave him the juice to drink. The strong earthy taste and smell of this extract of the raw potatoes at first produced a shuddering through his whole frame, and after drinking it, an acute pain, which ran through all parts of his body; but knowing by this that it was taking strong hold, he persevered, drinking a spoonful every hour or so, until by the effect of this drink, and of his own restored hope, he became so well as to be able to move about, and open his mouth enough to eat the raw potatoes and onions pounded into a soft pulp. This course soon restored his appetite and strength; and 10 days after we spoke to the *Solon* (the brigantine), so rapid was his recovery that, from lying helpless and almost hopeless in his berth, he was at the mast-head, furling a royal.

*

The worst story of scurvy that I know is that in the account of Anson's voyage round the world.

*

Soon after our passing Streights Le Maire, the scurvy began to make its appearance amongst us, and our long continuance at sea, the fatigue we underwent, and the various disappointments we met with, had occasioned its spreading to such a degree that at the latter end of April [1741] there were but few on board who were not in some degree afflicted with it, and in that month no less than forty-three died of it on board the *Centurion*. But though we thought that the distemper had then risen to an extraordinary height, and were willing to hope that as we advanced to the northward its malignity would abate, yet we found, on the contrary, that in the month of May we lost near double that number; and as we did not get to land till the middle of June, the mortality went on increasing, and the disease extended itself so prodigiously that, after the loss of above two hundred men, we could not at last muster more than six fore-mast men in a watch capable of duty.

This disease, so frequently attending long voyages, and so particularly destructive to us, is surely the most singular and unaccountable of any that affects the human body. Its symptoms are inconstant and innumerable, and its progress and effects extremely irregular; for scarcely any two persons have complaints exactly resembling each other, and where there hath been found some conformity in the symptoms, the order of their appearance has been totally different. However, though it frequently puts on the form of many other diseases, and is therefore not to be described by any exclusive and infallible criterions, yet there are some symptoms which are more general than the rest, and, occurring the oftenest, deserve a more particular enumeration. These common appearances are large discoloured spots dispersed over the whole surface of the body, swelled legs, putrid gums, and, above all, an extraordinary lassitude of the whole body, especially after any exercise, however inconsiderable; and this lassitude at last degenerates into a proneness to swoon, and even die, on the least exertion of strength, or even on the least motion.

This disease is likewise usually attended with a strange dejection of the spirits, and with shiverings, tremblings, and a disposition to be seized with the most dreadful terrors on the slightest accident. Indeed it was most remarkable, in all our reiterated experience of this malady, that whatever discouraged our people, or at any time damped their hopes, never failed to add new vigour to the distemper; for it usually killed those who were in the last stages of it, and confined those to their hammocks who were before capable of some kind of duty; so that it seemed as if alacrity of mind, and sanguine thoughts, were no contemptible preservatives from its fatal malignity.

But it is not easy to compleat the long roll of the various concomitants of this disease; for it often produced putrid fevers, pleurisies, the jaundice, and violent rheumatic pains, and sometimes it occasioned an obstinate costiveness, which was generally attended with a difficulty of breathing, and this was esteemed the most deadly of all the scorbutick symptoms; at other times the whole body, but more especially the legs, were subject to ulcers of the worst kind, attended with rotten bones, and such a luxuriancy of fungous flesh as yielded to no remedy. But a most extraordinary circumstance, and what would be scarcely credible upon any single evidence, is, that the scars of wounds which had been for many years healed were forced open again by this virulent distemper. Of this there was a remarkable instance in one of the invalids on board the *Centurion*, who had been wounded above fifty years before at the battle of the Boyne, for though he was cured soon after, and had continued well for a great number of years past, yet on his being attacked by the scurvy, his wounds, in the progress of his disease, broke out afresh, and appeared as if they had never been healed: nay, what is still more astonishing, the callus of a broken bone, which had been compleatly formed for a long time, was found to be hereby dissolved, and the fracture seemed as if it had never been consolidated. Indeed, the effects of this disease were in almost every instance wonderful; for many of our people, though confined to their hammocks, appeared to have no inconsiderable share of health, for they eat and drank heartily, were chearful, and talked with much seeming vigour, and with a loud strong tone of voice; and yet, on their being the least moved, though it was from only one part of the ship to the other, and that too in their hammocks, they have immediately expired; and others, who have confided in their seeming strength, and have resolved to get out of their hammocks, have died before they could well reach the deck; nor was it an uncommon thing for those who were able to walk the deck, and to do some kind of duty, to drop down dead in an instant, on any endeavours to act with their utmost effort, many of our people having perished in this manner during the course of this voyage.

With this terrible disease we struggled the greatest part of the time of our beating round Cape Horn; and though it did not then rage with its utmost violence, yet we buried no less than forty-three men on board the *Centurion* in the month of April, as hath been already observed.

*

Three of Anson's ships succeeded in reaching Juan Fernandes Island. They were the *Centurion*, the *Gloucester* and the *Tryall*. But by then, a year after leaving England, their combined crews of 961 were reduced to 335 after 626 had died chiefly through scurvy.

Laying in supplies of the right food to prevent scurvy for a short voyage of, say, up to a month seems simple; though it is probably a much easier operation for anyone who prefers vegetarian food, as I do. If I were going on a long voyage the length of an average clipper passage to Australia, 100 days, I would set relays of wheat grains to germinate and also grow a continuous crop of mustard and cress. After the fresh fruit and vegetables had come to an end, I feel confident that the wheat and cress should keep scurvy away.

Sailing ships before the nineteenth century appear to have had no idea of baking bread. I believe they considered that a 12 foot long brick baker's oven would be necessary for that. On my own Trans-Atlantic voyages I have carried a light camping oven made of tin which weighs only 5 pounds so that I could bake if necessary. When racing across to America in 1964, the wholemeal bread obtained in England lasted me for the 30 day crossing, but on the return journey the American bread did not last the voyage and I baked some of the wholemeal flour I had brought out from England. During the following winter this flour and dried yeast were stored in an unheated wooden shed and when I found them the following summer I baked more bread from them. The bread was delicious, and as both the flour and the yeast had been either on board the yacht or in a shed for 13 months there was no reason why the old sailing ships could not have carried flour on long voyages if it was stored correctly.

Captain James Cook was celebrated for the practical precautions he took against scurvy and he was regarded as the first seaman to prevent it. One of his greatest difficulties was to force his crew to accept anti-scorbutic food like scurvy grass as it was called. To encourage the others he finally had one of the crew flogged for refusing to eat his anti-scorbutic rations.

It appears that the first measures against scurvy were recommended by Dr James Lind of Haslar Hospital who was consulted by Captain Hugh Palliser in 1748. Palliser had been given the command of an expedition and wished to avoid the ghastly mortality of Anson's voyage. Broadly speaking Dr Lind recommended more fresh food and less salt meat. He said that a syrup from boiling lemons and oranges should be issued every day at sea. Lastly he stated that nothing was so important as lemon juice. It was not till 40 years after the publication of Lind's recommendations that the Admiralty issued a ration of lime juice to sailors, which unfortunately has not much anti-scorbutic value compared with lemon juice. The mistake arose because the West Indians called a lemon a lime. 170 years later ships are still carrying lime thinking it a good anti-scorbutic when they should be carrying lemon juice. Dr Lind's fresh vegetables would have been quite sufficient without lemon juice if only he could have persuaded the seamen to eat some of them raw. Cooking destroyed most of the anti-scorbutic vitamins.

Captain James Cook served under Palliser and almost certainly learned from him to take precautions against scurvy.

7

Speed

IT WAS while on passage through the Roaring Forties or Fifties from the Greenwich Meridian to Australia that the clippers made their fastest runs. They were built to stand up to a gale of wind [1] with a big area of sail set on their tall spars.

It is not easy to say which is the fastest sailing ship in the world. What is the yardstick to be? A run of an hour, a day, 6 days or a passage? For a sailing passage round the world I consider that a 6-day run is the best standard for comparison.

According to Basil Lubbock in *The Colonial Clippers*, the *Lightning* claimed the longest run for a day – 436 nautical miles – on her maiden voyage from Boston to Liverpool. Her captain and crew were Americans. I cannot be enthusiastic about this claim because she took 7 days to sail the next 345 miles. However, in March 1857, making a passage to Australia as a gold clipper (with a British crew), she sailed 790 miles in 2 days. To be exact, the period was only 46 hours 48 minutes because she lost 1 hour 12 minutes through the

1. During the last century and, in fact, until recently a Force 7 wind was rated a gale; that is, wind averaging between 28 and 33 knots at a height of 33 feet above sea level. Now nothing less than a Force 8 wind of 34–40 knots is rated a gale. This 34–40 knots is the average speed and this wind would probably be gusting up to 50 knots.

change of longitude while running down the easting. On one of these days her run was claimed to be 430 miles and I think that if this was correct it justified her claim to have made the fastest day's run of any sailing ship.

The *Lightning* was designed and built by Donald Mackay at Boston, USA. She had a registered tonnage of 1,468 tons, a length of 244 feet and a beam of 44 feet. She carried a big crew probably not less than 40. (Another Mackay ship, *The Sovereign of the Seas,* carried 105 crew on her maiden voyage.) Donald Mackay built a number of ships like the *Lightning* and they were all very fast. There were various reasons for this: such as broad beam and light construction, but they all add up to the fact that Mackay was a brilliant designer. The great characteristic of his ships was that they could carry full sail in a strong wind. Time after time their logs recorded passing another sailing ship which was reduced to double-reefed topsails while the Mackay-designed ship was running with all sail set including studding sails and a skysail. For this the ship needed stout spars and rigging and Mackay saw that it had them. For example, the *Lightning*'s lower rigging was hemp rope of 11½ inches circumference; in other words, the shrouds were approximately 4 inches in diameter. Her mainmast was 164 feet high with a mainyard of 95 feet across. She could set 54,000 square feet of sail. (An acre is 43,560 square feet. By comparison my yacht, *Gipsy Moth III*, of 9½ registered tons, could set 1,467 square feet when sailed single-handed. Ann Davison set 237 square feet.) The *Lightning* had a mainmast of 42 inches diameter which weighed 20 tons. Her planking was 5 inches thick. These ships were designed with a broad beam which helped them to stand up to a big area of sail. They were passenger-carrying ships with light loads of emigrants or diggers returning from the Australian gold-fields instead of dead-weight cargo. This would increase their speed. Also they were built of light American timber. These light woods were soft and because of this the American clippers did not last long.

In Lloyd's calendar of 1960 which gives a list of record sailing voyages it is stated that an even faster day's run was made in 1854 by *The Champion of the Seas,* which was then the biggest sailing ship of the world. She too was a Donald Mackay designed ship. This claim is based on a copy of the ship's gazette discovered a few years ago in Australia. According to this the *Champion of the Seas* made a run of 465 miles on December 12th, 1854, while running down her easting to Australia. I think this is a bogus claim for the following reasons:

1. Surely such an amazing day's run of 465 miles which was 29 miles more than the *Lightning*'s extreme claim, would have resounded all over the world.

2. On examining the daily runs for the whole of the week of the 12th December, I note that on the previous three days, the 9th, 10th and 11th December, the total distance run amounted to 808 miles. The next day's run was said to be 465 miles. The following day, the 13th, is marked 'no observations' and no mileage was given. Why was this? Was the captain not streaming a log and could he not give a distance run by the log or by dead reckoning? On the next day, the 14th, the distance run is given as 341 miles. Therefore the total distance run during the 12th, 13th and 14th amounted to 806 miles; which is exactly the same distance as was run during the previous three days. I think the observation on the 12th must have been a faulty one and that the ship is more likely to have run 300 miles that day instead of 465; 265 the following day instead of nothing; and 241 miles the third day instead of 341.

3. I discussed these speeds with Alan Villiers who is today the chief authority on full-rigged ships. He points out that seamen thought it odd that the big claims for record days' runs went out with the passing of the profitable sailing ship passenger business. It was a most valuable asset to achieve a record day's run; immigrants rushed to book a passage in that ship.

The day's run was decided by an astro-navigation fix, that is to say by observations of the sun or moon etc. with a sextant. The captain was the only navigator on board or at least the only man who took any sights. Some of these captains must have been bad navigators, judging by the number of ships which were wrecked due to faulty fixes. Certainly the value of a sun position line was not understood then as it is today, the instruments were not so accurate and there was no help to be obtained from radio beacons.

Although I have made thousands of observations with a sextant and am most interested in the art of astro-navigation, having written several text books on it, yet in 1964, while sailing across the Atlantic in *Gipsy Moth III*, all the sun observations I made during one day of the voyage were grossly erratic, up to 90 miles in error. I checked and rechecked all my working and the instruments used but could find no fault with any of them. Next day my results were again normal with the order of accuracy I usually expect which is such that it will enable me to check the course and speed of the ocean current by comparison with the day's dead reckoning. I think the only possible explanation of those errors was that a long ocean swell, due to a distant storm or hurricane, was underrunning the rough surface sea due to local conditions. It can be difficult to detect this swell if the surface is rough.

I remember an instance of this in 1931 when I was flying over the Tasman Sea between New Zealand and Australia in my *Gipsy Moth* seaplane. Having no blind flying instruments I was forced to fly a few feet above the surface so as to have a visible horizon to fly by in the rough weather. Suddenly I looked up and found the sea ahead was above the aeroplane. I was in the trough of a long big ocean swell and looking at the crest of a swell ahead. The art of using a sextant depends chiefly on being able to select a good horizon. This is usually a distant horizon; it is important not to use the crest of a nearby wave. Sometimes it is necessary to wait for more than five minutes before a usable horizon can be observed from a small yacht. If a half-mile-long 30-feet swell is running, the crest of a swell will be 30 feet above the trough so that if one takes the crest for the horizon when in the trough it will be 30 feet too high 1,500 feet away; the observed sun's elevation will be four fifths of a degree too small which will put the ship's position 50 miles in error. These conditions of a long, big swell underrunning the local sea must be expected in the Southern Ocean and I think a clipper navigator would need to be most careful never to make a serious error in his fix.

Finally, if this great sailing ship of 2,700 tons could make a run of 465 miles in a day, surely one could expect it to make a fast passage from Liverpool to Melbourne. Yet the *Champion of the Seas* does not feature among the twelve fastest passage-makers between Britain and Australia listed in Lloyd's Calendar. It was the British built *Thermopylae* of 950 tons which made the two fastest passages; yet she never claimed a day's run exceeding 375 miles.

As far as I know, the fastest ship in the world for a 6 days' run was the *Cutty Sark*. In 1876 she ran 2,163 miles in 6 days when sailing through the Roaring Forties on a passage from the English Channel to Sydney. In 1893 she ran 2,180 nautical miles in 6 days. I do not know of any sailing ship which has ever beaten either of these two runs. They were all the more remarkable because the *Cutty Sark* was only of 960 registered tons compared with the *Lightning*'s 1,468. The *Cutty Sark* was 224 feet long with a beam of 36 feet. She was built of fine, hard timber and can be seen 100 years after she was built lying in a dry dock at Greenwich near the National Maritime Museum.

The fastest passage from Britain to Australia was made by the *Thermopylae* in 1868–9 of 61 days from port to port, London to Melbourne. The sailing route distance would be about 13,150 miles – 600 miles less than to Sydney. The average speed was therefore 215 miles per day. It is difficult to decide the facts; according to Basil Lubbock in Lloyd's Calendar of 1960 the *Thermopylae*'s passage was 60 days, pilot to pilot. In his book, *The China Clippers*, he says the passage was of 63 days, port to port, and in another of his books, *The Colonial Clippers*, he gives the passage as 61 days, port to port. She made an equally fast passage in 1870–1. Fortunately, for the sake of avoiding controversy, any of these times was the fastest passage ever made.

The *Thermopylae*'s fastest passage from London to Sydney was 75 days, an average speed of 188 mpd, and her slowest 109 days at 129 mpd. Her fastest passage home from Sydney to London was 77 days, 15,100 miles at 196 mpd, and her slowest 105 days to the Lizard at 140 mpd.

The *Cutty Sark*'s passages out to Sydney varied between 72

and 82 days from the Lizard and between 84 and 94 days home.

The *Lightning* held the record for the passage from Melbourne to Liverpool. Her time from Port Phillip Heads, Melbourne, to the Mersey, Liverpool, in 1854–5 was 64 days 21 hours 10 minutes for a sailing route distance of 13,880 miles. This included a record passage from Melbourne to Cape Horn of 19 days 1 hour. Lubbock wrote in his book that the *Lightning*'s captain, Bully Forbes, carried on in a most daring manner, and on the ship's arrival at Liverpool her passengers told weird stories of his keeping his station at the break of the poop with a pistol in each hand in order to prevent his scared crew from letting go of the royal halyards. This, of course, is a nonsensical passenger's tale, but this was one of the few voyages on which a Mackay ship lost some spars. On August 28th, a violent squall carried away the fore-topmast stunsail boom and the fore-topmast, while three sails, the fore-royal, the fore-topgallant sail and the fore-topsail were blown out at the same time. Her total time for circumnavigating the globe on this occasion, including 20 days spent in port in Australia, was only 5 months, 8 days, 21 hours. She brought back a million pounds' worth of gold dust (at the 1854 valuation).

It is interesting to compare these speeds with the passages of small boats which have sailed along the route. In 1942–3 Vito Dumas in *Lehg II* circumnavigated the globe from Montevideo back to Montevideo in 1 year 9 days, a distance of 20,420 miles, compared with the 28,500 miles of the clipper route. Dumas, however, was sailing his yacht single-handed. Dumas' passage of 7,400 miles from Cape Town to Wellington, New Zealand, is the longest that has been made by a singlehanded yacht. Taking 104 days, his average speed was 71 mpd; and from Wellington to Valparaiso, 5,650 miles, he averaged 78½ mpd. I suppose that the registered tonnage of this Argentine boat, which had a keel of 3½ tons, would be 8 tons. It was a small boat with a waterline length of 29½ feet and an overall length of 31 feet.

Another man who circled the world singlehanded, Nance, an Australian, averaged 121 mpd for the 6,500-mile passage from Auckland to Buenos Aires, a great speed for a boat of only 21½ feet waterline and 3·4 tons registered tonnage. This is the second longest singlehanded passage that I know of. During this voyage in 1965 he beat a record which has stood for 70 years. After leaving Auckland, he sailed 2,000 miles in 13 days, an average speed of 154 mpd. This is the fastest solo passage of 1,200 miles or more that has been made since July 1895, when Joshua Slocum sailed 1,200 miles in 8 days on a west to east crossing of the Atlantic. The length of Nance's circumnavigation from Buenos Aires back to Buenos Aires and keeping between the latitudes of 35°S and 56°S – most of the time in the Roaring Forties as was Dumas' passage – was 17,500 miles according to his own reckoning.

Nance's yacht, *Cardinal Vertue*, had previously belonged to Doctor David Lewis who raced it across the Atlantic in the first singlehanded race of 1960. This race was east to west against the prevailing current and wind and along the Great Circle Route which is described in the Admiralty Chart of sailing routes as 'seldom possible' for sailing ships, meaning square-rigged ships. In that race *Cardinal Vertue* took 54 days for the 3,000 mile passage, an average 68 mpd. To illustrate how much faster it is to sail with the prevailing wind and current instead of against it, my yacht *Gipsy Moth III* averaged 100 mpd across the Atlantic east to west in the 1964 solo race, whereas on the return journey of 3,200 miles from Newport, RI, USA, to the Lizard she averaged 126 mpd. On the homeward passage I was not sailing her singlehanded; I had my son, Giles, on board as crew.

Conor O'Brien's *Saoirse* is the yacht which has come nearest to following the clipper way round the world. *Saoirse* kept just north of the Roaring Forties between South Africa and Australia – too far north, in my opinion, if he were seeking a fast passage – and his time of 56 days from Durban to Melbourne averaged 103 mpd for the 5,775-mile passage. This was with a crew of 4 in a yacht of 37 feet on the waterline and 9½ registered net tonnage. His passage from Auckland, New Zealand, round the Horn to the Falkland Islands took 43 days, an average of 125 mpd for the 5,500 miles. *Saoirse*, unlike the clippers which sailed non-stop to their Australian destination, called at a number of ports – Madeira, Canary Isles, Cape Verde Isles, Pernambuco, Cape Town, Durban – on the way to Australia, and at Auckland, the Falkland Islands, Pernambuco and Fayal in the Azores on the way home. His circumnavigation took 2 years. It was an outstanding voyage.

How do these ships and yachts compare in speed with modern racing yachts? In 1965 eleven offshore races of the Royal Ocean Racing Club totalled 3,133 miles round Britain and in the Bay of Biscay, an average of 285 miles per race. The average number of yachts entered in class II – the class in which my yacht, *Gipsy Moth III*, belongs – was 26 yachts per race. All these yachts were, of course, equipped with full racing crews and five of the eleven races were won by yachts belonging to one of the international teams picked for the Admirals Cup Race – that is to say, they were one of the three crack offshore racing yachts chosen to represent their country that year. It seems to me that this racing is equivalent to dividing a passage across the North Atlantic into eleven stages, with a fortnight's break between stages, and taking the fastest time of 26 yachts competing in each stage. In 1965 the winners averaged 126 mpd. In 1962 the winners of twelve similar RORC races averaged 107½ mpd. I think the increase in speed in 1965 is due to the competition of eight nations for the Admirals Cup then.

The theoretical maximum speed of a ship is dependent on the waterline length; it is, to be exact, equal in knots to 1⅓ multiplied by the square root of the waterline length in feet. This means that a clipper of 250 feet length on the waterline has a maximum theoretical speed of 21 knots or 504 mpd, compared with *Cardinal Vertue*'s theoretical maximum with a 21½ foot waterline, of 6⅙ knots or 148 mpd. It is rarely that a ship can be sailed at its maximum speed for a day or more. A calm, or even a drop in wind strength, greatly reduces the average speed for the day. Nance's achievement in averaging 154 mpd for 13 days is therefore all the more remarkable, even if a favourable current of 10–20 mpd is allowed for.

Some people think that because the maximum speed is a

function of the waterline length, it is only necessary to have a longer boat to go faster. If this were true then a singlehander would only need to own a boat the size of the *Cutty Sark* in order to win any singlehanded race, which is an obvious absurdity showing up the fallacy. The small boat sailed skilfully and efficiently by its skipper will beat a large boat which cannot be trimmed for changes of wind strength and wind direction, however much bigger the large boat may be.

The reason why a boat's theoretical maximum speed is a function of the waterline length is as follows: a ship creates a bow wave as it moves through the water. The length from the crest of the bow wave to the crest of the next wave lengthens as the speed increases. If a ship exceeds its theoretical maximum speed, the wave length is so long that the ship is climbing up the bow wave at a steep angle. This requires so much more driving force from the sails than does sailing level that in practice it is difficult if not impossible to achieve. The longer the boat the longer the wave length of the bow wave can be and the faster the speed can be before the boat begins climbing uphill.

After 1875 the new sailing ships seemed to get gradually, year by year, slower and make longer passages. After that date most of the passsages to Australia were taking more than 90 days, and by the end of the century about half the passages were 100 days or more.

One of the last races from Australia to the English Channel was in 1927 by seventeen big sailing ships with wheat cargoes. These ships had small crews compared with the passenger clippers and they were mostly crews of young fellows of twenty. The fastest, the *Herzogin Cecilie*, took 88 days and the slowest, the *Olivebank*, 167 days. Eight of them took more than 130 days and one was dismasted.

One of the slowest passages ever recorded must surely be that of the *Garthwray*. Alan Villiers writes about her in *Falmouth for Orders*:

*

Garthwray was a full-rigged ship of 1,937 tons, built at

Workington in 1889, and she always carried, like most of the old British sailors, a few apprentices. Some time in July 1922 she left the Firth of Forth with a cargo of coal for Iquique, in Chile. At the end of 1923 she was still on the way to Iquique. First she tried to round the Horn from east to west, but the Horn was exceptionally vicious that year and the end of a long battle saw her running back to Montevideo for repairs. She was five months out when she reached that port. A second time she set out; a second time she battled with the howling westerlies of the Horn in a vain attempt to get around. The loss of a tops'l-yard convinced the skipper at last of the fruitlessness of his efforts. He swore no vain oaths, but put up his helm and set the old ship before the wind to run around the world and make the Chilean coast from the other side. On the way from the Horn to Good Hope she again fell foul of the elements, to such an extent this time that, over a year out from Scotland, she had to put into Table Bay to refit. But that did not end the voyage. She was bound to Iquique, and she had to get there. So she set out again, and in the long run she did come to Iquique, after being something like 559 days on the voyage and sailing something like 30,000 miles. Clearing Iquique to load at Talcahuano for the homeward voyage, *Garthwray* struck headwinds and then ran into a fog that lasted three days. Groping blindly in that fog, she ran her bones ashore on Santa Maria Island, off Concepcion harbour and that was the end of her.

*

Alan also tells an amusing story of the *Garthneill*. In 1919 *Garthneill* was in Melbourne and she wanted to sail in ballast to Bunbury in West Australia, 2,000 sailing miles away (the shortest possible sailing route would have been 1,625 miles), to pick up a cargo of railway-sleepers. She left Melbourne on July 6th, 1919, but could not make any headway against the westerly gales and turned up on July 29th at Sydney in distress. Alan writes:

*

It was not until Thursday, August 14th, that she put to sea

again. This time it was intended, apparently, to attempt the passage around the north of Australia, through Torres Straits, but the wind would not allow that. All that it would do was to howl from the west, which it did with remarkable consistency and violence. So *Garthneill*'s Old Man decided that as the wind persisted in blowing from the west, the only thing that he could do was to make the best of a bad job and run before it. That was what he did, with such success that the little barque passed the Three Kings, off the northern end of New Zealand, on the fifth day out, and came to Cape Horn in thirty-three days. Twenty days later she was past the Cape of Good Hope – fifty-three days out from Sydney – and she ran across from the longitude of Cape Town to Bunbury in twenty-three days. The weather was very bad most of the way, with heavy gales, ice on the rigging, fog, and snow, and *Garthneill* had to be hove-to a good many times on that voyage. A tops'l-sheet carried away once and there was the devil to pay. In the end, very rusty and looking a bit the worst for wear, *Garthneill* sailed out of the list of the ships that were posted overdue and came into Bunbury, seventy-six days out from Sydney via Cape Hope and the Horn. It was a remarkable passage.

8

Ice and Storms

As soon as the clippers reached the Roaring Forties[1] and crossed the Greenwich Meridian there they were within the iceberg zone. There is a line on the hydrographic pilot charts of the South Atlantic ocean which marks the extreme limit of icebergs; they had sailed south of this line. The shortest distance from this meridian to, say, Sydney, was the Great

1. Vito Dumas says that the Roaring Forties got their name from the peculiar roaring noise which the strong winds made when blowing over the huge seas built up by gales and a long fetch of several thousand miles.

Circle between them. On a globe this is the shortest distance between the two points and can be represented by a piece of string stretched tautly between them. Unfortunately, it passes within 1,200 miles of the South Pole which is an impossible route because of the solid Antarctic continent there. However, if a ship could sail a Great Circle course down to the parallel of latitude 60°S and then up along another Great Circle course to Sydney, the passage would be roughly 1,000 miles shorter than if it sailed along the 40th parallel of latitude. Besides the southerly route being shorter it would be certain to provide stronger winds, probably gales for most of the way; and these big, heavily sparred clippers thrived on gales. Therefore the clipper captains steered as far south as they could or as they dared. Nearly every ship was out to make a fast passage if not to set up a record. The ship with the reputation for speed got the best of the passenger trade and carried most gold dust or wool. The gold clippers had big crews and they kept a good look-out port and starboard forward as well as from the mast and the poop. Curiously, ice was not feared as much along the clipper route as it was on the Grand Banks off Newfoundland in the North Atlantic. When I asked a Cape Horner why this was, he asserted that, 'You could smell ice ahead in the southern ocean well in advance, whereas the bergs on the Grand Banks gave no warning.' If they were right in their feelings, I suppose the only reason could be that down south a berg would be travelling downwind in the same direction as the ships. Therefore it would leave a trail of cold water behind it which might warn an oncoming ship; whereas on the Banks a berg would be travelling southwards, across the prevailing westerly wind and would not cool the water to leeward of it (nor, of course, the water to windward of it).

Any ship going down to 60°S would be up to 800 miles within the iceberg zone for 5,000 miles of the passage. Here is Joseph Conrad writing on the subject in his *The Mirror of the Sea*, a book of personal experiences and impressions. Conrad was a professional sailor of full-rigged ships, who served his time from boy to captain.

*

The unholy fascination of dread dwells in the thought of the last moments of a ship reported as 'missing' in the columns of the *Shipping Gazette*. Nothing of her ever comes to light – no grating, no lifebuoy, no piece of boat or branded oar – to give a hint of the place and date of her sudden end. The *Shipping Gazette* does not even call her 'lost with all hands'. She remains simply 'missing'; she has disappeared enigmatically into a mystery of fate as big as the world, where your imagination of a brother-sailor, of a fellow-servant and lover of ships, may range unchecked.

And yet sometimes one gets a hint of what the last scene may be like in the life of a ship and her crew, which resembles a drama in its struggle against the great force bearing it up, formless, ungraspable, chaotic and mysterious, as fate.

It was on a grey afternoon in the lull of a three days gale that had left the Southern Ocean tumbling heavily upon our ship, under a sky hung with rags of clouds that seemed to have been cut and hacked by the keen edge of a sou'-west gale.

Our craft, a Clyde-built barque of 1,000 tons, rolled so heavily that something aloft had carried away. No matter what the damage was, it was serious enough to induce me to go aloft myself with a couple of hands and the carpenter to see the temporary repairs properly done.

Sometimes we had to drop everything and cling with both hands to the swaying spars, holding our breath in fear of a terribly heavy roll. And, wallowing as if she meant to turn over with us, the barque, her decks full of water, her gear flying in bights, ran at some ten knots an hour. We had been driven far south – much farther that way than we had meant to go; and suddenly, up there in the slings of the foreyard, in the midst of our work, I felt my shoulder gripped with such force in the carpenter's powerful paw that I positively yelled with unexpected pain. The man's eyes stared close in my face, and he shouted, 'Look, sir! Look! What's this?' Pointing ahead with his other hand.

At first I saw nothing. The sea was one empty wilderness of black and white hills. Suddenly, half concealed in the tumult of the foaming rollers I made out awash, something enormous, rising and falling – something spread out like a burst of foam, but with a more bluish, more solid look.

It was a piece of an ice-floe melted down to a fragment, but still big enough to sink a ship, and floating lower than any raft, right in our way, as if ambushed among the waves with murderous intent. There was no time to get down on deck. I shouted from aloft till my head was ready to split. I was heard aft, and we managed to clear the sunken floe which had come all the way from the Southern ice-cap to have a try at our unsuspecting lives. Had it been an hour later, nothing could have saved the ship, for no eye could have made out in the dusk that pale piece of ice swept over by the white-crested waves.

And as we stood near the taffrail side by side, my captain and I, looking at it, hardly discernible already, but still quite close-to on our quarter, he remarked in a meditative tone:

'But for the turn of that wheel just in time, there would have been another case of a "missing" ship.'

Nobody ever comes back from a 'missing' ship to tell how hard was the death of the craft, and how sudden and overwhelming the last anguish of her men. Nobody can say with what thoughts, with what regrets, with what words on their lips they died. But there is something fine in the sudden passing away of these hearts from the extremity of struggle and stress and tremendous uproar – from the vast, unrestful rage of the surface to the profound peace of the depths, sleeping untroubled since the beginning of ages.

*

Some amazingly romantic stories have been left behind after the gold clipper era. How sailing ships would be staggering along through the huge southern seas with sail shortened to double-reefed topsails while one of Mackay's ships would slide past carrying full sail with studding sails as well in the gale and how, sometimes, if it was evening, the passengers would be dancing on the poop. There is another story of how the bosun was over the side of the ship on a cradle painting the stem while the ship was running in a gale. At least two of the gold clipper captains, the British Bully Forbes and the American Bully Waterman, were said to padlock their sheets (ropes controlling the corners of the square sails) so that sail could not be reduced and to overawe their terrified crew from the break of the poop with a pair of levelled revolvers. It makes a good story and there may have been good foundation for it but crack racing helmsmen of today do not like to cleat up the sheets even in 16-foot dinghies.

There are three notorious Capes in the world which were always treated with the greatest respect, if not fear, by the square-rigged sailors; Cape of Good Hope, always known as the Cape, Cape Leeuwin (the SW Cape of Australia) and Cape Horn.

Basil Lubbock tells the story of a famous sailing ship which nearly came to grief off the Cape on her maiden voyage. This was the *Loch Torridon* rated one of the most successful sailing ships of the nineteenth century. This story makes one wonder, however, how much is due to the ship and how much to the captain.

The *Loch Torridon* was a 4-masted barque of 2,000 tons burden, built in 1881. She was square-rigged except for a large fore-and-aft spanker set on the mizzen. Her mainmast was 152 feet from deck to truck and her mainyard 88 feet long. Captain Pattman who commanded her for 26 years after her maiden voyage said that, 'being perfectly sparred, the ship is easy to steer, and even in the worst weather the smallest boy on board can keep her on her course'.

Now I come to her maiden voyage. She sailed out to Hobson's Bay (Melbourne) from Glasgow in 105 days. She returned home westwards round the Cape and on the 9th October ran into a heavy WNW gale. The captain hove her to on the starboard tack, then, after a while, decided to wear her round on to the port tack (i.e. turn downwind), but the increasing gale heeded her over until her starboard rail was under water.

Basil Lubbock gives this account: "Thereupon Captain Pinder decided to wear her back on to the starboard tack. The mate besought him not to do this without setting the foresail, but unfortunately, having been lucky once, the captain insisted, with the result that when she got off before the wind she had not enough way on her and a tremendous sea came roaring over the stern and carried overboard the master, second mate, man at the wheel, sailmaker and a boy, all being drowned. The mate also was swept away but was saved by a hitch of the mainbrace getting round his leg. On the following day the weather moderated, and the men brought the ship home to Plymouth.'

The *Loch Torridon* was a fast ship; for instance, she ran out to Sydney in 1898 in 72 days 15 hours with 5,000 tons of cargo. She had an adventure with ice which I shall refer to in another chapter. She met her end in the English Channel in 1915 when she was torpedoed by a German submarine. Once she ran 2,119 miles in 7 days.

Fortunately for Conor O'Brien, he avoided running into a bad storm of this sort when he left South Africa for Melbourne. He writes:

*

I kept on within a few miles either side of the 37th parallel until the 4th January, 1924, when I went a little farther south to look for Amsterdam Island. I did not go there only to shoot wild cattle, or to look at the view, or to rescue castaways, or because I had a sentimental affection for the last milestone on the road to the Antipodes; I went primarily to check the rate of my chronometer. It seems rather ridiculous to divide a run of only fifty days into two periods of twenty-five for this purpose, but I had been told so often that a chronometer would not keep its rate in a small boat that I had regarded mine with suspicion; and since I had only one of them I had no means of telling whether it was going properly except by confirming the positions of islands and the like or by observing lunar distances. And when it comes to working lunars, as I did before making the land at the Cape, I think they suffer from the violent motion a great deal more than any chronometer.

That morning was not recommended for astronomical observations; it was thick with rain, and the ghost of the sun which rarely appeared was little use in the virtual absence of any horizon. However, the weather was not so thick nor the wind and sea so high at the time that I was afraid of hitting the island by daylight, and as I ought to see it early in the afternoon I sailed straight for it. I do not usually like to run downwind towards any land in thick weather, but I knew this particular land was quite small, quite round, and quite clear of danger. I had hardly realized the existence of Amsterdam Island till I got to Durban, when a friend to whom I was talking at the ship-chandlers said, for my benefit, I presume, that there was a store of provisions and clothing for shipwrecked mariners there. On my asking for further information the ship-chandler produced, to my astonishment, a whole drawerful of charts of Amsterdam and St Paul's Island; large-scale things that showed every stone and hotspring of them and were surrounded with pretty pictures. When I expressed my astonishment, he said so many vessels were lost between the Cape and Australia that anyone who found himself reasonably near the Islands called there for castaways, and he sold them the charts so that they should know where to look for distress signals and landing places.

St Paul's is the more interesting in the pictures; it is a breached volcanic crater with a bottomless lake in the middle, into which one can pull a boat, and any amount of hotsprings. But the only livestock appear to be penguins; anyway it was seventy miles farther south than I was going. Amsterdam is also a volcano, but quite extinct, and of the convex kind; it has no harbours, but is said to abound with cattle and cabbages.

At noon I was, according to my reckoning, thirty miles from the island, and approaching it at the rate of six and a half knots. At twenty minutes past one I saw, high up in the sky above the smother along the water, a streak of black becoming more defined and lenticular in shape; then the right-hand point was cut off by a patch of light which, advancing with a clear-cut vertical front, rapidly swallowed up the remainder, but before the last of the dark wedge had vanished, hung a little speck of black in front of it. What I had seen was obviously the upper part of a cliff in profile with the top of a rocky pinnacle standing near it, but I had not the least idea how far off it was.

There are few people who, if told while at sea to look for the top of a hill two thousand feet high, will look for it in anything like the right direction. Personally I always look somewhere near the horizon, and every time I wonder afresh how the thing gets such an absurd distance up in the air. I get so much accustomed to limiting my view to a few minutes of arc above the visible horizon, that is the water, wherever it may be, for to me on my low deck a very ordinary sea will encroach on many degrees of sky, and yet I have no difficulty in seeing the top of it. I can only guess roughly, for I had no opportunity of measuring the thing, that what I saw might have been 100 feet of cliff 5 miles away, or 400 feet 20 miles away, as improbable extremes; or anything in between. There was not evidence enough here to convict a dollar watch of perjury, let alone a very reputable chronometer. So I had failed in my primary object. It was also obvious that I was going to fail to see any view, or to shoot any cattle, and one can sentimentalize over the ideal far better than over the visible image of a milestone. It was my duty, however, if I could rediscover the island to look for castaways; and I therefore carried on, though the weather was getting thicker and the wind and sea no less. I went up and sat on the foreyard for a couple of hours – you gentlemen that perch precariously on cross-trees do not know how comfortable it is to have a nice substantial foresail sticking out in front of you to keep your legs from dangling – for the first thing I should see would probably be the surf along the shore, and though as the visibility had now decreased to about a mile, as I should guess, and the surf could be seen as soon from the deck, only from aloft could one tell at all the trend of the coast, or which way to steer to go clear of it. But either my helmsman was careless, or, as is more probable, I had set an unnecessarily wide course, for I never saw the land again; and to tell the truth, as the weather was getting thicker all the time, and it was impossible that the castaways should have seen me, I was very glad to miss it. Of course the next day was gloriously fine; this, and that day the previous week that we had spent hove-to, were the only really bad days of the whole passage.

Here I saw a dead penguin floating in the water, a thing,

you will say, that might happen to any penguin and was hardly worth comment. But it puzzled me that he should be floating there in this hungry southern ocean, and not inside the stomach of an albatross. For albatrosses eat salt beef, bread and jam, and raw potatoes, therefore why not penguins? And penguins are eaten by skua gulls and by seals, therefore why not by albatrosses? I looked over the stern to see if our albatross would be diverted from the very meagre contents of the slush-bucket to a tasty piece of fresh meat; and lo, our albatross was not there. That one I knew by the fact that he had three white feathers in a line on his port wing, and four in a diamond on his starboard, and he had followed us for 600 miles. He may have felt tired, though it is said that these birds sleep while on the wing; or he may have had an establishment on Amsterdam Island, and turned aside on urgent private affairs; but why were there no others in his place? Can it be that albatrosses do not eat penguins; and if so, what do they eat? They cannot dive after fish, they will not take a slice of bread if you hold it a foot above the water, and the amount of food which is to be found actually floating is negligible. Yet they are big birds and must take a lot of feeding. And the same question might be asked, and I cannot suggest an answer, in the case of all the larger gulls; very small birds like Mother Carey's Chickens no doubt can live on the minute organisms which inhabit the top layer of the sea, but one cannot imagine an albatross subsisting on plankton.

Last week's run had come to 982 miles, and it looked as if I had really at last struck the right conditions for pulling up our deplorable average from Durban; but not yet. Even here in 37½° S I had a day of calms, and logged 55 miles only, but in the evening a little breeze from the NNE, which is the best wind for making passages, sprang up. From noon of the 7th January the ship began to get her favourite weather, a moderate beam wind with a smooth sea. . . . But in the evening [of January 11th] the wind began to blow and we began to reef, and in spite of all the ship began to go more slowly and could not do any better than 145 miles by noon of the 12th. The wind was backing towards the north-west.

The barometer was falling more and more rapidly, and it

was clear that the depression which had been gradually overtaking us for the last six days had arrived. We could not go any faster, to keep ahead of it; if I had tried to set any more sail I should only have lost it, for a gale was blowing. Either the trough of the storm was moving irregularly, or it had well developed secondaries attached, for after a night from the south-west the wind ran back to the north-west next morning, gale force, and making a very rough sea of it. It was time to look out for squalls, so I took in the mainsail and kept my eyes open; and sure enough before long the wind flew back to the south-west and began blowing very hard. I was not at all prepared for what I saw. That wind just tore blocks out of the long ridges of the north-westerly sea, piled Pelion on Ossa and the resulting pyramid on top of the huge south-westerly swell that runs without ceasing round the Southern Ocean, often unnoticed, but rising in an instant at the touch of its normal wind; and the result was stupendous. I do not suppose it very often happened that all three sets of waves climbed up each other's backs, but it happened once within a ship's length of me. Of course the elevation of 40 feet, as I judged it to be, was quite momentary; the pile was entirely top-heavy and the upper 10 feet or so curled over as clean as if it had tripped up on a reef and tumbled all over the ocean. You need not believe it, but that is what it looked like. Where then was the storm-oil? In the forepeak, and it would have taken dangerously long to get it out. Where then was the sea-anchor? In a mess; at least the gear was; it would have taken impossibly long to clear it. Why then did I not heave-to? Well, we did not make that sea break, and if it wanted to break over us it would do so quite irrespective of which end on we lay to it, or whether we were sailing or stopped, and that would be the end of the story either way; so I thought I would make all speed out of that dangerous locality, and carried on in the direction of Australia at the very surprising speed – seeing that we generally do so poorly in a gale – of 7½ knots. The wind blew so hard that by noon it had flattened all the irregularities off the true swell, which was now immensely big, but long and easy. I put down 170 miles in the log and hoped for another day as good on the morrow.

But I was disappointed. The wind became lighter and the sea more irregular again, and the day's run was no more than 153 miles; this making 1,130 for the week, an average of 6.8 knots, allowing that the week was an hour and a half short on account of the change of longitude. It was considerably the best week's run I ever did, and rather unexpectedly so, seeing that it included three days of gales. I sometimes wonder whether it was because these were the best helmsmen I ever had.

The boy especially, because he had never steered by compass in his life, learned very soon to judge his course from the breath of the wind on his neck, and to balance himself in such a way that he unconsciously anticipated each swing of the ship's head from her heave and roll. Or perhaps the seas were not really as bad as I thought they were; always excepting that portentous breaker. That did me a lot of harm; it lost my best helmsman for me, for when it came along the boy was not in his bunk or in the galley, but had come on deck to look at the pretty view – in the Southern Hemisphere it is the south-west wind that clears up the weather – and he saw that breaker and swore he would never go to sea no more.

*

Conor O'Brien was lucky that he did not run into a cyclone like the whaler *Cachalot* experienced in the Indian Ocean. Although it was 2,000 miles north of the clipper way I am quoting Frank Bullen's account of it because it is one of the best descriptions of a real storm.

*

Hitherto, with the exception of a couple of gales in the North and South Atlantic, we had been singularly fortunate in our weather. It does happen so sometimes.

I remember once making a round voyage from Cardiff to Hong Kong and the Philippines, back to London, in ten months, and during the whole of that time we did not have a downright gale. The worst weather we encountered was between Beachy Head and Portland, going round from London to Cardiff.

But now a change was evidently imminent. Of course, we forward had no access to the barometer; not that we should have understood its indications if we had seen it, but we all knew that something was going to be radically wrong with the weather. For instead of the lovely blue of the sky we had been so long accustomed to by day and night, a nasty, greasy shade had come over the heavens, which, reflected in the sea, made that look dirty and stale also. That well-known appearance of the waves before a storm was also very marked, which consists of an undecided sort of break in their tops. Instead of running regularly, they seemed to hunch themselves up in little heaps, and throw off a tiny flutter of spray, which generally fell in the opposite direction to what little wind there was. The pigs and fowls felt the approaching change keenly, and manifested the greatest uneasiness, leaving their food and acting strangely. We were making scarcely any headway, so that the storm was longer making its appearance than it would have been had we been a swift clipper ship running down the Indian Ocean. For two days we were kept in suspense; but on the second night the gloom began to deepen, the wind to moan, and a very uncomfortable 'jobble' of a sea got up. Extra 'gaskets' were put upon the sails, and everything movable about the decks was made as secure as it could be. Only the two close-reefed topsails and two storm stay-sails were carried, so that we were in excellent trim for fighting the bad weather when it did come. The sky gradually darkened and assumed a livid green tint, the effect of which was most peculiar.

The wind blew fitfully in short gusts, veering continually back and forth over about a quarter of the compass. Although it was still light, it kept up an incessant mournful moan not to be accounted for in any way. Darker and darker grew the heavens, although no clouds were visible, only a general pall of darkness. Glimmering lightnings played continually about the eastern horizon, but not brilliant enough to show us the approaching storm-cloud. And so came the morning of the third day from the beginning of the change. But for the clock we should hardly have known that day had broken, so gloomy and dark was the sky. At last light came in the east, but such a light as no one would wish to see. It was a lurid glare, such as may be seen playing over a cupola of Bessemer steel when the spiegeleisen is added, only on such an extensive scale that its brilliancy was dulled into horror. Then, beneath it we saw the mountainous clouds fringed with dull violet and with jagged sabres of lightning darting from their solid black bosoms. The wind began to rise steadily but rapidly, so that by eight am it was blowing a furious gale from ENE. In direction it was still unsteady, the ship coming up and falling off to it several points. Now, great masses of torn, ragged cloud hurtled past us above, so low down as almost to touch the mast-heads. Still the wind increased, still the sea rose, till at last the skipper judged it well to haul down the tiny triangle of storm stay-sail still set (the topsail and fore stay-sail had been furled long before), and let her drift under bare poles, except for three square feet of stout canvas in the weather mizen-rigging. The roar of the wind now dominated every sound, so that it might have been thundering furiously, but we should not have heard it. The ship still maintained her splendid character as a sea-boat, hardly shipping a drop of water; but she lay over at a most distressing angle, her deck sloping off fully thirty-five to forty degrees. Fortunately she did not roll to windward. It may have been raining in perfect torrents, but the tempest tore off the surface of the sea, and sent it in massive sheets continually flying over us, so that we could not possibly have distinguished between fresh water and salt.

The chief anxiety was for the safety of the boats. Early on the second day of warning they had been hoisted to the topmost notch of the cranes, and secured as thoroughly as experience could suggest; but at every lee lurch we gave it seemed as if we must dip them under water, while the wind threatened to stave the weather ones in by its actual solid weight. It was now blowing a furious cyclone, the force of which has never been accurately gauged (even by the present elaborate instruments of various kinds in use). That force is, however, not to be imagined by any one who has not witnessed it...

The terrible day wore on, without any lightening of the tempest, till noon, when the wind suddenly fell to a calm.

Until that time the sea, although heavy, was not vicious or irregular, and we had not shipped any heavy water at all. But when the force of the wind was suddenly withdrawn, such a sea arose as I have never seen before or since. Inky mountains of water raised their savage heads in wildest confusion, smashing one another in whirlpools of foam. It was like a picture of the primeval deep out of which arose the new-born world. Suddenly out of the whirling blackness overhead the moon appeared, nearly in the zenith, sending down through the apex of a dome of torn and madly gyrating cloud a flood of brilliant light. Illumined by that startling radiance, our staunch and seaworthy ship was tossed and twirled in the hideous vortex of mad sea until her motion was distracting. It was quite impossible to loose one's hold and attempt to do anything without running the imminent risk of being dashed to pieces. Our decks were full of water now, for it tumbled on board at all points; but as yet no serious weight of a sea had fallen upon us, nor had any damage been done. Such a miracle as that could not be expected to continue for long. Suddenly a warning shout rang out from somewhere – 'Hold on all, for your lives!' Out of the hideous turmoil around arose, like some black, fantastic ruin, an awful heap of water. Higher and higher it towered, until it was level with our lower yards, then it broke and fell upon us. All was blank. Beneath that mass every thought, every feeling, fled but one – 'How long shall I be able to hold my breath?' After what seemed a never-ending time, we emerged from the wave more dead than alive, but with the good ship still staunch underneath us, and Hope's lamp burning brightly. The moon had been momentarily obscured, but now shone out again, lighting up brilliantly our bravely-battling ship. But, alas for others! – men, like ourselves, whose hopes were gone. Quite near us was the battered remainder of what had been a splendid ship. Her masts were gone, not even the stumps being visible, and it seemed to our eager eyes as if she was settling down. It was even so, for as we looked, unmindful of our own danger, she quietly disappeared – swallowed up with her human freight in a moment, like a pebble being dropped into a pond.

While we looked with hardly beating hearts at the place

where she had sunk, all was blotted out in thick darkness again. With a roar, as of a thousand thunders, the tempest came once more, but from the opposite direction now. As we were under no sail, we ran little risk of being caught aback; but, even had we, nothing could have been done, the vessel being utterly out of control, besides the impossibility of getting about. It so happened, however, that when the storm burst upon us again, we were stern on to it, and we drove steadily for a few moments until we had time to haul to the wind again. Great heavens! how it blew! Surely, I thought, this cannot last long – just as we sometimes say of the rain when it is extra heavy. It did last, however, for what seemed an interminable time, although any one could see that the sky was getting kindlier. Gradually, imperceptibly, it took off, the sky cleared, and the tumult ceased, until a new day broke in untellable beauty over a revivified world.

Years afterwards I read, in one of the hand-books treating of hurricanes and cyclones, that 'in the centre of these revolving storms the sea is so violent that few ships can pass through it and live.' That is true talk. I have been there, and bear witness that but for the build and sea-kindliness of the *Cachalot*, she could not have come out of that horrible cauldron again, but would have joined that nameless unfortunate whom we saw succumb. 'Never again heard of.' As it was, we found two of the boats stove in, whether by breaking sea or crushing wind nobody knows. Most of the planking of the bulwarks was also gone, burst outward by the weight of the water on deck. Only the normal quantity of water was found in the well on sounding, and not even the rope yarn was gone from aloft. Altogether, we came out of the ordeal triumphantly, where many a gallant vessel met her fate, and the behaviour of the grand old tub gave me a positive affection for her, such as I have never felt for a ship before or since.

*

Another story of a ship in a storm makes one consider what is the best design of vessel for avoiding serious damage in such a situation. It is reprinted in Basil Lubbock's book from the Melbourne *Argus*. In spite of journalistic over-emphasis infecting some of the sentences, the true story shines through:

*

The *Loch Vennachar* left Glasgow bound for Melbourne on 6th April 1892, with a crew of 33 all told and 12 passengers, 4 of whom were ladies. All went well with the ship until she reached latitude 39° 25′ S, longitude 27° 21′ E, when at eight o'clock on the evening of 3rd June the barometer began to fall ominously and sail was promptly shortened. Darkness lifted soon after five o'clock in the morning and break of day showed the terrific head seas that swept down upon the vessel, lashed by the north-east gale. (At this time both watches were aloft fighting to make the foresail fast.) Captain Bennett, who was on the poop, saw the danger of his crew and at once resolved to sacrifice the sail. He sang out to the mate to send the men aft and the hands, who had been lying out on the pitching foreyard, gained the deck in safety and reached the poop in time. As they did so, two enormous waves bore down upon the ship, which rode slowly over the first, and sank to an interminable depth in the trough at the other side. Whilst in this position, the second wave came on towering half-way up the foremast, and broke on board, filling the lower topsail 60 feet above the deck, as it came.

Hundreds of tons of water swept over the ship in a solid mass from stem to stern, thundering inboard on the port side of the foc's'le and racing away over the main deck and over the poop, where most of the crew were standing. Every man on the poop was thrown down, and when they regained their feet they perceived that the foremast and mainmast were over the side, and the mizzen topmast above their heads had disappeared. Not a man on board actually saw the spars go or heard the crash of the breaking rigging, so violent was the shock and so fierce the howling of the hurricane. The cook was washed out of his galley and swept overboard, the galley being completely gutted of everything it contained.

*

Thanks to the captain and crew this ship eventually reached

her destination. Incidentally, this ship seems to have been an unlucky one. Nine years later, when anchored, she was run down and sunk by a steamer. She was raised and repaired. Four years later she disappeared. An item of her cargo was found and it was decided that she had gone on the rocks near Kangaroo Island, near Adelaide.

Even the staunch little *Cutty Sark* was pooped in 1884 when she was making one of her regularly excellent fast passages of under 80 days. She was running her easting down when she was pooped by a big sea which jammed the helmsmen in the wheel, so that she came up in the wind and swept her decks clean, taking the boats off the afterskids, breaking in one side of the monkey poop and gutting the cabin. This was not a serious happening, but it is interesting to visit the *Cutty Sark* at Greenwich and see the actual deck, cabin, etc., where this took place.

I know of only 3 yachts which have sailed along this section of the clipper way from Meridian, as the clipper sailors called the Greenwich Meridian in the Roaring Forties, to Australia, but I am sure there must be others. These three are *Saoirse* and the two singlehanders, Dumas in *Lehg II* and Nance in *Cardinal Vertue*. I doubt whether *Cardinal Vertue* is a suitable yacht for sailing in these rough waters down south and I am sure that Nance was a brave man. *Cardinal Vertue* had previously lost the top of her mast in the Solo Trans-Atlantic Race of 1960. Fortunately for David Lewis who then owned her, this occurred just outside Plymouth after the start of the race and he was able to put back and have it repaired with the loss of only 2 days. This was the only case I know of where a yacht which has been dismasted has finished third in a race. When Lewis was sailing her back across the Atlantic after the race he was lucky to escape broaching to and capsizing in rough weather. On Nance's passage from Cape Town to Australia *Cardinal Vertue* had her mast broken above the first set of crosstrees and Nance was swept overboard when trying to recover the top of the mast. He was able to hold on to the rigging in the water and pull himself back on deck. This was near St Paul's Island about 50 miles south of Amsterdam Island and more than half-way between South

Africa and Australia. With a jury rig he sailed 1,900 miles on to Fremantle in south-western Australia in 36 days. After repairs he set sail again and, while rounding Cape Leeuwin, running under a staysail, a big sea crashed over the stern, bent the self-steering vane and damaged the yacht. Seven frames or ribs were cracked, also a deck beam and several planks in the bow. Nance stayed at the helm for two days until finally, overcome by fatigue, he handed all sail and left *Cardinal Vertue* lying a-hull under bare poles while he had a sleep. He was in his bunk when *Cardinal Vertue* capsized. The main boom was lost and the mainsail lashed to it. Later when Nance was again forced below for some sleep, the boat was knocked down onto her beam-ends, the cabin hatch was smashed and a lot of water came aboard. He made port again at Albany, Western Australia under a headsail and a trysail. After that he continued his voyage to Melbourne. His troubles on his voyage round the globe were over, and later he rounded Cape Horn with no incident or difficulty whatever; which was fortunate, because the high doghouse and long coach-roof of *Vertue* would be most vulnerable to the rough seas of a real Cape Horner. He had started from Buenos Aires in December 1962 and reached it again on the 22nd January 1964, just over 2 years later.

The Argentinian, Vito Dumas, in *Lehg II*, made the passage from Cape Town to Wellington, 7,400 miles in 104 days at an average speed of 71 mpd, without any trouble or incident except that he complained, after passing the meridian of Cape Leeuwin, that he was beginning to suffer from scurvy.
He writes in his book:

*

I was beginning to worry over the fresh water question; what I had left was getting dark and muddy and it was dwindling. My gums were painful; and that is the first symptom of scurvy. I knew well how this disease, which in former times would plough terrible gaps in a crew, begins with ulceration of the gums and skin, loosening of the teeth and softening of scar tissue. Common contributory factors are prolonged cold, damp, bad or insufficient food, but especially the lack of fresh vegetables. It usually appears after sixty days at sea; I had done sixty-five. Had I not been careful to dose myself with vitamin C throughout the voyage I might never have made any port at all. And in spite of my precautions the first symptoms had appeared.

*

He also records that during that night a cachalot (sperm whale) nearly 50 feet long made a couple of passes at *Lehg II*.

9

Mammals against Molluscs

THE SPERM whales live almost entirely on squid (molluscs) which they hunt on the ocean bed at incredible depths. From what Frank Bullen wrote one gets a good idea of how many sperm whales there must be in the world and, consequently, of how many squid there must be to feed them:

For the first time, I realized how numerous those gigantic denizens of the sea really are. As far as the eye could reach, extending all round one half of the horizon, the sea appeared to be alive with spouts – all sperm whales, all bulls of great size. Subsequent experience satisfied me that such a sight was by no means uncommon here; in fact, 'lone whales' or small 'pods' were quite the exception.

*

I was discussing this with Doctor Brian Grundy who used to sail with me as racing crew in *Gipsy Moth II*, and who spent a season in the Antarctic as doctor on a whaler factory ship. I suggested that now the sperm whale is nearly exterminated, the number of squid would increase to a terrifying extent if they were not cannibals. Brian said, however, that he had seen just as many whales at one time as Bullen described.

Bullen once had the unique experience of watching a large sperm whale and a squid fighting it out. This was in the north of the Indian Ocean near Sumatra, but it could have happened on the clipper way:

*

At about 11.00 pm I was leaning over the lee rail, gazing steadily at the bright surface of the sea, where the intense radiance of the tropical moon made a broad path like a pavement of burnished silver. Eyes that saw not, mind only confusedly conscious of my surroundings, were mine; but suddenly I started to my feet with an exclamation, and stared with all my might at the strangest sight I ever saw. There was a violent commotion in the sea right where the moon's rays were concentrated, so great that, remembering our position, I was at first inclined to alarm all hands; for I had often heard of volcanic islands suddenly lifting their heads from the depths below, or disappearing in a moment, and I felt doubtful indeed of what was now happening. Getting the night-glasses out of the cabin scuttle, where they were always hung in readiness, I focussed them on the troubled spot, perfectly satisfied by a short examination that neither volcano nor earthquake had anything to do with what was going on; yet so vast were the forces engaged that I might well have been excused for my first supposition. A very large sperm whale was locked in deadly conflict with a cuttle-fish, or squid, almost as large as himself, whose interminable tentacles seemed to enlace the whole of his body. The head of the whale especially seemed a perfect network of writhing arms – naturally, I suppose, for it appeared as if the whale had the tail part of the mollusc in his jaws and, in a businesslike, methodical way, was sawing through it. By the side of the black columnar head of the whale appeared the head of the great squid, as awful an object as one could well imagine even in a fevered dream. Judging as carefully as possible, I estimated it to be at least as large as one of our pipes, which contain 350 gallons; but it may have been, and probably was, a good deal larger. The eyes were very remarkable for their size and blackness, which, contrasted with the livid whiteness of the head, made their appearance all the more striking. They were, at least, a foot in diameter, and, seen under such conditions, looked decidedly eerie and hobgoblin-like. All around the combatants were numerous sharks, like jackals round a lion, ready to share the feast, and apparently assisting in the destruction of the great cephalopod. So the titanic struggle went on, in perfect silence as far as we were concerned, because, even had there been any noise, our distance from the scene of conflict would not have permitted us to hear it.

The conflict ceased, the sea resumed its placid calm, and nothing remained to tell of the fight but a strong odour of fish, as of a bank of seaweed left by the tide in the blazing sun. Eight bells struck, and I went below to a troubled sleep, wherein all the awful monsters that an over-excited brain could conjure up pursued me through the gloomy caves of ocean, or mocked my pigmy efforts to escape.

The occasions upon which these gigantic cuttle-fish appear at the sea surface must, I think, be very rare. From their construction, they appear fitted only to grope among the rocks at the bottom of the ocean. Their mode of progression is backward, by the forcible ejection of a jet of water from an orifice in the neck beside the rectum or cloaca. Consequently their normal position is head downward, and with tentacles spread out like the ribs of an umbrella – eight of them at least; the two long ones, like the antennae of an insect, rove unceasingly around, seeking prey.

The imagination can hardly picture a more terrible object than one of these huge monsters brooding in the ocean depths, the gloom of his surroundings increased by the inky fluid (sepia) which he secretes in copious quantities, every cup-shaped disc, of the hundreds with which the restless tentacles are furnished, ready at the slightest touch to grip whatever is near, not only by suction, but by the great claws set all round within its circle. And in the centre of this network of living traps is the chasm-like mouth, with its enormous parrot-like beak, ready to rend piecemeal whatever is held by the tentaculae. The very thought of it makes one's flesh crawl. Well did Michelet term them 'the insatiable nightmares of the sea.'

Yet, but for them how would such great creatures as the sperm whale be fed? Unable, from their bulk, to capture small fish except by accident and, by the absence of a sieve of baleen, precluded from subsisting upon the tiny crustacea which support the Mysticetae, the cachalots seem to be confined for their diet to cuttle-fish, and, from their point of view, the bigger the latter are the better. How big they may become in the depths of the sea, no man knoweth; but it is unlikely that even the vast specimens seen are full-sized, since they have only come to the surface under abnormal conditions, like the one I have attempted to describe, who had evidently been dragged up by his relentless foe.

*

The story of this fight between the whale and the squid makes one wonder how big giant squid grow. Sperm whales throw up the contents of their stomach when they are dying and Bullen once found a 'tentacle or arm as thick as a stout man's body, and with six or seven sucking discs on it. These were about as large as a saucer, and on their inner edge were thickly set with hooks or claws all round the rim, sharp as needles, and almost the shape and size of a tiger's.' Frank Lane, in his interesting book, *Kingdom of the Octopus*, says that according to Bullen's description this piece of squid belonged to an unknown kind. There must be many unknown squid, because already two different species have been found in the stomach of whales which have not been identified anywhere else. A squid caught off the coast of Ireland had arms 8 feet in length which were 5 inches in diameter at the base. It had tentacles 30 feet long. Bullen's piece as thick as a stout man's body would be 12 inches in diameter; it would have come from a very big squid indeed. Bullen also recorded that he had seen a squid with a body of 60 feet long. As the tentacles of the so-called giant squid which have been found are about eight times as long as the body, that squid of Bullen's could have been a huge creature, perhaps its tentacles could have spanned 360 feet. Scientists have been sceptical and critical of Bullen's statements, but Bullen was a whaler who hunted whales from an open ship's boat and was therefore close to them when they were dying so that he could see what they threw up. He was an extremely astute and keen observer of nature and I do not think he has been proved wrong in many of his other statements; why therefore should he be wrong about squid?

Is a squid dangerous to ships or men? It is well known that a sperm whale will attack a ship. Lane quotes in his book: 'The most famous sinking occurred on November 20th, 1820, when the 238-ton whale ship *Essex* was twice rammed by a huge sperm whale which afflicted such damage that she sank. This was the tragedy – most of the crew never reached land – that prompted Herman Melville to end his novel with the whale sinking the ship.'

Will a squid attack a ship? Lane quotes this account:

*

In *Naturen* (published by the Bergen Museum in Norway) for December 1946 there appeared one of the most remarkable reports about cephalopods that I have read. It was by Commander Arne Groenningsaeter of the Royal Norwegian Navy. In correspondence he has kindly given me further details which did not appear in his original report. I have included some of these in what follows.

When Groenningsaeter was Executive Officer of the 15,000-ton tanker *Brunswick*, she was attacked on three occasions during the years 1930-33 by giant squids, each time between Hawaii and Samoa in the South Pacific. Each attack occurred during the day in good light. On each occasion Groenningsaeter was on the bridge, about 50 feet above sea-level, and was able to see clearly what happened. He estimated that the length of the squids as they moved through the water was 30 feet or more. As the tentacles would then be partly retracted the squids' over-all length was probably about 60 feet.

Each attack followed the same pattern. The squid surfaced abaft the ship on the port side and rapidly overhauled her. Groenningsaeter tells me that the *Brunswick*'s speed was 12 knots, so the squid's speed was probably more than 20 miles per hour. The squid swam parallel to the ship until it nearly reached the bow, then turned in to attack, hitting the ship a third of her length from the stern. Groenningsaeter says: 'It certainly gave us a very determined thud as it hit us full speed.'

When the first attack occurred Groenningsaeter thought the animal was a sea serpent because 'it left behind a thick trail of ink during its run up, and this trail seemed to be one with the animal in the fresh trade wind sea. Its speed was so great that this inky water stayed behind and, with the choppy and rippled sea, it was difficult to distinguish, looking like a long snake. Only the fact that I was standing so high up on the steady bridge of a 15,000-tonner made it possible for me to see the whole manoeuvre. If it had been observed from a sailing ship's poop at about 15 feet it could easily have been mistaken for a sea serpent.'

As the squid slid alongside giant tentacles, 'equivalent to an 8 to 10 inch pipeline,' reared up, apparently trying to reach the main deck, but as the squid had struck the ship just ahead of the aft superstructure they could not stretch far enough. (It is possible that the writhing of the arms and tentacles was because the squid was wounded.) The squid could get no hold on the ship's smooth plates and slid to the stern, where it was churned to death by the propeller.

Groenningsaeter believes that the squids attacked because they mistook the ship for a sperm whale. He points out that in each attack the squid struck the ship at a point – a third of her length from the stern – which, in a sperm whale, would be equivalent to a position just behind the 'hump'. 'It was the fact that the squid was *overtaking* the ship which made this method of attack unusual. Otherwise I do not think that a collision between a ship and a marine animal was worth while reporting.'

It is, of course, generally believed that it is the sperm whale which attacks squids, but if Groenningsaeter's explanation of the attacks on the *Brunswick* is accepted, it would appear that sometimes it is the squid which attacks. The Russian teuthologist, Igor Akimushkin, tells me that when he was on the Kuril Islands in the North-West Pacific he investigated the stomach contents of some 700 sperm whales, but in none of them did he find any remains of very large squids. But the bodies of many of these whales bore fresh traces of struggles with such squids. Were these marks left by the squids 'that got away', or were they received by the whales after attacks by squids on the Groenningsaeter pattern? A squid would, of course, stand virtually no chance of killing an adult cachalot.

*

Lane also quotes an account from *The Times* of July 4th, 1874; but says that he does not know if the report is authentic.

*

A SUCCESSOR TO THE SEA SERPENT. – The following strange story has been communicated to the Indian papers: 'We had left Colombo in the steamer *Strathowen*, had rounded Galle, and were well in the bay, with our course laid for Madras, steaming over a calm and tranquil sea. About an hour before sunset on the 10th of May we saw on our starboard beam and about two miles off a small schooner lying becalmed. There was nothing in her appearance or position to excite remark, but as we came up with her I lazily examined her with my binocular, and then noticed between us, but nearer her, a long, low, swelling lying on the sea, which from its colour and shape I took to be a bank of seaweed. As I watched, the mass, hitherto at rest on the quiet sea, was set in motion. It struck the schooner, which visibly reeled, and then righted. Immediately afterwards the masts swayed sideways, and with my glass I could clearly discern the enormous mass and the hull of the schooner coalescing – I can think of no other term. Judging from their exclamations, the other gazers must have witnessed the same appearance. Almost immediately after the collision and coalescence the schooner's masts swayed towards us, lower and lower; the vessel was on her beam-ends, lay there a few seconds, and disappeared, the masts righting as she sank, and the main exhibiting a reversed ensign struggling towards its peak. A cry of horror rose from the lookers-on, and, as if by instinct, our ship's head was at once turned towards the scene, which was now marked by the forms of those battling for life – the sole survivors of the pretty little schooner which only 20 minutes before floated bravely on the smooth sea. As soon as the poor fellows were able to tell their story they astounded us with the assertion that their vessel had been submerged by a gigantic cuttle-fish or calamary, the animal which, in a smaller form, attracts so much attention in the Brighton Aquarium as the octopus. Each narrator had his version of the story, but in the main all the narratives tallied so remarkably as to leave no doubt of the fact. As soon as he was at leisure, I prevailed on the skipper to give me his written account of the disaster, and I have now much pleasure in sending you a copy of his narrative: "I was lately the skipper of the *Pearl* schooner, 150 tons, as tight a little craft as ever sailed the seas, with a crew of six men. We were bound from the Mauritius for Rangoon in ballast to return with paddy, and had put in at Galle for water. Three days out we fell becalmed in the bay (latitude 8.50 N, longiture 84 5 E). [This is about 600 miles from Car Nicobar where Bullen saw the fight between a giant squid and a sperm whale.] On the 10th of May, about 5 pm, – eight bells I know had gone, – we sighted a two-masted screw on our port quarter, about five or six miles off; very soon after, as we lay motionless, a great mass rose slowly out of the sea about half a mile off on our larboard side, and remained spread out, as it were, and stationary; it looked like the back of a huge whale, but it sloped less, and was of a brownish colour; even at that distance it seemed much longer than our craft, and it seemed to be basking in the sun. 'What's that?' I sung out to the mate. 'Blest if I knows; barring its size, colour, and shape, it might be a whale,' replied Tom Scott: 'and it ain't the sea sarpent,' said one of the crew, 'for he's too round for that ere crittur.' I went into the cabin for my rifle, and as I was preparing to fire, Bill Darling, a Newfoundlander, came on deck, and, looking at the monster, exclaimed, putting up his hand, 'Have a care, master; that ere is a squid, and will capsize us if you hurt him.' Smiling at the idea, I let fly and hit him, and with that he shook; there was a great ripple all round him, and he began to move. 'Out with all your axes and knives,' shouted Bill, 'and cut any part of him that comes aboard; look alive, and Lord help us!' Not aware of the danger, and never having seen or heard of such a monster, I gave no orders, and it was no use touching the helm or ropes to get out of the way. By this time three of the crew, Bill included, had found axes, and one a rusty cutlass, and all were looking over the ship's side at the advancing monster. We could now see a huge oblong mass moving by jerks just under the surface of the water, and an enormous train following; the oblong body was at least half the size of our vessel in length and just as thick; the wake or train might have been 100 feet long. In the time that I have taken to write this the brute struck us, and the ship quivered under the thud; in another moment, monstrous arms like trees seized the vessel and she heeled over; in another second the monster was aboard, squeezed in between the two masts, Bill screaming 'Slash for your lives'; but all our slashing was of no avail, for the brute, holding on by his arms, slipped his vast body overboard, and pulled the vessel down with him on her beam-ends; we were thrown into the water at once, and just as I went over I caught sight of one of the crew, either Bill or Tom Fielding, squashed up between the masts and one of those awful arms; for a few seconds our ship lay on her beam-ends, then filled and went down; another of the crew must have been sucked down, for you only picked up five; the rest you know. I can't tell who ran up the ensign. – JAMES FLOYD, late master, schooner *Pearl*."' – *Homeward Mail*. [This means the story was sent to London by a homeward-bound mail vessel.]

I have tried hard but unsuccessfully to find confirmation of this incident – from Lloyd's, the National Maritime Museum, the General Register of Shipping and Seamen, shipping lines and other likely sources. The reliability of the account must, therefore, be judged by internal evidence alone.

The opening of *The Times*' report indicates that the story was well-known in India. Where did it come from? Men and ships are named, date and time are given, the position is pin-pointed to minutes of latitude and longitude, and circumstantial accounts of the incident are recorded from both the onlooker's and the victim's points of view. If it were all fiction – and there seems no alternative to a complete hoax if the story is untrue – how did the hoaxer persuade newspapers to publish the baseless story? Evidently the Editor of *The Times* was satisfied it was not a hoax.

I sent a copy of *The Times*' report to Commander Groenningsaeter, the only man I know who has witnessed such an incident, and he replied that the 'method of attack' on the *Pearl* seemed to be identical to that on his own ship. He suggests that the *Pearl* may 'have had a very low stability being in ballast and with sails up. Its ballast may have shifted.'

Groenningsaeter's suggestion may explain why the squid, although so much lighter than the *Pearl* and without having a solid object to give it purchase, was able to capsize it. These two facts, the great disparity in weight and lack of support, are probably the strongest arguments against the authenticity of the report.

The Times' account shows evidence of being written by eyewitnesses. The appearance of the animal as it lay on the surface; the jerky movement as the squid propelled itself by jets from its funnel; the trailing arms ('the wake or train'); and the use of the word coalescing ('I can think of no other term') when the squid swarmed over the schooner – that is just the word to describe such an action – all these are exactly right, and indicate that the reports came from people who were describing what they actually saw.

To me, however, the most convincing evidence of authenticity is the casual remark that the man who warned the master of the *Pearl* not to molest the squid was a Newfoundlander. As the preceding pages have shown, at the time of this incident the one place in the world where men were most likely to know about large squids, and their ferocity if attacked, was Newfoundland.

Information travelled much more slowly then than now, and it is unlikely that Moses Harvey's accounts of two squids, which had been written only some six months before, would be common knowledge in India at the time of the alleged sinking of the *Pearl*. Moreover, at that time, May 1874, nobody knew that Newfoundland was to become famous during the next few years for its stranded giant squids. The most reasonable explanation seems to be that the account was a report of an actual incident, including the presence on the

Pearl, of a man from the one place where, at that time, giant squids and their behaviour were reasonably well-known.

It was all so long ago that the truth may never be known, but it is at least possible that on that calm summer evening in the Bay of Bengal the schooner *Pearl* was sunk by a gigantic kraken.

*

Will a squid attack man? Lane quotes one case where fishermen struck the first blow; and another where the squid with no provocation attacked men on a becalmed ship:

*

On October 26th, 1873, two fishermen, Theophilus Piccot and Daniel Squires, and Piccot's twelve-year-old son, Tom, were fishing for herring off Portugal Cove, Newfoundland. They saw a large object floating on the surface and, thinking it was a piece of wreckage, rowed over to it. One of the men struck it with a boat-hook. Instantly the supposedly dead mass reared up, and the fishermen saw what they had attacked – a kraken.

With its huge eyes flashing, the animal lunged towards them and struck the gunwhale with its horny beak. A long thin tentacle shot out and instantly coiled round the boat. A shorter but thicker arm followed, and held it fast. The body of the kraken sank beneath the surface, and began to drag the boat with it.

The fishermen were almost paralysed with fear. Water was pouring into the boat as it settled in the water and they thought it was only a matter of seconds before they would all drown. But if the men were resigned to die young Tom Piccot was not. He picked up a small tomahawk from the bottom of the boat and smashed at the arm and tentacle. He severed them just in time. The boat righted itself but the kraken was still alongside. It discharged pints of ink which darkened the water all round them. But it did not renew the fight. The beast's huge bulk seemed to slide off and disappear. The last the men saw of it were the huge fins at the end of its body which, they said, measured six or seven feet.

Fearing pursuit, the fishermen rowed for the shore with all their strength.

*

The boy still had the part of the tentacle which he had cut off and this was found to be 19 feet long with a circumference of $3\frac{1}{2}$ inches.

In this second case the squid was definitely the attacker, but Lane says that Denys de Montfort, who recorded the story, was not a trustworthy naturalist.

*

Denys de Montfort recounts the story of Capt. Jean Magnus Dens of Dunkirk. While crossing the Atlantic his ship was becalmed, and the crew started to scrape and paint her.

'The men were standing on stages suspended near the water's edge, scraping with iron scrapers, when suddenly a huge cuttlefish [squid] appeared and, throwing one of his arms about two of the men, tore the unfortunates, with their stage, from the side of the vessel and dragged them into the water. At the same time it threw another arm about a man who was just mounting the main rigging; but here its arm became entangled with the shrouds and ratlines, and it was unable to disentangle itself. The man, who was being severely squeezed, cried out for help, and the crew immediately ran to his assistance. Several threw harpoons into the body of the beast, which was now rising along the ship's side; others with axes cut in pieces the arm which held the man to the rigging and took the unfortunate down on deck.

'This done, the cuttle sank down, but the captain payed out on the lines which were fast to the harpoons, in the hope that presently he would be able to drag the beast up again and recover the two men who had been dragged down. In fact, at first he was able to drag the animal toward the surface; but presently the huge beast again sank down, and they were obliged to pay out line after line, till at last, having but a little left, they were forced to hold on; and now four of the harpoons drew out, while the fifth line broke, and thus all hope of saving the unfortunates or killing the monster was lost.'

Bartsch quotes this story with apparent approval and Lee

(1875) says: 'I believe the old sea-captain's narrative of the incident to be true.'

*

Lane's book, *Kingdom of the Octopus*, is a scientific work, the life history of the Cephalopoda. In it he deals thoroughly with all the known species of these creatures and includes a chapter on the poison sacs which some of them have and the way in which they inject it into their victims. The chapter from which these accounts come was titled 'KRAKEN', and I assume the author does not regard it as part of the scientific content of the book.

For my part, I believe these stories though I think that there is some exaggeration of details here and there.

I admit I do not like the thought of giant squid and on a calm night in tropical seas I would always like to have a sharp knife handy in case the tentacles of a monster began feeling round inside the boat. My own paltry experiences with cephalopods are only two:

While living at Wellington, New Zealand, in the 1920s I used to go for a sea-water swim every morning on waking. The swimming bath was a piece of Wellington Harbour enclosed by woodwork rising a few feet above high water. One morning in winter I arrived in the twilight to find an octopus with a spread of 17 feet hanging up in the changing shed. A swimmer earlier than myself had been about to dive in when he noticed a whitish patch beneath him which turned out to be the octopus which they had killed. It must have crawled into the swimming bath during the night.

An even smaller adventure was in 1964. When sailing back across the Atlantic with Giles, in *Gipsy Moth III*, we were both asleep in the cabin one afternoon, and when I awoke I found a small squid lying on the engine deck inside the cabin. The woodwork all around was splashed with dense sepia. I put this squid into a bucket, hoping to revive it, but it was dead. It seemed amazing that it should have hurtled through the companionway into the cabin, especially as the entrance to the cabin from the cockpit would present a small target to a squid flying in from abeam.

Bullen describes another fight which he saw. This time the central character in the drama was a bowhead whale, bigger, more clumsy and tame by comparison with a sperm whale:

*

While all the boats were away a large bowhead rose near the ship, evidently being harassed in some way by enemies, which I could not at first see. He seemed quite unconscious of his proximity to the ship, though, and at last came so near that the whole performance was as near as if it had been got up for my benefit. Three 'killers' were attacking him at once, like wolves worrying a bull, except that his motions were far less lively than those of any bull would have been.

The 'killer', or Orca gladiator, is a true whale, but, like the cachalot, has teeth. It differs from that great cetacean, though, in a most important particular; i.e. by having a complete set in both upper and lower jaws, like any other carnivore. For a carnivore indeed he is, the very wolf of the ocean, and enjoying, by reason of his extraordinary agility as well as comparative worthlessness commercially, complete immunity from attack by man. By some authorities he is thought to be identical with the grampus, but whalers all consider the animals quite distinct.

Not having had very long acquaintance with them both, I cannot speak emphatically upon this difference of opinion; so far as personal observation goes, I agree with the whalers in believing that there is much variation both of habits and shape between them.

But to return to the fight. The first inkling I got of what was really going on was the leaping of a killer high into the air by the side of the whale, and descending upon the victim's broad, smooth back with a resounding crash. I saw that the killer was provided with a pair of huge fins – one on his back, the other on his belly – which at first sight looked as if they were also weapons of offence. A little observation convinced me that they were fins only. Again and again the aggressor leaped into the air, falling each time on the whale's back, as if to beat him into submission.

The sea around foamed and boiled like a cauldron, so that it was only occasional glimpses I was able to catch of the two killers, until presently the worried whale lifted his head clear out of the surrounding smother, revealing the two furies hanging – one on either side – to his lips, as if endeavouring to drag his mouth open – which I afterwards saw was their principal object, as whenever during the tumult I caught sight of them, they were still in the same position. At last the tremendous and incessant blows, dealt by the most active member of the trio, seemed actually to have exhausted the immense vitality of the great bowhead, for he lay supine upon the surface. Then the three joined their forces, and succeeded in dragging open his cavernous mouth, into which they freely entered, devouring his tongue. This, then, had been their sole object, for as soon as they had finished their barbarous feast they departed, leaving him helpless and dying.

*

It is a different matter, however, when a sperm whale is attacked. Here is Bullen writing about another fight:

*

The sperm whale needs no shelter at such periods (when with young) or, at any rate, does not avail herself of any. Schools of cows with recently-born young gambolling about them are met with at immense distances from land, showing no disposition to seek shelter either. For my part, I firmly believe that the cachalot is so terrible a foe, that the great sharks never dare to approach a sperm cow on kidnapping errands, or any other if they can help it, until their unerring guides inform them that life is extinct. When a sperm whale is in health, nothing that inhabits the sea has any chance with him; neither does he scruple to carry the war into the enemy's country, since all is fish that comes to his net, and a shark fifteen feet in length has been found in the stomach of a cachalot.

The only exception he seems to make is in the case of man. Instances have several – nay, many times occurred when men have been slain by the jaws of a cachalot crushing the boat in which they were; but their death was, of course, incidental to the destruction of the boat. Never, as far as I have been able to asertain, has a cachalot attacked a man swimming or clinging to a piece of wreckage, although such opportunities have occurred innumerably. I once saw a combat between a bull cachalot and so powerful a combination of enemies that even one knowing the fighting qualities of the sperm whale would have hesitated to back him to win.

Two 'killers' and a swordfish, all of the largest size. Description of these warriors is superfluous, since they are so well known to museums and natural history; but unless one has witnessed the charge of a Xiphias, he cannot really realise what a fearful foe it is. Still, as a practice, these creatures leave the cachalot respectfully alone, knowing instinctively that he is not their game. Upon this memorable occasion, however, I guess the two Orcas were starving, and they had organised a sort of forlorn hope with the Xiphias as an auxiliary who might be relied upon to ensure success if it could be done. Anyhow, the syndicate led off with their main force first; for while the two killers hung on the cachalot's flanks, diverting his attention, the swordfish, a giant some sixteen feet long, launched himself at the most vulnerable part of the whale, for all the world like a Whitehead torpedo. The wary eye of the whale saw the long, dark mass coming, and, like a practised pugilist, coolly swerved, taking for the nonce no notice of those worrying wolves astern. The shock came; but instead of the sword penetrating three, or maybe four feet just where the neck (if a whale has any neck) encloses the huge heart, it met the mighty impenetrable mass of the head, solid as a block of thirty tons of india rubber.

So the blow glanced, revealing a white streak running diagonally across the eyes, while the great Xiphias rolled helplessly over the top of that black bastion. With a motion so rapid that the eye could scarcely follow it, the whale turned, settling withal, and, catching the momentarily motionless aggressor in the lethal sweep of those awful shears, crunched him in two halves, which writhing sections he swallowed seriatim. And the allied forces aft – what of them? Well, they had been rash – they fully realised that fact, and would have fled, but one certainly found that he had lingered on the scene too long. The thoroughly-roused leviathan, with a reversal of his huge bulk that made the sea boil like a pot, brandished his tail aloft and brought it down upon the doomed 'killer', making him at once the 'killed'. He was crushed like a shrimp under one's heel.

The survivor fled – never faster – for an avalanche of living, furious flesh was behind him, and coming with enormous leaps half out of the sea every time. Thus they disappeared, but I have no doubts as to the issue.

*

If a swordfish will attack a sperm whale, it can be expected to attack a boat. In 1955, Eric Hiscock was sailing home after a voyage round the world in *Wanderer* when a rude shock brought him up from below. He saw the head and spear of a swordfish appear above the stern. This was on the Equator at 23° W longitude. Later I saw the gash, 12 inches long by half an inch deep, which this fish had gouged out of the rudder stock. Hiscock mentions in his book that there is a piece of timber 20 inches thick in the British Museum which has been pierced by the sword of a swordfish. I do not think that a swordfish is to be feared but a sailor in a small yacht must always beware of sharks. Davenport, owner of the Australian yacht *Waltzing Matilda*, which sailed from Australia to Cape Raper, 600 miles north of the Horn, before proceeding through the west-coast channels and the Magellan Strait into the Atlantic, records that a yacht which had been sailed single-handed was found drifting off the Great Barrier Reef of Australia with the owner lying dead on deck still gripping the shrouds by which he had pulled himself out of the water after he had his legs bitten off by a shark. As I see it, the only security against a man-eating shark is to avoid being in the sea when the shark is there.

10

The Romantic Landfall

AFTER 13,000 miles of sailing on the open ocean since leaving Plymouth, and 6,500 miles of sailing nearly in a straight line from where 'Meridian' crossed the Roaring Forties, the clipper captain found the prospect of a landfall looming ahead of him. This was not a pleasing prospect for a man who liked plenty of sea room and no worry about meticulous navigation.[1] Coastwise inshore pilotage and navigation were irksome to him. If bound for Melbourne he must pass between Cape Otway and King Island, a gap 47½ miles wide, to enter Bass Strait, which lies between SE Australia and Tasmania. Navigation in Bass Strait can be tricky. Near King Island westerly gales can build up the east-going tidal stream to 5 knots instead of the normal maximum of 2 knots; and the Admiralty Pilot warns vessels 'approaching King Island from the westward, especially during thick or hazy weather, to exercise caution and sound frequently'. Thirty-six sailing ships are known to have been wrecked on the island.

The hard truth is that most ship losses are due to errors in navigation. It is the navigator's job to allow for every factor which can affect a ship's position. If it is claimed that allowing for the vagaries of current is a matter of sea sense then I assert that sea sense *is* navigation; at least a navigator must have sea sense to be successful. In most cases of shipwreck it is simply that the ship would not have been run aground if it had been known that the ground was there or, in other words, if the ship's position had been known. The navigator in the square-rigged ships was usually the captain and he was often a capricious man.

In 1854 Captain Bully Forbes, celebrated, or notorious, as

1. This was not always so. For instance Captain Woodget used to take the *Cutty Sark* through Bass Strait in any weather with no landfall since the Lizard.

the captain of the *Lightning*, was transferred to the new *Schomberg* which James Baines had ordered a British firm to build in competition with the Mackay ships. Her registered tonnage was 2,284 tons and her length overall 288 feet. Her hull was built of three skins. Bully Forbes left Liverpool in October 1855 with a signal hoisted: 'Sixty days to Melbourne'. On December 27th she was tacking against a headwind 35 miles west of Cape Otway. It was a moonlight night and Bully Forbes was below playing whist when the mate reported that the ship was closing the land and he suggested going about. Bully Forbes was in a bad temper because he was losing and he insisted on playing another rubber before tacking the ship. When they came on deck and gave the order to tack the wind had died away and there was a strong west-going current. The *Schomberg* refused to tack. Bully Forbes tried to wear her round. The ship, stranded on a sandbank, could not be got off and later went to pieces. At a court of enquiry Bully Forbes was cleared of blame because the sandbank was uncharted, but some passengers declared that he was so disgusted with the *Schomberg*'s slowness compared with the *Lightning* that he let the ship strand on purpose. Bully Forbes' career was ruined.

Joseph Conrad, who was a sailor from the age of 17 to 36, knew what stranding meant to a captain. He wrote in *The Mirror of the Sea*:

*

Stranding is as if an invisible hand had been stealthily uplifted from the bottom to catch hold of her keel as it glides through the water.

More than any other event does 'stranding' bring to the sailor a sense of utter and dismal failure. There are strandings and strandings, but I am safe to say that ninety per cent of them are occasions in which the sailor, without dishonour, may well wish himself dead; and I have no doubt that of those who have had the experience of their ship taking the ground, ninety per cent did actually for five seconds or so wish themselves dead.

'Taking the ground' is the professional expression for a

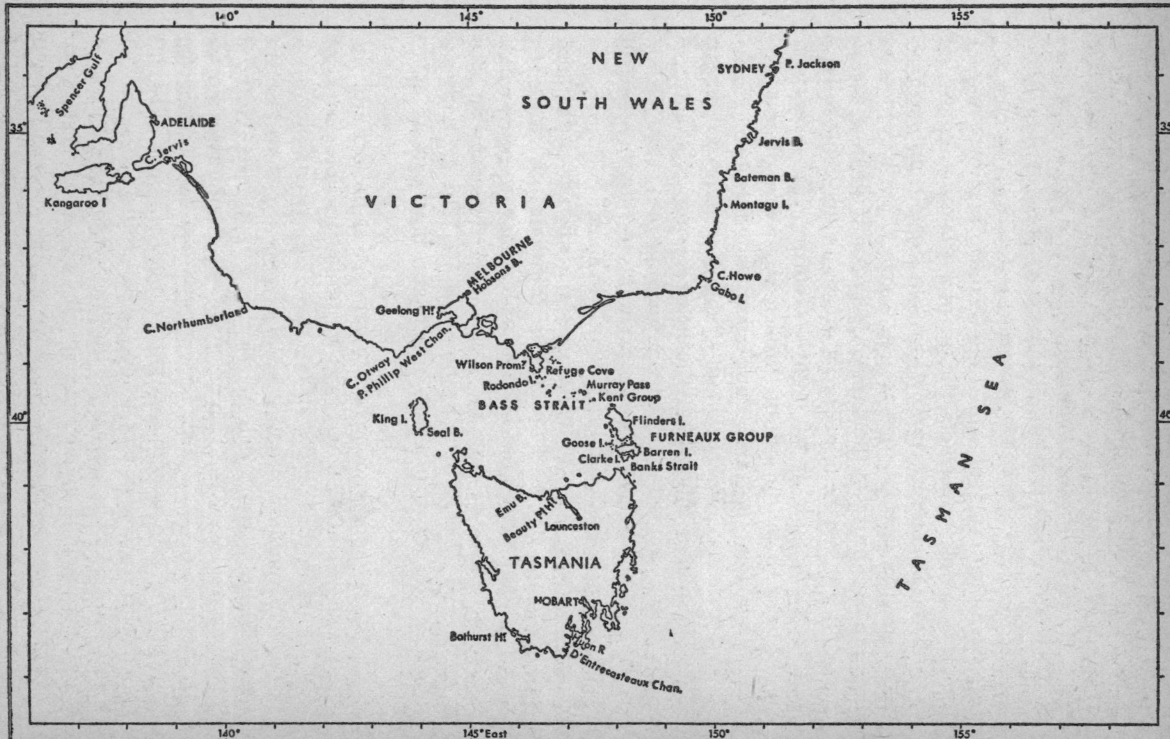

NEW
SOUTH WALES
VICTORIA
TASMANIA
TASMAN SEA
SYDNEY
P. Jackson
Jervis B.
Bateman B.
Montagu I.
C. Howe
Gabo I.
Spencer Gulf
ADELAIDE
C. Jervis
Kangaroo I
C. Northumberland
MELBOURNE
Hobsons B.
Geelong Hr.
C. Otway
P. Phillip West Chan.
Wilson Prom?
Refuge Cove
Rodondo I.
Murray Pass
Kent Group
BASS STRAIT
King I.
Seal B.
Flinders I.
FURNEAUX GROUP
Goose I.
Barren I.
Clarke I.
Banks Strait
Emu B.
Beauty Pt. Hr.
Launceston
HOBART
Bathurst Hr.
Huon R
D'Entrecasteaux Chan.
140°
145°
150°
155°
145° East
35°
40°

ship that is stranded in gentle circumstances. But the feeling is more as if the ground had taken hold of her. It is for those on her deck a surprising sensation. It is as if your feet had been caught in an imponderable snare; you feel the balance of your body threatened, and the steady poise of your mind is destroyed at once. This sensation lasts only a second, for even while you stagger something seems to turn over in your head, bringing uppermost the mental exclamation, full of astonishment and dismay, 'By Jove! she's on the ground!' ...

'Strandings' are all unexpected, except those heralded by some short glimpse of the danger, full of agitation and excitement, like an awakening from a dream of incredible folly.

The land suddenly at night looms up right over your bows, or perhaps the cry of 'Broken water ahead!' is raised and some long mistake, some complicated edifice of self-delusion, over-confidence, and wrong reasoning is brought down in a fatal shock, and the heart-searing experience of your ship's keel scraping the scrunching over, say, a coral reef. It is a sound, for its size, far more terrific to your soul than that of a world coming violently to an end.

Years ago I was concerned as chief mate in a case of stranding which was not fatal to the ship. We went to work for ten hours on end, laying out anchors in readiness to heave off at high water. While I was still busy about the decks forward I heard the steward at my elbow saying: 'The captain asks whether you mean to come in, sir, and have something to eat today.'

I went into the cuddy. My captain sat at the head of the table like a statue. There was a strange motionlessness of everything in that pretty little cabin. The swing-table which for seventy odd days had been always on the move, if ever so little, hung quite still above the soup tureen. Nothing could have altered the rich colour of my commander's complexion, laid on generously by wind and sea; but between the two tufts of fair hair above his ears, his skull, generally suffused with the hue of blood, shone dead white, like a dome of ivory. And he looked strangely untidy. I perceived he had not shaved himself that day; and yet the wildest motion of the ship in the most stormy latitudes we had passed through never made him miss one single morning ever since we left the Channel. The fact must be that a commander cannot possibly shave himself when his ship goes aground. I have commanded ships myself, but I don't know; I have never tried to shave in my life.

He did not offer to help me or himself till I had coughed markedly several times. I talked to him professionally in a cheery tone, and ended with the confident assertion:

'We shall get her off before midnight, sir.'

He smiled faintly without looking up and muttered as if to himself:

'Yes, yes; the captain puts the ship ashore and we get her off.'

Then, raising his head, he attacked grumpily the steward, a lanky anxious youth with a long pale face and two big front teeth.

'What makes this soup so bitter? I am surprised the mate can swallow the beastly stuff. I am sure the cook's ladled some salt water into it by mistake.'

The charge was so outrageous that the steward for all answer only dropped his eyelids bashfully.

*

It is only fair to point out that the difficulty of navigating a nineteenth-century clipper was far greater that that of navigating a yacht today. The clipper had no echo sounder and, going at 12 knots, it could not use a lead. It must heave-to and take all way off in order to make a sounding in anything but the shallowest water. The captain, who was nearly always racing against time, would not dare to do such a thing – he would be laughed at by the fleet. The ship of today can get bearings of marine radio beacons and a fairly accurate fix from them in thick weather, or even in thick fog for that matter. The clipper had no direction-finding equipment, nor did it have radar, which can be a valuable aid in picking up land ahead. However, I will not say much about radar because of the great increase in collisions since ships were equipped with radar and began sailing at full speed through dense fog because of it.

Also, a clipper was unwieldy to manoeuvre. Tacking with about 20 square sails to handle was a big operation. Each of these sails had ropes to all four corners and every one of them had to be manhandled and trimmed. Therefore a clipper needed to know of land ahead in plenty of time to manoeuvre. To tack or bear away on seeing land ahead not too distant, she needed smart handling. If she failed to stay or, in other words, failed to come about and was left pointing dead into wind with no way on her she was liable to go aground before she was got under control; she would drift astern fast. A yacht, on the other hand, only needs 10 seconds to tack. Similarly in a storm, if a clipper was not tacked fast enough and was left broadside-on to wind and waves, the wind would heel her far over and the pressure on the tall masts and huge area of sail was so great that it was extremely difficult to regain control.

The clipper way I am following in this book does not stop at Melbourne but continues on to Sydney. Why is this, you may well ask, when Melbourne is a much easier landfall, 420 miles closer to Plymouth; when the passage to Sydney after passing Melbourne requires tricky navigation through Bass Strait, followed by the need to keep inshore along the coast of New South Wales in order to avoid the contrary south-going current. Clipper navigators never liked inshore sailing where most accurate navigation was essential in case one of the variable currents pushed the ship into a bay. Besides this, the winds would be variable after leaving Bass Strait which meant frequent tacking and constant trimming of yards and sails and there was always the risk of being becalmed and set on to the shore by the current.

Many sailing ships were bound for Sydney, mostly carrying passengers and general cargo. But I confess that I chose Sydney because of its personal appeal for me. Four times I have found my way to Sydney, each time on some exciting romantic venture. On my first visit I steamed into the magnificent harbour from New Zealand; I was a blighted swain who had jumped on board the steamer in Wellington, New Zealand, because of an ice-blooded, heartless and haughty maiden travelling in the ship to Sydney. Though I had the usual profound belief that it was impossible, my bleeding heart survived this ordeal. My next visit was when I flew my Gipsy I Moth plane there to complete the second solo flight made from England to Australia. That was in January 1930. I was escorted in by a flight of planes and was so agitated at the sight of all the crowds on Mascot Aerodrome that I landed like a rabbit lolloping over a rough meadow. It was all a great thrill – with the uproarious, friendly Sydney welcome – which must surely be unique.

The third time I came to Sydney was from the east after I had made the first solo flight across the Tasman Sea from New Zealand to Australia. This was in my Gipsy I Moth seaplane and it was another thrilling experience to be alighting and taking off in that little seaplane in the great Sydney Harbour. The fourth visit was to start a flight from Sydney in a Puss Moth monoplane to Peking and then on to London: this was in 1936.

And so I like to imagine sailing ships from England passing through Sydney Heads to drop anchor in the peaceful waters of Sydney Harbour after the 13,750-mile passage from Plymouth.

II

Across the Tasman Sea

THE CLIPPER captains, rather than make a passage to Sydney through the narrow waters of Bass Strait, preferred to lengthen the voyage by 500 miles and sail round south and east of Tasmania. After spending a month or more in port, they would set off from Sydney, loaded up with wool and more passengers, to traverse the Tasman Sea before entering the Southern Ocean on the way to Cape Horn. The sailing distance to Plymouth by way of the Horn was 14,750 miles. Sometimes a ship would call at Wellington, New Zealand, or pass through Cook Strait between the North and South Islands of New Zealand.

It is only 1,200 miles across the Tasman Sea from Sydney to Wellington. This sounds a short hop compared with the other stretches of the voyage, but it is two-thirds the width of the North Atlantic between Ireland and Newfoundland. And the Tasman Sea is notorious for vicious little storms which blow up suddenly without warning; it can be formidable and dangerous. Although a number of yachts sail across the Tasman Sea in summer and there have been eight races across from New Zealand to Australia without loss, many ships have foundered there. My friend, Gower Wilson, who helped me rebuild my seaplane on Lord Howe Island in the Tasman Sea and who was one of the most competent hands in a boat I ever saw, was lost with all the crew of a yacht on passage from Lord Howe Island to Sydney.

I experienced this Tasman Sea weather in 1931 when I was flying my Gipsy Moth seaplane from New Zealand to Australia. During the night a vicious squall capsized and sank the seaplane at her mooring in the Lord Howe Island lagoon. After rebuilding the seaplane I was flying on to Sydney, 420 miles to the west, when I spotted a steamer; I described how she looked from above:

What an awesome sight from above! The bows, sliding off one roller, crashing into the next to churn up a wide spreading patch of frothing water. Then, as the cross-swell struck her, she lurched heavily, appeared to slide into a hollow and sink into the trough, decks awash as if waterlogged; but she wallowed out and rolled first on to one beam and then on to the other, discharging water from her decks as if over a weir. Not a sign of life was visible. – From *Alone over the Tasman Sea.*

Most passages across the Tasman Sea, however, are delightful fair-weather sailing. Conor O'Brien, when he left Melbourne, did not sail round to Sydney but headed direct for New Zealand, leaving Bass Strait by its south-east entrance, Banks Strait, between Tasmania and Clark Island of the Furneaux group of islands where there is a clear passage 7¾ miles wide. He had none of the new-fangled navigation aids which we racing yachtsmen value today, only his sextant and compass. He writes:

*

For a day all went well; then I was stricken down by some sort of poisoning; a distressing malady, which, however, saved the ship. For on the night of the 1st April, after passing Goose Island (of the Furneaux group; and who shall say that in such circumstances something foolish is not likely to happen?) I set a course, an obviously imprudent course on such a dark night, for Banks Straits, and went below. But not for long; my malady compelling me, I came on deck, went over to the lee rail, and saw a ghastly pyramid of black rock sticking up well on my lee bow. Fortunately my mate was quick in action, the vessel quick on her helm, the wind offshore, and the water smooth, or the cruise would have ended then and there on Clark Island. I did not cut any more corners fine that night, and I darkened the ship; for the foolish thing I had done was to leave the gas blazing away in the cabin with the skylight open, so that the helmsman could see nothing; and there was no look-out forward as there should have been in such narrow waters.

*

Brigadier Miles Smeeton, in *Tzu Hang*, was having a fair-weather passage too; we shall be hearing more from him later:

*

We all slept a glorious and undisturbed sleep that night and woke up to find that the sails were flapping uselessly.

While we worked a seal played around us, popping his whiskery nose out of the oily sea, and looking like a bald-headed old man peering over the morning paper; then he turned over on his back and waved a flipper across his chest as if he was fanning himself. After a time he went on his way. Perhaps he was bound for the Snares (a notoriously deadly uninhabited islet sixty miles south-west of the South Cape of New Zealand), anyway he didn't seem to be at all perturbed about his landfall.

While the seal played around us the albatrosses came visiting. They came gliding over the swell, apparently using the cushion of air, raised by the lift of the waves, to support them. There seemed to be no breeze at all, and from time to time they were forced to give a few slow strokes with their wings. They always seemed to look rather furtive and ashamed when they did so, as if they hoped that no other albatross had seen them. It was obviously something that they did not want talked about in the albatross club. They glided so close to the smooth water that sometimes an end wing feather would draw a skittering line across the surface as they turned. One after another they came up to the ship and thrusting their feet out in front of them, they tobogganned to a halt and as they settled down, they held their wings together high above their bodies, until they folded them one after the other, on a curious double fold, against their backs.

They paddled round the ship as we worked, coming close under the counter, and all the time Pwe (the Siamese cat) pursued them on deck. She crouched under the rail and then raised her head, with her ears flattened sideways, so that she showed as little of herself as possible when she looked over. Then she crouched down and crawled along the deck until she thought that she was directly over one of the big birds, when she looked again. But she could get no further, and her jaw used to chatter with rage and frustration.

Sometimes the albatrosses used to dip their bills in the water and then snap them together with a popping sound. We never found out what they ate. They trifled with pieces of bread, but never swallowed them.

*

Though Conor O'Brien had an easy passage, he had other troubles on board:

*

Unfortunately, someone left a fishing line towing astern all night, and at dawn I found that it had hooked and drowned an unfortunate mollyhawk, which is a small kind of albatross. Superstition apart, it is an infamous thing to kill an albatross, for they are such friendly birds and one does not have much company in the Southern Ocean; this one of course died an accidental death, but before long retribution descended on the cause of the accident. G. knocked his elbow on a bulkhead, and it swelled up and got sore. We others suffered incidentally, for in a day we were head-reaching under short canvas as uncomfortably as might be expected in the Tasman Sea, which is notoriously the roughest bit of water in the world, and all the time getting driven farther and farther to the northwards. However, if one can't pass New Zealand on one side, one must go on the other; there is only about 800 miles of it. By the time a fair wind came along the best course was through the middle of it, through Cook Strait; it would have been undesirable on account of the temptations of the seductive harbours that lie on either side of it, were it not that G's arm was becoming worse and it might be necessary to go into one of those harbours for a doctor. I was by now all right again.

We did not lose much time over this part of the passage and on the 14th day out I took the morning watch in order to see New Zealand. I was rather anxious about the stage-managing of this; I might have sailed too slowly during the night and seen the land only as a pimple on the horizon, or it might have been less fine, with only a dark mass showing under a bank of cloud; but it turned out all right, the clouds were lying low on the water and high above them the sun was emerging from behind the colossal cone of Mount Egmont, which I had approached within 40 miles.

I think this was the most impressive mountain scenery I ever saw.

In the course of time I began to see more rather attractive-looking mountains to the southward, but I was slow cnough about getting there. There had been floods up the Wanganui River, and Cook Strait was full of floating logs quite enough to do damage and requiring us to keep a good look-out by day and to heave-to at night.

*

Vito Dumas also records his impressions of Mount Egmont

when he visited Wellington on his solo voyage round the bottom of the world:

*

It was cold on Christmas morning and I suffered from the 11° C and especially from my caloric deficiency. Cook Strait is about sixty-five miles wide. Being at the foot of Mount Egmont, which is 8,260 feet high, I was surprised not to see it. But no matter; I was sure of my navigation.

The day passed by. At four in the afternoon I was absorbed by the battle of Titans going on around Mount Egmont, which had shown itself for a few seconds. The low clouds, striking the foot of the mountain and jostled on by those following, were whirling at a fantastic speed. The clouds rushed, rolling, boiling and twisting to the summit of the mountain. I could imagine what a roaring inferno it was up there, and by analogy I caught an inkling of the incandescent stages of the earth's formation. Everything here spoke of primeval times, the more so as no sign of animal life appeared. Drifting along the current was the wreckage of forests, roots and broken branches that tossed and beckoned to the sky as they rolled. The latter was overcast with an indescribable pallette of tattered clouds, black, blue and red, casting strange shadows on the sea. Wherever I looked I was aware of the harsh exuberance of cold, hostile nature; of cold that pierced into the marrow of my bones – the dark vindictive cold of inaccessible spaces, without pity or mercy for any creatures. And I, with my unfortunate *Lehg II*, was sailing into this hell. I would not give up. Hope and some tiny inward glow sustained and heartened me. I was firmly convinced that whatever lay before me, sinister though it might be, must be mild in comparison with my sufferings on the ocean I had just crossed.

12

High Winds and Rough Seas around New Zealand

THE CLIPPERS sailing from Australia would not pass through Cook Strait if they could avoid it; in other words, unless they were calling at Wellington or because winds and weather pushed them there. The mountain ranges of the North and South Islands of New Zealand force the winds into Cook Strait and, as Wellington is at latitude 41° 20′ S, these are the winds of the Roaring Forties which are forced through a narrow funnel.

Wellington is notorious for being one of the windiest cities in the world. In Wellington Harbour I have seen the wind blowing on the sea surface at 60 mph from the north, while only 50 yards away it was blowing as hard from the opposite direction, from the south. This was in an eddy, or small cyclone, caused by the hills obstructing a gale.

Once I was flying my Gipsy Moth plane across North Island to keep an appointment. It was rough weather and clouds were low on the hills. The only way I could cross the mountains, having no blind flying instruments, was to fly through a gorge. The plane was tossed out of that gorge, bowled over and over like a dead leaf in a gale. When I had recovered from the excitement of that I felt annoyed and tried again. This time I managed to force a passage by diving into the entrance of the gorge and flying just above the water.

Captain Cook in the midsummer of 1769 took 5 weeks to sail round the North Cape of New Zealand going westwards. During this period he only made good 150 miles, an average of 4½ miles a day. Referring to the gale, he recorded in his log, 'which for its strength and continuance was such as I hardly was ever in before'. Most of New Zealand lies in the Roaring Forties and Cook's bark *Endeavour*, a 368-ton Whitby-built collier, could not be sailed to windward in a gale. Yet Cook, exploring and surveying New Zealand, coasted all along the western side of both North and South Islands, a lee shore to the fierce westerly winds – another proof of his great seamanship, because he knew that he would be lucky to escape to windward if embayed by a gale. Frank Bullen draws a true picture of the New Zealand scene. His ship was hunting whales at the south end of New Zealand between Stuart Island and South Island. In his book he told the story of New Zealand's only whaler, the *Chance*, which, with a mixed crew, chiefly Maoris, was competing on the Solander ground with a fleet of crack Yankee whalers. Bullen described the New Zealand ship:

*

I am bound to confess that there was a great difference in appearance between the Yankee and the colonial – very much in favour of the former. She was neat, smart, and seaworthy, looking as if just launched; but the *Chance* looked like some poor old relic of a bygone day, whose owners, unable to sell her, and too poor to keep her in repair, were just letting her go while keeping up the insurance, praying fervently each day that she might come to grief, and bring them a little profit at last. She looked what she really was – the sole survivor of the once great whaling industry of New Zealand.

In many of the preceding pages I have, though possessing all an Englishman's pride in the prowess of mine own people, been compelled to bear witness to the wonderful smartness and courage shown by the American whale men, to whom their perilous calling seems to have become a second nature. Therefore, it is the more pleasant to me to be able to chronicle some of the doings of Captain Gilroy, familiarly known as 'Paddy', master of the *Chance*, who was unsurpassed as a whale-fisher or a seaman by any Yankee that ever sailed from Martha's Vineyard. Such whaling skippers as our late commander hated him with ferocious intensity; and but for his Maori and half-breed bodyguard, I have little doubt he would have long before been killed.

New Zealand is pre-eminently a country of grand harbours; but I think those that are least used easily bear the palm for grandeur of scenery and facility of access. The wonderful harbour, or rather series of harbours, into which we were now entering for the first time (Preservation Inlet at the south-west extremity of New Zealand) greatly resembled in appearance a Norwegian fjord, not only in the character of its scenery, but from the interesting, if disconcerting, fact that the cliffs were so steep-to that in some places no anchorage is found alongside the very land itself. There are, however, many places where the best possible anchorage can be obtained, so securely sheltered that a howling south-wester may be tearing the sea up by the roots outside, and you will know nothing of it within, except what may be surmised from the clouds overhead. It was an ideal place for a whaling station, being right on the Solander.

During the grey of dawn the anchor was weighed. There was no breath of wind from any quarter, so that it was necessary to lower boats and tow the old girl out to her field of duty. Before she was fairly clear of the harbour, though, there came a 'snifter' from the hills that caught her unprepared, making her reel again, and giving us a desperate few minutes to scramble on board and hoist our boats up. As we drew out from the land, we found that a moderate gale was blowing, but the sky was clear, fathomless blue, the sun rose kindly, a heavenly dream of soft delicate colour preceding him; so that, in spite of the strong breeze, all looked promising for a good campaign. At first no sign could be seen of any of the other ships, though we looked long and eagerly for them. At last we saw them, four in all, nearly hull down to seaward, but evidently coming in under press of sail. So slow, however, was their approach that we had made one 'leg' across the ground and half-way back before they were near enough for us to descry the reason of their want of speed. They had each got a whale alongside, and were carrying every rag of canvas they could spread, in order to get in with their prizes.

Our old acquaintance, the *Chance*, was there, the three others being her former competitors, except those who were disabled, still lying in Port William. Slowly, painfully they laboured along, until well within the mouth of the Straits, when, without any warning, the wind which had been bringing them in suddenly flew round into the northward, putting them at once in a most perilous position. Too far within the Straits to 'up helm' and run for it out to sea; not far enough to get anywhere that an anchor might hold; and there to leeward, within less than a dozen miles, loomed grim and gloomy one of the most terrific rock-bound coasts in the world. The shift of wind had placed the *Chance* farther to leeward than all the rest, a good mile and a half nearer the shore; and we could well imagine how anxiously her movements were being watched by the others, who, in spite of their jealousy of his good luck, knew well and appreciated fully Paddy's marvellous seamanship, as well as his unparalleled knowledge of the coast.

Having no whale to hamper our movements, besides being well to windward of them all, we were perfectly comfortable as long as we kept to seaward of a certain line and the gale was not too fierce, so for the present all our attention was concentrated upon the labouring ships to leeward. The intervention of the land to windward kept the sea from rising to the awful height it attains under the pressure of a westerly or a south-westerly gale, when, gathering momentum over an area extending right round the globe, it hurls itself upon those rugged shores. Still, it was bad enough. The fact of the gale striking across the regular set of the swell and current had the effect of making the sea irregular, short, and broken, which state of things is considered worse, as far as handling the ship goes, than a much heavier, longer, but more regular succession of waves.

As the devoted craft drifted helplessly down upon that frowning barrier, our excitement grew intense. Their inability to do anything but drift was only too well known by experience to every one of us, nor would it be possible for them to escape at all if they persisted in holding on much longer. But it was easy to see why they did so. While Paddy held on so far to leeward of them, and consequently in so much more imminent danger than they were, it would be derogatory in the highest degree to their reputation for seamanship and courage were they to slip and run before he did. He, however, showed no sign of doing so, although they all neared, with an accelerated drift, that point from whence no seamanship could deliver them, and where death inevitable, cruel, awaited them without hope of escape. The part of the coast upon which they were apparently driving was about as dangerous and impracticable as any in the world. A gigantic barrier of black, naked rock, extending for several hundred yards, rose sheer from the sea beneath, like the side of an ironclad, up to a height of seven or eight hundred feet. No outlying spurs of submerged fragments broke the immeasurable landward rush of the majestic waves towards the frowning face of this world-fragment. Fresh from their source, with all the impetus accumulated in their thousand-mile journey, they came apparently irresistible. Against this perpendicular barrier they hurled themselves with a shock that vibrated far inland, and a roar that rose in a dominating diapason over the continuous thunder of the tempest-riven sea. High as was the summit of the cliff, the spray, hurled upwards by the tremendous impact, rose higher, so that the whole front of the great rock was veiled in filmy wreaths of foam, hiding its solidity from the seaward view. At either end of this vast rampart nothing could be seen but a waste of breakers seething, hissing, like the foot of Niagara, and effectually concealing the *chevaux de frise* of rocks which produced such a vortex of tormented waters.

Towards this dreadful spot, then, the four vessels were being resistlessly driven, every moment seeing their chances of escape lessening to vanishing-point. Suddenly, as if panic-stricken, the ship nearest to the *Chance* gave a great sweep round on to the other tack, a few fluttering gleams aloft showing that even in that storm they were daring to set some sail. What the manoeuvre meant we knew very well – they had cut adrift from their whale, terrified at last beyond endurance into the belief that Paddy was going to sacrifice himself and his crew in the attempt to lure them with him to inevitable destruction. The other two did not hesitate longer. The example once set, they immediately followed; but it was for some time doubtful in the extreme whether their resolve was not taken too late to save them from destruction. We watched them with breathless interest, unable for a long time to satisfy ourselves that they were out of danger. But at last we saw them shortening sail again – a sure sign that they considered themselves, while the wind held in the same quarter, safe from going ashore at any rate, although there was still before them the prospect of a long struggle with the unrelenting ferocity of the weather down south.

Meanwhile, what of the daring Irishman and his old barrel of a ship? The fugitives once safe off the land, all our interest centred in the *Chance*. We watched her until she drew in so closely to the seething cauldron of breakers that it was only occasionally we could distinguish her outline; and the weather was becoming so thick and dirty, the light so bad, that we were reluctantly compelled to lose sight of her, although the skipper believed that he saw her in the midst of the turmoil of broken water at the western end of the mighty mass of perpendicular cliff before described. Happily for us, the wind veered to the westward, releasing us from the prospect of another enforced visit to the wild regions south of the island. It blew harder than ever; but being now a fair wind up the Straits, we fled before it, anchoring again in Port William before midnight. Here we were compelled to remain for a week; for after the gale blew itself out, the wind still hung in the same quarter, refusing to allow us to get back again to our cruising station.

But on the second day of our enforced detention a ship poked her jib-boom round the west end of the little bay. No words could describe our condition of spellbound astonishment when she rounded-to, cumbrously as befitting a ship towing a whale, and revealed to us the well-remembered outlines of the old *Chance*. It was like welcoming the first-fruits of the resurrection; for who among sailor men, having seen a vessel disappear from their sight, as we had, under such terrible conditions, would ever have expected to see her again? She was hardly anchored before our skipper was alongside, thirsting to satisfy his unbounded curiosity as to the unheard-of means whereby she had escaped such apparently inevitable destruction. I was fortunate enough to accompany him, and hear the story at first-hand.

It appeared that none of the white men on board, except

the redoubtable Paddy himself, had ever been placed in so seemingly hopeless and desperate a position before. Yet when they saw how calm and free from anxiety their commander was, how cool and business-like the attitude of all their dusky shipmates, their confidence in his ability and resourcefulness kept its usual high level. It must be admitted that the test such feelings were then subjected to was of the severest, for to their eyes no possible avenue of escape was open. Along that glaring line of raging, foaming water not a break occurred, not the faintest indication of an opening anywhere wherein even so experienced a pilot as Paddy might thrust a ship. The great black wall of rock loomed up by their side, grim and pitiless as doom – a very door of adamant closed against all hope. Nearer and nearer they drew, until the roar of the baffled Pacific was deafening, maddening, in its overwhelming volume of chaotic sound. All hands stood motionless, with eyes fixed in horrible fascination upon the indescribable vortex to which they were being irresistibly driven.

At last, just as the fringes of the back-beaten billows hissed up to greet them, they felt her motion ease. Instinctively looking aft, they saw the skipper coolly wave his hand, signing to them to trim the yards. As they hauled on the weather braces, she plunged through the maelstrom of breakers, and before they had got the yards right round they were on the other side of that enormous barrier, the anchor was dropped and all was still. The vessel rested, like a bird on her nest, in a deep, still tarn, shut in, to all appearance, on every side by huge rock barriers. Of the furious storm but a moment before howling and raging all around them, nothing remained but an all-pervading, thunderous hum, causing the deck to vibrate beneath them, and high overhead the jagged, leaden remnants of twisted, tortured cloud whirling past their tiny oblong of sky. Just a minute's suspension of all faculties but wonder, then, in one spontaneous, heartfelt note of genuine admiration, all hands burst into a cheer that even overtopped the mighty rumble of the baffled sea.

Here they lay, perfectly secure, and cut in their whale as if in dock; then at the first opportunity they ran out with fearful difficulty a kedge with a whale-line attached, by which means they warped the vessel out of her hiding-place – a far more arduous operation than getting in had been. But even this did not exhaust the wonders of that occasion. They had hardly got way upon her, beginning to draw out from the land, when the eagle-eye of one of the Maoris detected the carcass of a whale rolling among the breakers about half a mile to the westward. Immediately a boat was lowered, a double allowance of line put into her, and off they went to the valuable flotsam. Dangerous in the highest degree was the task of getting near enough to drive harpoons into the body; but it was successfully accomplished, the line run on board, and the prize hauled triumphantly alongside. This was the whale they had now brought in. We shrewdly suspected that it must have been one of those abandoned by the unfortunate vessels who had fled, but etiquette forbade us saying anything about it. Even had it been, another day would have seen it valueless to any one, for it was by no means otto of roses to sniff at now, while they had certainly salved it at the peril of their lives.

When we returned on board and repeated the story, great was the amazement. Such a feat of seamanship was almost beyond belief; but we were shut up to believing, since in no other way could the vessel's miraculous escape be accounted for. The little, dumpy, red-faced figure, rigged like any scarecrow, that now stood on his cutting-stage, punching away vigorously at the fetid mass of blubber beneath him, bore no outward visible sign of a hero about him; but in our eyes he was transfigured – a being to be thought of reverently, as one who in all those qualities that go to the making of a man had proved himself of the seed royal, a king of men, all the more kingly because unconscious that his deeds were of so exalted an order.

I am afraid that, to a landsman, my panegyric may smack strongly of gush, for no one but a seaman can rightly appraise such doings as these; but I may be permitted to say that, when I think of men whom I feel glad to have lived to know, foremost among them rises the queer little figure of Paddy Gilroy.

*

Frank Bullen's classic story was a favourite of mine in 1914 when I was at a preparatory school at the age of 13.

A few days after the adventure of the *Chance*, the *Cachalot* was ready to sail from New Zealand for home. Bullen wrote:

*

All sail was set to a strong, steady north-wester, and with yards canted the least bit in the world on the port tack, so that every stitch was drawing, we began our long easterly stretch to the Horn, homeward bound at last.

Favoured by wind and weather, we made an average run of one hundred and eighty miles per day for many days, paying no attention to 'great circle sailing', since in such a slow ship the net gain to be secured by going to a high latitude was very small, but dodging comfortably along on about the parallel of 48° S, until it became necessary to draw down towards 'Cape Stiff', as that dreaded extremity of South America, Cape Horn, is familiarly called by seamen. As we did so, icebergs became numerous, at one time over seventy being in sight at once. Some of them were of immense size – one, indeed, that could hardly be fitly described as an iceberg, but more properly an ice-field, with many bergs rising out of it, being over sixty miles long, while some of its towering peaks were estimated at from five hundred to one thousand feet high. Happily, the weather kept clear; for icebergs and fog make a combination truly appalling to the sailor, especially if there by much wind blowing.

Needless, perhaps, to say, our look-out was of the best, for all hands had a double interest in the safety of the ship. Perhaps it may be thought that any man would have so much regard for the safety of his life that he would not think of sleeping on his look-out; but I can assure my readers that, strange as it may seem, such is not the case. I have known men who could never be trusted not to go to sleep, no matter how great the danger. This is so well recognized in merchant ships that nearly every officer acts as if there was no look-out at all forward, in case his supposed watchman should be having a surreptitious doze.

Stronger and stronger blew the brave west wind; dirtier, gloomier, and colder grew the weather, until, reduced to two topsails and a reefed foresail, we were scudding dead before the gale for all we were worth. This was a novel experience for us in the *Cachalot*, and I was curious to see how she would behave. To my mind, the supreme test of a ship's sea-kindliness is the length of time she will scud before a gale without 'pooping' a sea or taking such heavy water on board over her sides as to do serious damage. Some ships are very dangerous to run at all. Endeavouring to make the best use of the gale which is blowing in the right direction, the captain 'hangs on' to all the sail he can carry, until she ships a mighty mass of water over all, so that the decks are filled with wreckage, or, worse still, 'poops' a sea. The latter experience is a terrible one, even to a trained seaman. You are running before the wind and waves, sometimes deep in the valley between two liquid mountains, sometimes high on the rolling ridge of one. You watch anxiously the speed of the sea, trying to decide whether it or you are going the faster, when suddenly there seems to be a hush, almost a lull, in the uproar. You look astern, and see a wall of water rising majestically higher and higher, at the same time drawing nearer and nearer. Instinctively you clutch at something firm, and hold your breath. Then that mighty green barrier leans forward, the ship's stern seems to settle at the same time, and, with a thundering noise as of an avalanche descending, it overwhelms you. Of course the ship's way is deadened; she seems like a living thing overburdened, yet struggling to be free; and well it is for all hands if the helmsman be able to keep his post and his wits about him. For if he be hurt, or have fled from the terrible wave, it is an even chance that she 'broaches to'; that is to say, swings round broadside on to the next great wave that follows relentlessly its predecessor. Then, helpless and vulnerable, she will most probably be smashed up and founder. Many a good ship has gone with all hands to the bottom just as simply as that.

In order to avoid such a catastrophe, the proper procedure is to 'heave-to' before the sea has attained so dangerous a height; but even a landsman can understand how reluctant a shipmaster may be to lie like a log just drifting, while a more seaworthy ship is flying along at the rate of, perhaps, three hundred miles a day in the desired direction. Ships of the *Cachalot*'s bluff build are peculiarly liable to delays of this kind from their slowness, which, if allied to want of buoyancy, makes it necessary to heave-to in good time, if safety is at all cared for.

To my great astonishment and delight, however, our grand old vessel nobly sustained her character, running on without shipping any heavy water, although sometimes hedged in on either side by gigantic waves that seemed to tower as high as her lowermast-heads. Again and again we were caught up and passed by the splendid homeward-bound colonial packets, some of them carrying an appalling press of canvas, under which the long, snaky hulls, often overwhelmed by the foaming seas, were hardly visible, so insignificant did they appear by comparison with the snowy mountain of swelling sail above.

*

Bullen was as proud of his ugly old-fashioned whaler as if it had been a racing clipper. Conrad writes in *The Mirror of the Sea:*

*

There are ships which bear a bad name, but I have yet to meet one whose crew for the time being failed to stand up angrily for her against every criticism. One ship which I call to mind now had the reputation of killing somebody every voyage she made. This was no calumny, and yet I remember well, somewhere far back in the late seventies, that the crew of that ship were, if anything, rather proud of her evil fame, as if they had been an utterly corrupt lot of desperadoes glorying in their association with an atrocious creature. We, belonging to other vessels moored all about the Circular Quay in Sydney, used to shake our heads at her with a great sense of the unblemished virtue of our own well-loved ships.

I shall not pronounce her name. She is 'missing' now, after a sinister but, from the point of view of her owners, a useful career extending over many years, and, I should say, across every ocean of our globe. Having killed a man for every voyage, and perhaps rendered more misanthropic by the infirmities that come with years upon a ship, she had made up her mind to kill all hands at once before leaving the scene of her exploits. A fitting end, this, to a life of usefulness and crime – in a last outburst of an evil passion supremely satisfied on some wild night, perhaps, to the applauding clamour of wind and wave.

How did she do it? In the word 'missing' there is a horrible depth of doubt and speculation. Did she go quickly from under the men's feet, or did she resist to the end, letting the sea batter her to pieces, start her butts, wrench her frame, load her with an increasing weight of salt water, and, dismasted, unmanageable, rolling heavily, her boats gone, her decks swept, had she wearied her men half to death with the unceasing labour at the pumps before she sank with them like a stone?

However, such a case must be rare. I imagine a raft of some sort could always be contrived; and even if it saved no one, it would float on and be picked up, perhaps conveying some hint of the vanished name. Then that ship would not be, properly speaking, missing. She would be 'lost with all hands', and in that distinction there is a subtle difference – less horror and a less appalling darkness.

*

Bullen was describing how a ship should be hove-to, to slow her down or take the way off her, when the seas become too dangerous. Conrad describes the importance of hearing for gauging the time to reduce sail:

*

I had been some time at sea before I became aware of the fact that hearing plays a perceptible part in gauging the force of the wind. It was at night. The ship was one of those iron wool-clippers that the Clyde had floated out in swarms upon the world during the seventh decade of the last century. It was a fine period of ship-building, and also, I might say, a period of over-masting. The spars rigged up on the narrow hulls were indeed tall then, and the ship of which I think, was certainly one of the most heavily-sparred specimens. She was built for hard driving, and unquestionably she got all the driving she could stand. Our captain was a man famous for the quick passages he had been used to make in the old *Tweed*, a ship famous the world over for her speed. In the middle sixties she had beaten by a day and a half the steam mail-boat from Hong-Kong to Singapore. There was something peculiarly lucky, perhaps, in the placing of her masts – who knows? Officers of men-of-war used to come on board to take the exact dimensions of her sail-plan. Perhaps there had been a touch of genius or the finger of good fortune in the fashioning of her lines at bow and stern. It is impossible to say. The *Tweed* had been a wooden vessel, and the captain brought the tradition of quick passages with him into the iron clipper. I was the junior in her, a third mate, keeping watch with the chief officer; and it was just during one of the night watches in a strong, freshening breeze that I overheard two men in the sheltered nook of the main deck exchanging these informing remarks. Said one:

'Should think 'twas time some of them light sails were coming off her.'

And the other, an older man, uttered grumpily:

'No fear! not while the chief mate's on deck. He's that deaf he can't tell how much wind there is.'

And, indeed, poor B—, quite young, and a smart seaman, was very hard of hearing. At the same time, he had the name of being the very devil of a fellow for carrying on sail on a ship. He was wonderfully clever at concealing his deafness, and, as to carrying on heavily, though he was a fearless man, I don't think that he ever meant to take undue risks. I can never forget his naïve sort of astonishment when remonstrated with for what appeared a most dare-devil performance....

I am sure that he would not have got off scot-free like this but for the god of gales, who called him away early from this earth, which is three parts ocean, and therefore a fit abode for sailors. A few years afterwards in an Indian port,

I asked after B—. Had he got a command yet? And the other man answered carelessly:

'No; but he's provided for, anyhow. A heavy sea took him off the poop in the run between New Zealand and the Horn.'

13

Running down the Easting

A CLIPPER making its departure from Wellington would have a run of 5,200 nautical miles to Cape Horn if it kept on the latitude of 42½° S until it reached the meridian of 110° W longitude, and then headed south-east to the latitude of Cape Horn, 56° S. If it sailed along a great circle track from Wellington to the Horn, which would take it down to 65° S, the passage would be about 920 miles shorter. The first of these routes should keep the ship clear of icebergs the whole way – at least in the summer months of January, February and March; whereas the great circle route would be through the iceberg zone the whole way. But usually it would be impossible to go as far south as 65° S, because south of 60° S would be pack ice. There have been many ice dramas along this route. It may seem surprising that a clipper captain should take the risk of sailing through ice in order to cut his voyage short by, say, 700 miles, but one's attitude changes when racing against time on a broad ocean. 'The chance of hitting a mile-wide iceberg when sailing through an area of 500,000 square miles is negligible,' one thinks. Besides that, a look-out was kept on the clippers and it was expected to sight ice before hitting it.

The story of the *Indian Queen* was an amazing ice drama. Here is Basil Lubbock's account of it in his book, *The Colonial Clippers:*

*

The *Indian Queen*, 1,041 tons, the most notable Black Baller launched in 1853, and advertised as *Marco Polo*'s sister ship, was a very fast vessel, her first voyage to Australia [and on round the world back to England] being made in 6 months 11 days, and in 1855 she came home from Hobart in 78 days. In 1859 she narrowly escaped the fate of *Guiding Star*. [The *Guiding Star* was lost with all hands between January and April 1854 and it was generally supposed that this was caused by a huge ice island in about 44° S, 25° W.] The 13th March 1859, she sailed from Melbourne for Liverpool under Captain Brewer, with 40 passengers and the usual cargo of wool and gold dust. All went well until she was half-way to the Horn when on the 27th March the weather became thick with a strong NW wind and heavy westerly swell.

On the 31st March she was in 58° S, 151° W by account; the day was wet, foggy and very cold and the ship logged a steady 12 knots with the wind strong at NW. At 2 am on the following morning those below were aroused by a violent shock, the crash of falling spars and a grinding sound along the port side, and the first of the frightened passengers to arrive on the poop found the ship lying broadside to broadside with an immense iceberg. All her spars and sails above the lower masts were hanging over the starboard side, the foremast was broken off close to the deck and was held at an angle by its rigging, the mainyard was in half, the bowsprit was washing about under the bows, and though the mizzen topmast was still standing the topsail yard was in two, broken in the slings.

The night was dark and rainy and at first the watch below and passengers thought that all was lost. They found no one at the wheel, the port lifeboat gone, and not a soul on the poop, but they were somewhat reassured by the appearance of the carpenter who had been sounding the pumps and pronounced the ship to be making no water. Then the second mate appeared aft and announced that the captain, mate and most of the crew had gone off in the port lifeboat. Apparently there had been a disgraceful panic which involved even the captain, who actually left his own son, an apprentice, behind on the ship.

However, those who had been so shamefully deserted began to buckle to with a will, headed by the second mate, Mr

Leyvret, and the cool-headed carpenter, a man named Thomas Howard. Passengers, cooks, stewards and those of the crew left on board were promptly divided into watches, the captain's son was sent to the wheel, and whilst some set about clearing up the raffle of gear and getting things ship-shape as far as possible, others shovelled the ice, which lay in masses on the decks, overboard. With some difficulty the crossjack was backed and the head of the spanker hauled in. At the same time the boat was perceived tossing in the swell on the port beam and apparently endeavouring to regain the ship, and faint cries for help could be heard against the wind. She seemed to be without oars and with sea after sea washing over, she was soon swept past the ship by the back-wash off the ice and lost sight of in the fog, never to be seen again. The ship, though, with the backed crossjack, began to drift along the side of the berg and presently dropped clear of it into smoother water to leeward.

Day now began to break and all hands set about cutting away the wreck, but the mainyard and the rest of the raffle hanging from the stump of the masthead was hardly clear before the terrible cry of 'Ice to leeward!' arose and a huge berg appeared looming out of the mist. The crossjack was at once braced up, the spanker set and the foresail trimmed in some fashion or other, then in a tense silence the survivors watched the ship slowly forge ahead and, dragging the wreck of masts and spars and torn sails along with her, weather the new danger by a bare hundred yards. And scarcely had she done so when the foremast fell crashing on to the lifeboat, the other boats having already been stove in by falling spars. The business was to get the wreck of the foremast over the side and clear of the ship. Here the carpenter displayed the greatest coolness and skill, being ably backed up by the second mate and the four seamen left on board. With the last of the wreck overside, time was found to muster the survivors, when it was discovered that the captain, chief mate and 15 men had been lost in the port lifeboat, leaving behind the second mate, carpenter, bosun, 4 AB's, 1 OS and 2 boys, besides the cooks, stewards, doctor, purser and passengers who numbered 30 men, 3 women and 7 children.

A course was now steered for Valparaiso, some 3,800 miles away. It was not until the 7th April when the ship got finally clear of the scattered ice, but on the 3rd the wind came out of the south and with a lower stunsail and main staysail set on the main, the ship began to make 3 or 4 knots through the water. One iceberg of huge size and square like a mountainous box was only just cleared before it broke in two, the smaller portion bursting into the sea like an avalanche and, sweeping a huge wave in front of it, did not bring up until it was 2 to 3 miles away from the rest of the berg. The last ice was seen in 54°S, it being reckoned that the accident had happened in 60° S.

As soon as 49° S was reached, a direct course was shaped for Valparaiso, sheers were now rigged and a topmast secured to the stump of the foremast, then topsail yards were crossed on the jury foremast and mainmast which improved the ship's progress another knot. In this condition the *Indian Queen* slowly wandered north, weathering out gale after gale. On the 7th May a welcome sail was sighted. This proved to be the new Bedford whaler, *La Fayette*, whose captain boarded them, offered them every assistance and corrected their longitude, which was 3° out. On the following day the French Man of War, *Constantine*, appeared and promised to convoy them in. On the 9th May land was made some 20 miles south of Valparaiso, and on the morning of the 10th, as the crippled *Indian Queen* approached the bay, the boats of HMS *Ganges*, 84 guns, came out to her aid and towed her into the roads, where she anchored safely, just 40 days after her collision with the iceberg.

*

There are several incidents in this story which I find incredible. I can understand the watch below sleeping through any noise if conditions on deck were tough and if they were doing 4 hours on watch, 4 hours off. But the story says that 'At 2 am those below were aroused by a violent shock, crash of falling spars and a grinding sound along the port side.' How could the captain, first mate and the whole watch on deck have already left the ship in the port lifeboat before the crew or frightened passengers arrived on the poop? Yet they had not only left the ship but there was then no sign of them. I may be looking at this from a singlehander's viewpoint; if sailing alone, a simple increase of the wind strength or even a change in the noise made by the sea striking the ship's hull will wake a singlehander and have him on deck at once. Even if the watch below slept through the noise made by the ice I should have expected them to jump awake when a mast 9 feet in circumference broke.

Secondly, 'The night was dark and rainy,' also foggy. Later it says, 'The boat was perceived tossing in the swell on the port beam.' To be seen in such conditions, the boat must have been close. Why could it not return to the ship if it had been able to pull away from it?

Thirdly, I cannot understand why the boat did not remain near until the ship sank, hoping to get some food and water from it.

Lastly, it is incredible to me that any captain could deliberately leave his ship without warning those below, even if his son were not one of them.

I wonder what really happened?

Many ships simply disappeared without any sign of them or their cargo ever being seen again. This is no longer surprising when you read accounts such as that of the *Ben Voirlich* in 1878. She was on passage for Britain and running in heavy weather westward of the Horn on November 18th. This is how Basil Lubbock records what happened:

*

A very big sea was running, and the helmsman, a Dutchman, let go the wheel from sheer fright. As the ship broached to a huge wave broke over her quarter. This avalanche of water smashed in the break of the poop, gutted the cabin, and took nine men overboard. For an hour the ship lay over on her beam ends dragging her lower yards in the water, entirely out of control. Two men who happened to be at work on the lee fore yard arm were actually washed off it. One of them was lost overboard, but the other caught the rail and lay there head downwards, being held from going further by the chain fore sheet. An apprentice managed to get to him and grab hold, but the next moment a sea swept over them, and whilst the apprentice was washed inboard, the man was never seen again. The same apprentice happened to be washed up against the winch, to which he clung like a limpet; and then, as the old white-bearded sailmaker was hurled by him in the cross wash of the sea, caught the old man and held on to him or he would have gone overboard.

The brave ship struggled gamely; three times she brought her spars to windward, and three times she was laid flat again. The whole of her topgallant rail and bulwarks were washed away, together with everything of a movable nature on the deck. At last after a whole hour of desperate fighting, they managed to get the wheel up and the clipper slowly righted herself as she fell off and brought the wind astern.

*

The *Ben Voirlich* which was built in 1874 was fast; she made a passage from Plymouth to Port Phillip in 64 days. She had a similar experience to the one described above off the Cape of Good Hope in 1885.

Why did these ships take such a pounding while the Donald Mackay-designed gold clippers never appeared to suffer? It would not be surprising if, in similar circumstances the *Lightning* would have been running at 12 knots in comparative comfort with a lot of sail set. Because the Mackay ships were travelling with almost no cargo but only a light load of passengers and because they were built of light wood their displacement was much lighter than the British ships. Only recently have the yacht designers begun to think that a light displacement yacht will stand up to rough seas better than one of heavy displacement. Also, the American design, being broader in the beam, was more buoyant and stable, which enabled it to carry more sail, with an easier roll which, in turn, imposed less strain on the rigging and masts. Another factor, as I said before, was that Mackay designed much stronger rigging and spars than was usual at that time. All this adds up to saying that the Mackay ships of the 1850's were better designed for stability than the British ships.

14

The Southern Ocean

WHAT WAS life really like on the clippers and square-rigged ships? Alan Villiers is the man to tell us; he has sailed in many square-rigged ships both as crew and master; has owned one: has written many books about the sailing life: and is today the chief authority on square-riggers. In 1928 he was in the *Herzogin Cecilie*, a big four-masted barque, a ship square-rigged on the forward three masts and with fore-and-aft sails on the jigger mast at the stern. This ship was of 3,000 tons displacement and sailing from Port Lincoln, Australia, to Falmouth with a cargo of 4,500 tons of wheat. She was racing two other similar ships, probably the last race of its kind. The *Herzogin Cecilie* won this race in 96 days. The second ship, the *C. B. Pedersen*, took 104 days and the third, the *Beatrice*, 114 days (but she chose to sail home via the Cape of Good Hope instead of the Horn). After passing New Zealand the *Herzogin Cecilie* had not got enough wind to suit her. Alan Villiers writes in his book, *Falmouth for Orders*:

*

Fog, head wind, calm, rain – so they came, and after two weeks at sea we were not at Campbell Island. The ship loyally did her best, but she could not sail without wind, and there was little progress.

If there was not much of progress, there was never any scarcity of work. Fog, head wind, calm, rain – all meant work for our nineteen boys and the officers who commanded them. Head winds brought frequent puttings about, in the endeavour to make as much of what wind there was as possible; fog brought weary hours on the focs'l head, braying away with the fog-horn at the world of grey sea, albatrosses, and thick-hanging, clammy fog; and the yards are never hauled around so much as in a calm. The odd moments of fresh wind brought torn sails, and hard work high aloft getting them down and bending new ones....

Fooling about with rain-swollen ropes and rain-sodden sails in a calm is one of the most miserable aspects of sailing-ship life. In a calm the sailer lies dead, an encumbrance to herself and a source of worry to her crew; it is then, by the perversity of life, that the yards have to be hauled around more than under any other conditions. Often in our watch on deck in a rainy night of calm the mate's two whistles – he called us from our quarters by two shrill blasts on a whistle that everybody cursed – would summon us out to mess about with braces or with sails. It was a muttering band of discontents that followed the mate about and hauled half-heartedly on ropes in heavy rain, and said 'Satan!' with a malevolent vehemence. The uselessness of the operation takes the heart out of the watch, and they take four times as long as they usually would to swing around the yards. Every rope is foul, every block too small, every yard heavy as a six-wheeled omnibus. We pull and haul on every rope in the darned ship, and shift every darned sail, and utter every curse we know; and the competence of the officers is hotly criticised. Everybody is wet through; oilskins will not stand up to heavy continuous rain, and becoming thoroughly wet are more a hindrance than a help. To raise one's arms to haul upon some thickened rope is to invite a stream of cold water to pour down between clothes and skin; the watch swears that the wind is not coming from the quarter to which the mate is hauling around the yards, that it never has come from that quarter, and that it will never come from that quarter so long as *Herzogin Cecilie* is at sea. As a matter of fact, a faint breeze is perceptible from that quarter and the move of the mate is thoroughly justified. We know it and grin up our rain-soaked sleeves as we swear the more. For what is life without a growl?...

Give us wind, we said. Wind, wind!

The sixteenth day out from Australia they had their wind:

Not very long after we had made the t'gallant-stays'ls fast, the leach of the mizzen-royal blew out with a wild boom of canvas and quivering of the yard. It was a matter of great difficulty to mount the royal-yards, high above the reeling deck; to look into the wind up there was to have one's breath taken away. Fierce as the wind rushed across the decks, it was peaceful there to the fury aloft. How the wind roars through the sailing ship's rigging! How magnificent is its sound! Though it brings to us only work – hard, dangerous, tremendous, Herculean work of a kind people ashore can never know – we yet can feel the glory of the roar of the wind in the sailer's steel rigging, A score-odd notes are here, if you listen closely, if you listen carefully into the sullen great roaring that drowns everything at first. There is the plaintive moaning at the rigging screws, each with a different note; the sighing through the slackened running gear, and the mad roar at the wet and powerful backstays. Out on the yards there is a different note again, the noise of powerful winds meeting powerful canvas, and sending the good ship on; and down there on deck, far, far below, where puny figures haul on ropes and a big figure that is the mate stares aloft, is the crashing and the booming of the seas that break aboard. The great seas – the sea is gale-high now – come thundering at the ship like breakers at a rock-clad ocean beach, and break all around her and all over her as if they are bent upon breaking her, too; and here aloft the wind sweeps unchecked upon us, and tears the coats from our backs, and snatches the caps from our heads, and blinds us with rain, and cuts us with hail, and tears at the grip of our numbed hands upon the weather rigging, and brings the moisture to our eyes and the spirit to our souls, and we fight on! It is all very grand – very grand indeed. But it is also very hard . . .

Before the night was out we had one of the hardest fights upon a tops'l-yard of *Herzogin Cecilie* that I had ever experienced at sea . . .

We got the tops'l fast in the end; and just as we passed the last gasket on the lee side a mad roar above the noise of wind and sea for'ard told us that something was amiss. It was! The lee sheet of the fore upper tops'l – a chain with links three inches long made of steel half an inch through – had carried away and the lee side of the sail had blown to glory.

There had not been time to clew up that tops'l. We hastened on deck and joined the band that was trying to get the sail clewed up, but as soon as we tried to haul upon the buntlines they carried away. They were heavy steel wire, quite new, and had been sent aloft only in Port Lincoln. Every buntline carried away – there were five – and one of the clewlines with them. We did not waste any more time trying to haul the sail up in gear that it no longer possessed, but crowded into the rigging and fought our way aloft. It was a little after midnight then. The first sullen light of day was high in the storm-swept sky before we came down again.

It was a terrible business. To have made the sail fast, with all its gear, properly clewed up and everything in order, would have been a big job for all hands in conditions like that. But with no gear at all! Some of us thought we were going up to cut it away.

It was a matter of great difficulty and some danger to get aloft at all. The whole mast was shivering and shaking violently with the furious flapping of the sail; the great steel yard which held it quivered and bent; the rigging trembled fearfully, as if the ship were grinding upon some rock; and through it all was the roar of the mad wind, the lashing of the mad rain, and the fury of the mad sea. Slowly, slowly, steadily and surely, we worked our way aloft. Green seas fell upon the lower rigging as we climbed; the sprays drove over us high aloft. Every now and then the ship lay so far over and the wind blew so terrifically that we could not climb at all; we had to hang on for our lives, and wait our chance. Then up we went up again; up, up, always up. Nobody looked down upon the reeling decks that they were leaving; eyes strained aloft at the thick black murk overhead, and saw the shape of the flying tops'l bulking huge before them. So we fought on, over the futtock-shrouds and on into the topmast rigging that led to the yard. Here the job looked utterly impossible. As the ship rolled to lee and back to windward the rigging alternately tautened so that we thought it would break, and slackened so that it flung round turns in itself, and in us too. It seemed to be doing its utmost to prevent us from accomplishing its ascent; maybe it was trying to warn us not to go on the yard. But we had not time to think of that then, and we fought on.

It looked as if it were walking into the arms of death to go on that yard. Maybe it was, in a way, though one by one we went out, and nobody thought of that. The loose end of the chain-sheet, flying insanely around, swished through the air with a mad s-s-s-s, threatening murder to us all and every now and then thwacking the steel lower tops'l-yard with a crash that shook it, setting up an awful display of electric sparks. It tore a hole in the canvas of the lower tops'l, and the lee side of that went, too. The loose ends of the wire buntlines that had carried away were up to the same game, coiling through the air like steel snakes, writhing around us, just missing us, flying into the air and entwining around the rigging. These were only some of the things that we had to face to lay out on that yard. The whole of the tops'l – and it was 95 feet wide by 25 feet deep of best storm-canvas – flapped back over the yard every now and then, seeming to say to us that if we were mad enough to go out there – well, it would know what to do with us, that was all. We went; it bellied back upon us so that we had to slip down on the foot-ropes and lie there for our lives; it flung itself over that yard in a furious attempt to dislodge the puny humans who had come to fight it. Pieces of it that had carried away were flying around in the air like the loose buntline ends, and if any of these had caught us around the neck it would have been the end. We fought out our way, step by step, to the weather yardarm where we knew that we must begin our battle with the sail. There we hung for over an hour, now clawing desperately at the canvas, trying to get it in as there came a momentary lull, now hanging on even more desperately for our lives as the lull passed and the fury of the gale was worse than ever. Now we fought the sail from the weather leach and could do nothing; now we moved – slowly, tortuously, dangerously, grimly – into the middle of the yard, to try there with even less result; now we stumbled out to the lee side and renewed our desperate energies there, while the demon that was in that gale shrieked deafeningly into our ears, 'You will never do it; best cut it away!' We could not help hearing that shriek, but we took no notice. We fought on, always on; maybe a boy thought, wildly for an instant now and then when the banging back of the sail all but knocked him from the yard, of giving in – but only for an instant, fleetingly.

I do not know how we managed, in the end, to get what was left of that sail fast. No one who was on that yard knew; no one will ever know. There were times – many of them – when we feared that we should never manage it, when our tired muscles and torn hands found it a little hard to carry on, when the wind literally tore the long since useless oilskins from our backs and the hail just as literally cut right into our flesh. It was hell! It was madness! It was a desperate, losing fight, this struggle between a score-odd boys and a man or two, and all the fury of that down-south gale. But if we knew only too well that it was desperate, we were not prepared to admit that we had lost. We fought on.

We went back to the weather leach; shifted again to the middle of the yard; tried to get ropes around the sail; tried to pass a wire around it – and accomplished nothing. A score-odd times we got something of that 2,000-odd square feet of insane canvas up on the yard, and lay over it in the hope that we should get a little more. And just as many times with one mighty flap the sail took it all from us and we had to begin again. We dug our fingers – or tried to dig our fingers – into that canvas until it was wet with our blood in parts, as well as with the sprays and the rain; and always we had to try again. It was impossible to hold that canvas. Sitting quietly by some fireside ashore, can any who read this imagine what we faced? Perhaps it took a little courage to carry on up there, with a suspicion of ice about the rigging, and hands that were blue with cold and red with blood. We had not time to think of courage then; we had only time to fight on. We fought on, and lost; but there came a time, in a temporary lull that was a little longer than most, that we fought and won....

Once a steel buntline, writhing back over the yard, caught Zimmerman in the head and brought the swift blood. He reeled a bit, but carried on. Then after a while we saw that he had fainted, and lay in imminent peril across the yard. For one awful moment the canvas stayed still while we fought to him, and then because we could not take him down we lashed him there. And when we had time to remember him again we found that he had come to, and was working. Game? I don't know; it was no use any being in the ship-of-sails who was not like that.

Nyman, too, was fortunate to come from that tops'l-yard with his life. There is an old adage concerning working aloft that says something about one hand for the ship and one hand for yourself. If we had believed in that we never would have got that tops'l fast. It was two hands for the ship when the gale gave us a chance; and two hands for ourselves at times, when the only thing that we could do was hang on. Nyman was strong – very strong – but the grip of his two powerful hands was flung out of that canvas once, and he fell back over the yard. Somebody must have been looking after us up there; he caught the after-jackstay, and swinging up again, worked on. He looked down once at where he would have fallen, but did not say anything. I was next to him on the yard; it is doubtful if he would have fallen into the sea or on the decks. Either would have meant the same.

Once, while we fought, the moon broke through the flying storm clouds for an instant – a sight magnificent! Below, the ship crashing through the great black sea at fifteen knots, flying blindly onward for Cape Horn; all around her the white foam boiling madly; here aloft a score-odd boys – little sixteen-year-old apprentices and seventeen-year-old ABs – fighting for their lives.

And when, long after the moon had set and the sun had risen again, they came on deck, they smiled.

The *Herzogin Cecilie* had grand sailing from New Zealand to the Horn, 5,000 miles in 17 days.

The morning of the day we passed the Horn was bright and beautiful, with clear sunlight that, though it gave no actual warmth, yet disguised the cold a bit; and our great fair wind blew us on. It was splendid to be in a sailing ship then, and to walk the decks – with several coats on – and hear the music of it all, to look aloft at the white sails and whiter clouds far overhead – there was a hint of storm in those clouds, despite the sun – and to lean over the side and watch the broken water flying swiftly by. We were doing a steady thirteen knots then, fairly roaring along, rolling heavily now and then as the old ship dipped her rusty sides in answer to the caressing of the foam. It was all very grand, and rather pleasant, and infinitely beautiful – in the morning. Who would not be here, we thought, in a great sailing ship racing around Cape Horn? . . .

In *Herzogin Cecilie* there was a concert in the starboard focs'l on the night that we came around Cape Horn. All the boys were there, and the ship's orchestra played beautiful sad Finnish music, and Swedish music, and German. Schmidt of Weimar was the leader with the violin, of which he was a master, and his players were Fyhrqvist with another violin, Nyman with a mandolin, and Ringe with his drums. Ringe had been hurt at the wheel a night or two before. It was very hard to hold *Herzogin Cecilie* to her course in strong winds – too hard. It should have been the work of two boys, and not one.

But Ringe was not hurt so much that he would not have his drums brought to him, and play. What a memorable concert it was down there! Schmidt, his body swaying with the motion of the ship and the light of the focs'l lamp falling fitfully on his fine face, standing there with his violin, leading his little orchestra with the ability of a genius – I never heard such music in a ship before as Schmidt could get from that orchestra; it was lifeless without him – Fyhrqvist beside him, playing as if he loved it (and he did); Nyman swaying on a form with his back crouched against the focs'l table; Ringe struggling with the drums in his bunk, with the photographs of his home and his ships around him. Lying in their bunks, huddled on their sea-chests or on the forms, the boys gathered around and listened. The lamp swayed from side to side with the roll of the ship; outside was the roar of wind, and the pelting of rain overhead, and the swish of water on the fore-deck; and now and then there came the thunder of a sea smashing on the steel side so close, and the whole ship shuddered violently.

What did we care? We listened to the music, and thought. And predominant in our thoughts was the knowledge that Falmouth was not just a name upon the map any more. For we had come around Cape Horn.

*

Vito Dumas, during his solo passage from Wellington to Valparaiso during February and March of 1943, records two items of interest. On February 1st, after crossing the 180° meridian, 256 miles from Wellington, he wrote that he narrowly escaped disaster, passing very close to the floating trunk of an enormous tree. On February 8th he had a strange adventure. When he came on deck he was paralysed with fright; he thought that *Lehg II* had run on the rocks. He found the yacht had run into two whales, climbed up a shining back and then slipped off again. He wrote:

The seconds were interminable. What was the whales' reaction going to be? Perhaps the creature being jostled by my hull thought that his companion was being playful. They seemed to be asleep. I did not dare to move for fear of startling the monsters.

*

With exasperating slowness the boat pushed through between the whales and Dumas' heart resumed its normal beat.

Miles Smeeton, in his book, *Once is Enough*, describes the lonely feeling caused by the great Southern Ocean between New Zealand and the Horn.

*

A sailor, or at least a navigator, is always conscious of the land about him. The sea may be empty and clear from horizon to horizon, yet he will know that just here or just over there, is the land. Sometimes, when no land is visible, he will feel hemmed in by it, and sometimes he will be conscious of the sea's great deserted loneliness. I had never had the feeling of loneliness in the Atlantic or the Pacific. Here was a steamship route, there an island, and over us an aircraft might pass. Although for days and days we had seen nothing, we had always been aware of man moving or living not too far away. Now, as we entered the Southern Ocean, with New Zealand behind us, there was a feeling of desertion and loneliness. The Chilean coast was over 4,000 miles away, and in all that sea probably no ships at all. The only living things above the waters were the wheeling, wandering birds. Because we had just been struggling with the wind together, and because we had achieved what we were trying to do, and the ship was flying along on her course, we felt at one with the ship and at one with each other. This feeling of companionship was strong between us.

*

Conor O'Brien seemed happy enough in the Southern Ocean:

*

We had not seen land or land animals for a month, and this incursion of life, even of pelagic life [a really enormous quantity of prions and Cape pigeon which they had come upon], was welcome. Most conspicuous of course on account of his great size was the wandering albatross. That is what I call him when he is sweeping in wide circles around the ship without moving a muscle. But when he is afloat, or comes very near one, the sailors' name of 'Cape Sheep' seems more appropriate, for he is a woolly beast and clothed with very untidy ragged wool at that, while his face is, except for a beak more than a foot long, distinctly ovine. All this woolliness makes him very light for his bulk, and in consequence he drifts about in a ridiculous manner on the water and occasionally capsizes in a rough sea. He seemed to me to be singularly careless about the set of his feathers: one would suppose that a bird which spent most of his life in the air would be very particular about his wings, and I was much surprised to see him boxing his wife's ears with them. But he does not beat the water with them when he rises from it, which he does in this wise. He turns head to wind, spreads his wings, slowly lifts his right foot and places it on the surface, then does the same with his left, and lastly draws both up under him, and there he is. No need to flap or kick as lesser fowls do, his system of levitation supersedes the cruder methods. And in some marvellous manner, for the secret of which I am sure any aeroplane builder would give his fortune, he goes on rising or travelling in any direction without moving his wings for an apparently endless period. For a long time I believed that the Mother Carey's Chicken, at the other end of the scale of size, had the power of levitation even more developed, and never used the sea at all except to walk upon; whence his name of stormy petrel, or little Peter. But I saw these butterflies of the sea sharing the refuse of a whale factory with the Cape pigeon, and then they could not even walk on the water, much less fly. Still in normal conditions I never saw one swimming, out of all the thousands that accompanied us. It must be a very wearing life, for they never rise more than a few inches above the surface, and as the waves may be rising twenty feet and moving with corresponding speed in any direction, great vigilance and agility is required to avoid getting knocked over by the breaking crests, though of course the birds can walk up the unbroken slopes. But all the oceanic birds are wonderfully skilful at dodging seas, even the albatross sometimes comes down to amaze one by his swoops along the narrow rolling valleys. The low flying habit seems to be proportionate to the smallness of the birds; next to the Mother Carey's Chicken comes the prion, who keeps about the height of an average flying-fish, which he would resemble greatly but for his erratic zigzag flight. I think they feed on things so small that even their keen sight could not pick them out from a considerable elevation; and it is even said that the reason the stormy petrel likes a good breeze is that he picks animalculæ out of the spindrift.

15

Cape Horn

Now the clipper way is approaching the dreaded Cape Horn and in the seas around it, surely, far more drama has occurred than in any other ocean.

Why has the Horn got such an infamous reputation? Anyone reading about the storm winds and waves near Cape Horn must wonder why they should be so much more fearsome there than in the rest of the world.

The prevailing winds in the Forties and Fifties, between 50° S and 60° S, are westerly and pretty fresh on the average. For instance, off the Horn there are gales of Force 8 or more on one day in four in the spring and one day in eight in the summer. Winds have a lazy nature in that they refuse to climb over a mountain range if they can sweep past the end of it. South America has one of the greatest mountain ranges of the world, the Andes, which blocks the westerlies along a front of 1,200 miles from 35° S right down to Cape Horn. All this powerful wind is crowding through Drake's Strait between Cape Horn and the South Shetland Islands, 500 miles to the south. The normal westerlies pouring through this gap are interfered with by the turbulent, vicious little cyclones rolling off the Andes. The same process occurrs in reverse with the easterly winds which, though more rare than the westerlies, blow when a depression is passing north of the Horn.

As for the waves, the prevailing westerlies set up a current flowing eastwards round the world at a mean rate of 1 to 20 miles per day. This current flows in all directions at times due to the passing storms, but the result of all the different currents is this 10 to 20 miles per day flowing eastwards. As the easterly may check this current or even reverse it for a while, the prevailing stream flowing eastwards may sometimes amount to as much as 50 miles a day. As with the winds, this great ocean river is forced to pass between South America and the South Shetland Islands. This in itself tends to make the stream turbulent.

But there is another factor which greatly increases the turbulence. The bottom of the ocean shelves between the Horn and the Shetland Islands and this induces the huge seas to break. It is like a sea breaking on the beach at Bournemouth in a gale, except that the waves, instead of being 4 feet high, are likely to be 60 feet high.

There is yet another factor to make things worse. Anyone who has sailed out past the Needles from the Solent when the outgoing tide is opposing a Force 6 wind knows what a hateful short steep sea can result. A yacht will seem to be alternately standing on its stem and its stern with a lot of water coming inboard. The same thing happens at the Horn on a gigantic scale if there is an easterly gale blowing against the current flowing past the Horn.

What size are these notorious waves? No one has yet measured them accurately in the Southern Ocean, but the oceanographers have been measuring waves in the North Atlantic for some years. The British Institute of Oceanography have invented a wave measuring instrument which they use at the weather ships stationed in the Atlantic. Recently one instrument with a 60-foot scale recorded a wave of which the trace went off the scale. This wave was estimated at 69 feet in height, higher than our five-storey house in London. An American steamship in the South Pacific is said to have encountered a wave 112 feet high. Brian Grundy who used to sail with me in *Gipsy Moth II* told me that when he was in the Southern Ocean in a big whaling steamer he reckoned that one wave was 120 feet high. L. Draper of the Institute of Oceanography says that, according to *Statistics of a Stationary Random Process*, if a sea of average height 30 feet is running, then one wave out of every 300,000 can be expected to be four times that height, i.e. 120 feet.

Drake's Strait between the Horn and the South Shetland Islands was discovered by Sir Francis Drake in 1578. Previous to that it was thought that the land on the south side of the Magellan Strait was part of a southern continent. Drake had quite an adventure leading to this great discovery and we are lucky in having two different accounts of it; one was from Francis Fletcher, Chaplain on Drake's ship, the *Golden Hind*; the other account is from Nuno da Silva, a Portuguese captured by Drake and carried along by him as a sort of pilot. The account of Nuno da Silva the seaman is interestingly different from that of Fletcher the parson.

Francis Fletcher's story which I quote is from a manuscript in the British Museum setting out to be a literal copy of Fletcher's notes. The script was dated 1577, but this must be a mistake for 1578 because records show that the expedition did not leave Plymouth till November 1577.

Nuno da Silva was the pilot of a Portuguese ship which Drake took in the Cape Verde Islands. Drake freed all the crew and passengers of this ship except da Silva who was a man 'well travelled in Brasilia' and was said to be most willing to go with them into the South Sea. Da Silva wrote an account of the voyage in 1579 for the viceroy of New Spain in Mexico City. The Hakluyt Society of London printed these accounts in 1854 in a volume entitled *The World Encompassed by Sir Francis Drake*.

Drake's squadron had sailed through the Magellan Straits and emerged on the Pacific side. Da Silva wrote:

*

Being out of the Streight on the other side, upon the sixt of September of the aforesaid yeere, they held their course Northwest for the space of three dayes, and the third day they had a Northeast wind, that by force drave them West south west, which course they held for the space of ten or twelve dayes with few sailes up: and because the wind began to be very great, they tooke in all their sailes, and lay driving till the last of September.

The 24. day of the same moneth having lost the sight of one of their shippes, which was about an hundred tunne [this was the *Elizabeth*, 80 tons, under the command of Captain John Winter], then againe they hoised saile because the winde came better, holding their course Northeast for the space of seven dayes, and at the end of the sayde seven dayes, they had the sight of certayne Islands, which they made towards for to anker by them, but the weather would not permit them: and being there, the wind fell Northwest: whereupon they sailed West Southwest.

The next day they lost sight of another ship of their company, for it was very foule weather, so that in the ende the admirals shippe was left alone, for the ship of Nuno da Silva was left in the Bay where they wintered before they entred into the Streights: and with this foule weather they ranne till they were under seven and fiftie degrees, where they entred into a haven of an Island, and ankered about the length of the shot of a great piece from the land, at twentie fathome deepe, where they stayed three or foure dayes, and the wind comming Southward, they weyed anker, holding their course Northward for the space of two daies, and then they espied a small inhabited Island, where being arrived, they stroke sailes, and hoised out their boate, and there they tooke many birds and seales.

*

That is da Silva's bald account of the navigation. Here now is parson Fletcher's account of the same events after they had emerged from the Magellan Straits:

*

[The wind] being boath right against us and so violent that it was intollerable, wee were enforced back againe with the lee shoare of the Southerly Ilands from whence wee departed, with a fearfull look for destruction that night before day. The day being come, the light and sight of sonn and land was taken from us, so that here followed as it were a palpable darknes by the space of 56 dayes without the sight of sonn, moone, or starrs, the moone only excepted, which we see in eclipse the space of a quarter of an houre or there abouts. About which tyme, the storme being so outragious and furious, the bark *Marigold*, wherein Edward Bright, one of the accusers of Thomas Doubty, was captayne, with 28 soules, were swallowed up with the horrible and unmercifull waves, or rather mountanes of the sea, which chanced in the second watch of the night, wherein myself and John Brewer, our trumpeter, being in watch, did heare their fearefull cryes, when the hand of God came upon them. We thus deprived of our hand maid, continued without hope at the pleasure of God in the violent force of the winds, intollerable workeing of the wrathful seas, and the grisely beholding (sometymes) of the cragged rocks and fearfull height and monstrous mountaines, being to us a leeshoare, where unto we were continually driven by the winds, and carried by the mountaine-like billows of the seas, to looke every moment to have the lyke end as our other shipp had...

[They were driven into a large bay which I guess to be Bahia Otway on the south side of Isla Desolacion at the western entrance of Magellan Strait.] Our cables brake, our ankers came home, our ships were separated, and our spirits fainted as with the last gasp unto death, and though the Lord sett both our shipps from perishing, and spared our limbs, yet wee in the Admirall were fully perswaded the Vice Admirall was perished; and the Vice Admirall had the same opinion of us (as since it hath been confessed). [The Vice Admiral shot off for England which he reached in June of the following year. They had entered the South Sea on September 6th 1578. The Vice Admiral in the *Elizabeth* probably worked a passage through the narrow channel at the south-east end of Isla Desolacion into the Magellan Strait and from there made his way back into the Atlantic.] Notwithstanding, when it seemed good to God, after so long tryall of so long a tyme as 56 days of so unspeakable setting of the heavens, earth, seas, and wind against us, to the enforcing of us to confesse that God had met jumpe with us 'in Mari Pacifico' with so mighty a hand, as was told us, I doubt not by the Spirit of God, at Port Julian, as hath beene sayde, it pleased him againe for His Name's sake to heare the prayers of them which unfeignedly called up His most holly and reverend name, and for their sakes to deliver the rest, in the onely mediation of Christ Jesus, wherefore Hee caused the sunn by day and the moon and stars by night to shine upon us. He changed the sterne lookes of the grisely mountains to yeeld a favourable countenance, the heavens to laugh, the seas to obey, and the winds to cease; yea, every place we looked upon to yeeld us kind entertainment to refresh our weather beaten bodyes and lives, discomforted in so greavous miserye and forlorn state, which thing fell out most happily in His Providence that the uttmost Island of 'Terra Incognita', to the Southward of America, whereat wee ariveing, made both the seas to be one and the self same sea and that there was no farther land beyond the heights of the Iland, being to the Southward of the Aequinoctiall 55° and certain minutes to divide them; but that the way lay open for shipping in that height without lett or stay, being the main sea . . . In this Island were growing wonderfull plenty of the small berry with us named currants, or as the common sort call them small raisins. Myselfe being landed, did, with my bag, travell to the southernmost point of the Iland, to the sea on that syde where I found that Iland to be more Southerly three parts of a degree than anny of the rest of the Ilands. Where, haveing sett up on end a stone of som biggness, and with such tooles as I hadd of purpose ever about mee when I went on shoare, had engraven Her Majestyes name, her kingdom, the yeare of Christ, and the day of the moneth, I returned againe in som reasonable tyme to our company. Wee departing hence . . . altered the name of those Southerly Ilands from 'Terra Incognita' (for so it was before our coming thither, and so should have remained still with our good wills) to 'Terra Nunc Bene Cognita', that is, Broken Ilands . . . At our departure from this Iland, this one thing wee observed: the night was but two houres long, and yet the sonn was not in the tropick by eight degrees, whereoff we gatherd that when the sonn should be in the tropick, they should have no night at all, neither would the sonn be out of their sight at anny tyme for certaine dayes, by reason of its Easterly and Westerly course, as it falleth out in Russia and other the Northerly countryes, when the sonn is in our tropic, as our country men travellers in those parts can witness and myself in my former travels have seen.

*

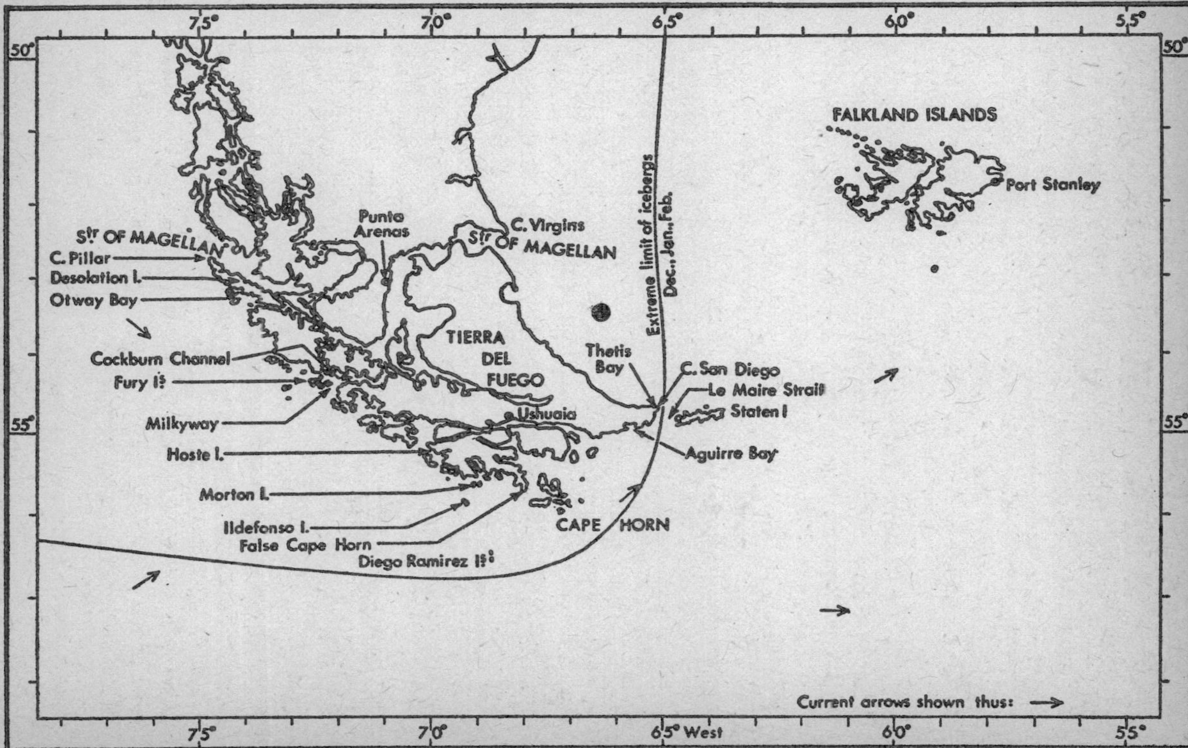
75°
70°
65°
60°
55°
50°
55°
FALKLAND ISLANDS
Port Stanley
Sᵗʳ OF MAGELLAN
C. Pillar
Desolation I.
Otway Bay
Punta Arenas
C. Virgins
Sᵗʳ OF MAGELLAN
Extreme limit of icebergs Dec., Jan., Feb.
TIERRA DEL FUEGO
Cockburn Channel
Fury Iˢ
Milkyway
Ushuaia
Thetis Bay
C. San Diego
Le Maire Strait
Staten I
Aguirre Bay
Hoste I.
Morton I.
Ildefonso I.
False Cape Horn
Diego Ramirez Iˢ
CAPE HORN
65° West
Current arrows shown thus:

Drake's nephew in his account of 1628, based on the Chaplain's notes, described Drake's Passage south of the Horn more clearly: 'The uttermost cape or hedland of all these Ilands, stands neere in 56 deg, without which there is no maine nor Iland to be seene to the Southwards, but that the Atlanticke Ocean and the South Sea, meete in a most large and free scope.'

*

This is the account of the traditional discovery of Drake's Strait. Drake did not discover Cape Horn, but was either at the Diego Ramirez Islands or at the Ildefonso Islands. Let us examine the evidence; Fletcher says that the island was 55 degrees and certain minutes south of the Equinoctial and that there was no land beyond it. This description could apply to the Ildefonsos 55° 50′ S, or to Horn Island which is from 55° 55′ to 55° 59′ S. However, he goes on to say that he found that the island was three parts of a degree south of any of the rest of the islands, which is 45 miles. This rules out Horn Island which is one of a group of about twenty islands and islets, all so close together that you cannot get a clear view through in any direction north of Horn Island. On the other hand the Ildefonsos do not fit well either because there are many islands 15 miles to the north and one, Morton Island, only 13 miles to the NNE.

Fletcher says that he did, with his bag, travel to the southernmost point of the island, to the sea, where he engraved a stone etc. Now Horn Island runs 5 miles in a NW-SE direction. It has high black cliffs towards the south and the cape rises to 1,330 feet. The soil consists mostly of hard turf and the vegetation is luxuriant. Surely parson Fletcher would have recorded that he had been mountaineering if he had traversed the island. Also I cannot associate Cape Horn with a wonderful plenty of small raisins growing on it, but perhaps that is only prejudice.

It seems to me that they were at the Diego Ramirez Islands. These lie a degree or 60 miles south-west by west of the Horn group and three-quarters of a degree or 45 miles SE by S of the Ildefonso Islands which seems to fit in with one of Mr

Fletcher's statements. The Diego Ramirez are in latitude 56½° S exactly, and although that does not agree with Fletcher's statement of 55 degrees and some minutes, it does agree with the pilot Nuno da Silva's statement that the island was 'under seven and fiftie degrees'. Da Silva says they anchored in 20 fathoms at the range of a big gun from the land. The Admiralty Pilot states there is an anchorage close eastward of the middle of one island in a depth of 16 fathoms with a sandy bottom. I am convinced that Drake never saw Cape Horn but discovered the Diego Ramirez Islands and correctly deduced that there was a passage south of them between the Atlantic and Pacific Oceans.

*

One of the worst cases of savaging by the elements off Cape Horn is that of Anson's Squadron during his voyage round the world in 1741 – 163 years after Drake's passage. Anson was rounding the Horn the hard way – from east to west – against the prevailing gales and the strong ocean current. His ships were poorly built according to our modern standards; the hulls rose high above the water, causing great wind resistance – so great that they could not beat to windward against strong winds and rough seas; the best they could do in such conditions was to proceed at right angles to the direction of the wind. They suffered a frightful hundred days trying to beat round the Horn. They left England a squadron of 8 ships of which 4 reached Juan Fernandes Island in the Pacific. Of these the *Gloucester* had only 82 left out of 374 crew. Most of the men still alive were too ill to work the ship. Captain Saunders had only himself and 4 crew to work the *Tryall*. The story was written by Richard Walter who sailed in the flagship *Centurion* with Anson:

*

On the 7th of March, in the morning, we opened Streights Le Maire, and soon after, or about ten o'clock, the *Pearl* and the *Tryall* being ordered to keep ahead of the squadron, we entered them with fair weather and a brisk gale, and were hurried through by the rapidity of the tide in about two hours, though they are between seven and eight leagues in length. As these streights are often esteemed to be the boundary between the Atlantic and Pacific Oceans, and as we presumed we had nothing before us from hence but an open sea, till we arrived on those opulent coasts where all our hopes and wishes centered, we could not help perswading ourselves that the greatest difficulty of our voyage was now at an end, and that our most sanguine dreams were upon the point of being realised; and hence we indulged our imaginations in those romantic schemes which the fancied possession of the Chilian gold and Peruvian silver might be conceived to inspire. These joyous ideas were considerably heightened by the brightness of the sky and serenity of the weather, which was indeed most remarkably pleasing; for though the winter was now advancing apace, yet the morning of this day, in its brilliancy and mildness, gave place to none we had seen since our departure from England. Thus animated by these flattering delusions, we passed those memorable streights, ignorant of the dreadful calamities which were then impending, and just ready to break upon us; ignorant that the time drew near when the squadron would be separated never to unite again, and that this day of our passage was the last chearful day that the greatest part of us would ever live to enjoy. We had scarcely reached the southern extremity of the Streights Le Maire, when our flattering hopes were instantly lost in the apprehensions of immediate destruction: for before the sternmost ships of the squadron were clear of the streights, the serenity of the sky was suddenly obscured, and we observed all the presages of an impending storm; and presently the wind shifted to the southward, and blew in such violent squalls that we were obliged to hand our top-sails, and reef our main-sail; whilst the tide, too, which had hitherto favoured us, at once turned furiously against us, and drove us to the eastward with prodigious rapidity, so that we were in great anxiety for the *Wager* and the *Anna* pink, the two sternmost vessels, fearing they would be dashed to pieces against the store of Staten-land: nor were our apprehension without foundation, for it was with the utmost difficulty they escaped.

From the storm which came on before we had well got clear of Streights Le Maire, we had a continual succession of such tempestuous weather as surprized the oldest and most experienced mariners on board, and obliged them to confess that what they had hitherto called storms were inconsiderable gales compared with the violence of these winds, which raised such short, and at the same time such mountainous waves, as greatly surpassed in danger all seas known in any other part of the globe: and it was not without great reason that this unusual appearance filled us with continual terror; for, had any one of these waves broke fairly over us, it must, in all probability, have sent us to the bottom. Nor did we escape with terror only; for the ship rolling incessantly gunwale to, gave us such quick and violent motions that the men were in perpetual danger of being dashed to pieces against the decks or sides of the ship. And though we were extremely careful to secure ourselves from these shocks by grasping some fixed body, yet many of our people were forced from their hold, some of whom were killed, and others greatly injured; in particular, one of our best seamen was canted overboard and drowned, another dislocated his neck, a third was thrown into the main hold and broke his thigh, and one of our boatswain's mates broke his collar-bone twice; not to mention many other accidents of the same kind.

On the 23rd, we had a most violent storm of wind, hail, and rain, with a very great sea; and though we handed the main topsail before the height of the squall, yet we found the yard sprung; and soon after the foot rope of the main-sail breaking, the main-sail itself split instantly to rags, and, in spite of our endeavours to save it, much the greater part of it was blown overboard. On this, the commodore made the signal for the squadron to bring-to; and the storm at length flattening to a calm, we had an opportunity of getting down our main top-sail to put the carpenters to work upon it, and of repairing our rigging; after which, having bent a new mainsail, we got under sail again with a moderate breeze; but in less than twenty-four hours we were attacked by another storm more furious than the former; for it proved a perfect hurricane, and reduced us to the necessity of lying-to under our bare poles. As our ship kept the wind better than any of the rest, we were obliged, in the afternoon, to wear ship, in order to join the squadron to the leeward, which otherwise we should have been in danger of losing in the night; and as we dared not venture any sail abroad, we were obliged to make use of an expedient which answered our purpose; this was putting the helm a weather, and manning the fore-shrouds: but though this method proved successful for the end intended, yet in the execution of it one of our ablest seamen was canted overboard; we perceived that, notwithstanding the prodigious agitation of the waves, he swam very strong, and it was with the utmost concern that we found ourselves incapable of assisting him; indeed we were the more grieved at his unhappy fate, as we lost sight of him struggling with the waves, and conceived from the manner in which he swam that he might continue sensible, for a considerable time longer, of the horror attending his irretrievable situation.

Before this last-mentioned storm was quite abated, we found two of the main-shrouds and one mizzen-shroud broke, all of which we knotted, and set up immediately.

*

The classic story of sailing round Cape Horn comes from Richard Henry Dana who wrote *Two Years Before the Mast*, first published in 1840.

Dana was born in Massachusetts in 1815. While at Harvard he had measles which damaged his eyesight so severely that he had to leave the university. He shipped as crew in a windjammer for two years. Anyone reading the account of his voyage could well be astonished to learn that he finished his university course on return and became a lawyer.

Dana's writing is so good that, 130 years later, it leads me to criticize the captain's navigation; but here is the story first:

Dana was sailing in the barque *Alert* from San Diego on the west coast of the United States, round the Horn to the east coast. The ship was burdened with a dead weight cargo of 40,000 hides and 30,000 horns and therefore must take a worse pounding from the seas than if she had been light in ballast with passengers.

*

We were short handed for a voyage round Cape Horn in the dead of winter. Besides S— and myself there were only five in the forecastle; who, together with four boys in the steerage, sailmaker, carpenter, etc. composed the whole crew. In addition to this, we were only three or four days out, when the sailmaker, who was the oldest and best seamen on board, was taken with the palsy, and was useless for the rest of the voyage . . . By the loss of the sailmaker, our watch was reduced to five, of whom two were boys, who never steered but in fine weather, so that the other two and myself had to stand at the wheel four hours apiece out of every twenty-four; and the other watch had only four helmsmen. 'Never mind – we're homeward bound!' was the answer to everything; and we should not have minded this were it not for the thought that we should be off Cape Horn in the very dead of winter. It was now the first part of May; and two months would bring us off the Cape in July, which is the worst month in the year there; when the sun rises at 9.00 and sets at 3.00, giving 18 hours night, and there is snow and rain, gales and high seas, in abundance.

The prospect of meeting this in a ship half manned, loaded so deep that every heavy sea must wash her fore and aft, was by no means pleasant. The *Brandywine* frigate, in her passage round, had 60 days off the Cape, and lost several boats by the heavy seas. All this was for our comfort; yet pass it we must; and all hands agreed to make the best of it. . . .

Sunday, June 19th, were in lat. 34° 15′ S, and long. 116° 38′ W.

There began now to be a decided change in the appearance of things. The days became shorter and shorter; the sun running lower in its course each day, and giving less and less heat, and the nights so cold as to prevent our sleeping on deck; the Magellan Clouds in sight, of a clear, moonless night; the skies looking cold and angry; and, at times, a long heavy, ugly sea, setting in from the southward, told us what we were coming to. Still, however, we had a fine, strong breeze, and kept on our way under as much sail as our ship would bear. Toward the middle of the week, the wind hauled to the southward, which brought us upon a taut bowline, made the ship meet, nearly head-on, the heavy swell which rolled from that direction; and there was something not at all encouraging in the manner in which she met it. Being still so deep and heavy, she wanted the buoyancy which should have carried her over the seas, and she dropped heavily into them, the water washing over the decks; and every now and then, when an unusually large sea met her fairly upon the bows, she struck it with a sound as dead and heavy as that with which a sledge-hammer falls upon the pile, and took the whole of it in upon the forecastle, and, rising, carried it aft in the scuppers, washing the rigging off the pins, and carrying along with it everything which was loose on deck. She had been acting in this way all of our forenoon watch below; as we could tell by the washing of the water over our heads, and the heavy breaking of the seas against her bows, only the thickness of a plank from our heads, as we lay in our berths, which are directly against the bows. At eight bells, the watch was called, and we came on deck, one hand going aft to take the wheel, and another going to the galley to get the grub for dinner. I stood on the forecastle, looking at the seas, which were rolling high, as far as the eye could reach, their tops white with foam and the body of them of a deep indigo blue, reflecting the bright rays of the sun. Our ship rose slowly over a few of the largest of them, until one immense fellow came rolling on, threatening to cover her, and which I was sailor enough to know, by the 'feeling of her' under my feet, she would not rise over. I sprang upon the knight-heads, and, seizing hold of the forestay, drew myself up upon it. My feet were just off the stanchion when the stem struck fairly into the middle of the sea, and it washed the ship fore and aft, burying her in the water. As soon as she rose out of it, I looked aft, and everything forward of the mainmast, except the long-boat, which was griped and double-lashed down to the ring-bolts, was swept clear. The galley, the pigsty, the hencoop, and a large sheep-pen, which had been built upon the fore-hatch, were all gone in the twinkling of an eye, – leaving the deck as clean as a chin new reaped, – and not a stick left to show where anything had stood. In the scuppers lay the galley, bottom up, and a few boards floating about, – the wreck of the sheep-pen, – and half a dozen miserable sheep floating among them, wet through, and not a little frightened at the sudden change that had come upon them. As soon as the sea had washed by, all hands sprang up out of the forecastle to see what had become of the ship; and in a few moments the cook and Old Bill crawled out from under the galley, where they had been lying in the water, nearly smothered, with the galley over them. Fortunately, it rested against the bulwarks, or it would have broken some of their bones. When the water ran off, we picked the sheep up, and put them in the long-boat, got the galley back in its place, and set things a little to rights; but, had not our ship had uncommonly high bulwarks and rail, everything must have been washed overboard, not excepting Old Bill and the cook. Bill had been standing at the galley-door, with the kid of beef in his hand for the forecastle mess, when away he went, kid, beef, and all. He held on to the kid to the last, like a good fellow, but the beef was gone, and when the water ran off, we saw it lying high and dry, like a rock at low tide, – nothing could hurt *that*. We took the loss of our beef very easily, consoling ourselves with the recollection that the cabin had more to lose than we; and chuckled not a little at seeing the remains of the chicken-pie and pancakes floating in the scuppers. 'This will never do!' was what some said, and every one felt. Here we were, not yet within a thousand miles of the latitude of Cape Horn, and our decks swept by a sea not one half so high as we must expect to find there. Some blamed the captain for loading his ship so deep when he knew what he must expect; while others said that the wind was always southwest, off the Cape, in the winter, and that, running before it, we should not mind the seas so much. When we got down into the forecastle, Old Bill, who was somewhat of a croaker, – having met with a great many accidents at sea, – said that, if that was the way she was going to act, we might as well make our wills, and balance the books at once, and put on a clean shirt. ''Vast there, you bloody old owl! you're always hanging out blue lights. You're frightened by the ducking you got in the scuppers, and can't take a joke! What's the use in being always on the lookout for Davy Jones?' 'Stand by!' says another, 'and we'll get an afternoon watch below, by this scrape;' but in this they were disappointed, for at two bells all hands were called and set to work, getting lashings upon everything on deck; and the captain talked of sending down the long top-gallant masts; but as the sea went down toward night, and the wind hauled abeam, we left them standing, and set the studding-sails.

The next day all hands were turned-to upon unbending the old sails, and getting up the new ones; for a ship, unlike people on shore, puts on her best suit in bad weather.

The wind continued westerly, and the weather and sea less rough since the day on which we shipped the heavy sea, and we were making great progress under studding-sails, with our light sails all set, keeping a little to the eastward of south; for the captain, depending upon westerly winds off the Cape, had kept so far to the westward that, although we were within about five hundred miles of the latitude of Cape Horn, we were nearly seventeen hundred miles to the westward of it. Through the rest of the week we continued on with a fair wind, gradually, as we got more to the southward, keeping a more easterly course, and bringing the wind on our larboard quarter, until —

Sunday, June 26th, when, having a fine, clear day, the captain got a lunar observation, as well as his meridian altitude, which made us in lat. 47° 50′ S, long. 113° 49′ W; Cape Horn bearing, according to my calculations, ESE ½ E, and distant eighteen hundred miles.

Monday, June 27th. During the first part of this day the wind continued fair, and, as we were going before it, it did not feel very cold, so that we kept at work on deck in our common clothes and round jackets. Our watch had an afternoon watch below for the first time since leaving San Diego; and, having inquired of the third mate what the latitude was at noon, and made our usual guesses as to the time she would need to be up with the Horn, we turned-in for a nap. We were sleeping away, 'at the rate of knots', when three knocks on the scuttle and 'All hands, ahoy!' started us from our berths. What could be the matter? It did not appear to be blowing hard, and, looking through the scuttle, we could see that it was a clear day overhead; yet the watch were taking in sail. We thought there must be a sail in sight, and that we were about to heave-to and speak her; and were just congratulating ourselves upon it, – for we had seen neither sail nor land since we left port, – when we heard the mate's voice on deck (he turned-in 'all-standing', and was always on deck the moment he was called) singing out to the men who were taking in the studding-sails, and asking where his watch were. We did not wait for a second call, but tumbled up the ladder; and there, on the starboard bow, was a bank of mist, covering sea and sky, and driving directly for us. I had seen the same before in my passage round in the *Pilgrim*, and knew what it meant, and that there was no time to be lost. We had nothing on but thin clothes, yet there was not a moment to spare, and at it we went.

The boys of the other watch were in the tops, taking in the top-gallant studding-sails and the lower and topmast studding sails were coming down by the run. It was nothing but 'haul down and clew up,' until we got all the studding-sails in, and the royals, flying jib, and mizzen top-gallant-sail furled, and the ship kept off a little, to take the squall. The fore and main top-gallant-sails were still on her, for the 'old man' did not mean to be frightened in broad daylight, and was determined to carry sail till the last minute. We all stood waiting for its coming, when the first blast showed us that it was not to be trifled with. Rain, sleet, snow, and wind enough to take our breath from us, and make the toughest turn his back to windward! The ship lay nearly over upon her beam-ends; the spars and rigging snapped and cracked; and her top-gallant-masts bent like whip-sticks. 'Clew up the fore and main top-gallant sails!' shouted the captain, and all hands sprang to the clew-lines. The decks were standing nearly at an angle of forty-five degrees, and the ship going like a mad steed through the water, the whole forward part of her in a smother of foam. The halyards were let go, and the yard clewed down, and the sheets started, and in a few minutes the sails smothered and kept in by clewlines and buntlines. 'Furl 'em, sir?' asked the mate. 'Let go the topsail halyards, fore and aft!' shouted the captain in answer, at the top of his voice. Down came the topsail yards, the reef-tackles were manned and hauled out, and we climbed up to windward, and sprang into the weather rigging. The violence of the wind, and the hail and sleet, driving nearly horizontally across the ocean, seemed actually to pin us down to the rigging. It was hard work making head against them. One after another we got out upon the yards. And here we had work to do; for our new sails had hardly been bent long enough to get the starch out of them and the new earrings and reef-points, stiffened with the sleet, knotted like pieces of iron wire. Having only our round jackets and straw hats on, we were soon wet through, and it was every moment growing colder. Our hands were soon stiffened, which, added to the stiffness of everything else, kept us a good while on the yard.

No sooner did the mate see that we were on deck than – 'Lay aloft there, four of you, and furl the top-gallant-sails!' This called me again, and two of us went aloft up the fore rigging, and two more up the main, upon the top-gallant-yards. The shrouds were now iced over, the sleet having formed a crust round all the standing rigging, and on the weather side of the masts and yards. When we got upon the yard, my hands were so numb that I could not have cast off the knot of the gasket to have saved my life. We both lay over the yard for a few seconds, beating our hands upon the sail until we started the blood into our fingers' ends, and at the next moment our hands were in a burning heat. My companion on the yard was a lad about sixteen years old, who came out in the ship a weak, puny boy, from one of the Boston schools, – 'no larger than a spritsail-sheet knot,' nor 'heavier than a paper of lamp-black,' and 'not strong enough to haul a shad off a gridiron,' but who was now 'as long as a spare topmast, strong enough to knock down an ox, and hearty enough to eat him.' We fisted the sail together, and, after six or eight minutes of hard hauling and pulling and beating down the sail, which was about as stiff as sheet-iron, we managed to get it furled; and snugly furled it must be, for we knew the mate enough to be certain that if it got adrift again we should be called up from our watch below, at any hour of the night, to furl it.

I had been on the lookout for a chance to jump below and clap on a thigh jacket and southwester; but when we got on deck we found that eight bells had been struck, and the other watch gone below, so that there were two hours of dog watch for us, and plenty of work to do. It had now set in for a steady gale from the southwest; but we were not yet far enough to the southward to make a fair wind of it, for we must give Terra del Fuego a wide berth. The decks were covered with snow, and there was a constant driving of sleet. In fact, Cape Horn had set in with good earnest. In the midst of all this, and before it became dark, we had all the studding-sails to make up and stow away, and then to lay aloft and rig in all the booms, fore and aft, and coil away the tacks, sheets, and halyards. This was pretty tough work for four or five hands, in the face of a gale which almost took us off the yards, and with ropes so stiff with ice that it was almost impossible to bend them. I was nearly half an hour out on the end of the foreyard, trying to coil away and stop down the topmast studding-sail tack and lower halyards. It was after dark when we got through, and we were not a little pleased to hear four bells struck, which sent us below for two hours, and gave us each a pot of hot tea with our cold beef and bread, and, what was better yet, a suit of thick, dry clothing, fitted for the weather, in place of our thin clothes, which were wet through and now frozen stiff.

This sudden turn, for which we were so little prepared, was as unacceptable to me as to any of the rest; for I had been troubled for several days with a slight toothache, and this cold weather and wetting and freezing, were not the best things in the world for it. I soon found that it was getting strong hold, and running over all parts of my face; and before the watch was out I went aft to the mate, who had charge of the medicine-chest, to get something for it. But the chest showed like the end of a long voyage, for there was nothing that would answer but a few drops of laudanum, which must be saved for an emergency; so I had only to bear the pain as well as I could.

When we went on deck at eight bells, it had stopped snowing, and there were a few stars out, but the clouds were still black, and it was blowing a steady gale. Just before midnight, I went aloft and sent down the mizzen royal yard, and had the good luck to do it to the satisfaction of the mate, who said it was done 'out of hand and ship-shape.' The next four hours below were but little relief to me, for I lay awake in my berth the whole time, from the pain in my face, and heard every bell strike, and, at four o'clock, turned out with the watch, feeling little spirit for the hard duties of the day. Bad weather and hard work at sea can be borne up against very well if one only has spirit and health; but there is nothing brings a man down, at such a time, like bodily pain and want of sleep. There was, however, too much to do to allow time to think; for the gale of yesterday, and the heavy seas we met with a few days before, while we had yet ten degrees more southing to make, had convinced the captain that we had something before us which was not to be trifled with, and orders were given to send down the long top-gallant masts. The top-gallant and royal yards were accordingly struck, the flying jib-boom rigged in, and the top-gallant masts sent down on deck, and all lashed together by the side of the long-boat. The rigging was then sent down and coiled away below, and everything made snug aloft. There was not a sailor in the ship who was not rejoiced to see these sticks come down; for, so long as the yards were aloft, on the least sign of a lull, the top-gallant-sails were loosed, and then we had to furl them again in a snow-squall, and *shin* up and down single ropes caked with ice, and send royal yards down in the teeth of a gale coming right from the south pole. It was an interesting sight, too, to see our noble ship, dismantled of all her top-hamper of long tapering masts and yards, and boom pointed with spear-head, which ornamented her in port; and all that canvas, which a few days before had covered her like a cloud, from the truck to the water's edge, spreading far out beyond her hull on either side, now gone; and she stripped, like a wrestler for the fight. It corresponded, too, with the desolate character of her situation – alone, as she was, battling with storms, wind, and ice, at this extremity of the globe, and in almost constant night.

Friday, July 1st. We were now nearly up to the latitude of Cape Horn, and having over forty degrees of easting to make, we squared away the yards before a strong westerly gale, shook a reef out of the fore top-sail, and stood on our way, east-by-south, with the prospect of being up with the Cape in a week or ten days. As for myself, I had had no sleep for forty-eight hours; and the want of rest, together with constant wet and cold, had increased the swelling, so that my face was nearly as large as two, and I found it impossible to get my mouth open wide enough to eat. In this state, the steward applied to the captain for some rice to boil for me, but he only got a – 'No! d— you! Tell him to eat salt junk and hard bread like the rest of them.' This was just what I expected. However, I did not starve, for the mate, who was a man as well as a sailor, and had always been a good friend to me, smuggled a pan of rice into the galley, and told the cook to boil it for me, and not let the 'old man' see it. Had it been fine weather, or in port, I should have gone below and lain by until my face got well; but in such weather as this, and short-handed as we were, it was not for me to desert my post; so I kept on deck, and stood my watch and did my duty as well as I could.

Saturday, July 2nd. This day the sun rose fair, but it ran too low in the heavens to give any heat, or thaw out our sails and rigging; yet the sight of it was pleasant; and we had a steady 'reef-topsail breeze' from the westward. The atmosphere, which had previously been clear and cold, for the last few hours grew damp, and had a disagreeable, wet chilliness in it; and the man who came from the wheel said he heard the captain tell 'the passenger' that the thermometer had fallen several degrees since morning, which he could not account for in any other way than by supposing that there must be ice near us; though such a thing was rarely heard of in this latitude at this season of the year. At twelve o'clock we went below, and had just got through dinner, when the cook put his head down the scuttle and told us to come on deck and see the finest sight that we had ever seen. 'Where away, Cook?' asked the first man who was up. 'On the larboard bow.' And there lay, floating in the ocean, several miles off, an immense, irregular mass, its top and points covered with snow, and its centre of a deep indigo colour. This was an iceberg, and of the largest size, as one of our men said who had been in the Northern Ocean. As far as the eye could reach, the sea in every direction was of a deep blue colour, the waves running high and fresh, and sparkling in the light, and in the midst lay this immense mountain-island, its cavities and valleys thrown into deep shade, and its points and pinnacles glittering in the sun. All hands were soon on deck, looking at it, and admiring in various ways its beauty and grandeur. But no description can give any idea of the strangeness, splendour, and, really, the sublimity of the sight. Its great size – for it must have been from two to three miles in circumference, and several hundred feet in height – its slow motion, as its base rose and sank in the water, and its high points nodded against the clouds; the dashing of the waves upon it, which, breaking high with foam, lined its base, with a white crust; and the thundering sound of the cracking of the mass, and the breaking and tumbling down of huge pieces; together with its nearness and approach, which added a slight element of fear – all combined to give to it the character of true sublimity. The main body of the mass was, as I have said, of an indigo colour, its base crusted with frozen foam; and as it grew thin and transparent toward the edges and top, its colour shaded off from a deep blue to the whiteness of snow. It seemed to be drifting slowly toward the north, so that we kept away and avoided it. It was in sight all the afternoon; and when we got to leeward of it the wind died away, so that we lay-to quite near to it for a greater part of the night. Unfortunately, there was no moon, but it was a clear night, and we could plainly mark the long, regular heaving of the stupendous mass, as its edges moved slowly against the stars, now revealing them, and now shutting them in. Several times in our watch loud cracks were heard, which sounded as though they must have run through the whole length of the iceberg, and several pieces fell down with a thundering crash, plunging heavily into the sea. Toward morning a strong breeze sprang up, and we filled away, and left it astern, and at daylight it was out of sight. The next day, which was —

Sunday, July 3rd, the breeze continued strong, the air exceedingly chilly, and the thermometer low. In the course of the day we saw several icebergs of different sizes, but none so near as the one which we saw the day before. Some of them, as well as we could judge, at the distance at which we were, must have been as large as that, if not larger. At noon we were in latitude 55° 12′ S and supposed longitude 89° 5′ W. Toward night the wind hauled to the southward, and headed us off our course a little, and blew a tremendous gale; but this we did not mind, as there was no rain nor snow, and we were already under close sail.

Monday, July 4th. This was 'Independence Day' in Boston. What firing of guns, and ringing of bells, and rejoicings of all sorts, in every part of our country! The ladies (who have not gone down to Nahant, for a breath of cool air and sight of the ocean) walking the streets with parasols over their heads, and the dandies in their white pantaloons and silk stockings! What quantities of ice-cream have been eaten, and what lumps of ice brought into the city from a distance, and sold out by the lump and the pound! The smallest of the islands which we saw today would have made the fortune of poor Jack, if he had had it in Boston; and I dare say he would have no objection to being there with it. This, to be sure, was no place to keep the Fourth of July. To keep ourselves warm, and the ship out of the ice, was as much as we could do. Yet no one forgot the day; and many were the wishes and conjectures and comparisons, both serious and ludicrous, which were made among all hands. The sun shone bright as long as it was up, only that a scud of black clouds was ever and anon driving across it. At noon we were in latitude 54° 27′ S and longitude 85° 5′ W, having made a good deal of easting, but having lost in our latitude by the heading off of the wind. Between daylight and dark – that is, between nine o'clock and three – we saw thirty-four ice islands of various sizes; some no bigger than the hull of our vessel, and others apparently nearly as large as the one that we first saw; though, as we went on, the islands became smaller and more numerous; and at sundown of this day, a man at the mast-head saw large fields of floating ice, called 'field-ice', at the south-east. This kind of ice is much more dangerous than the large islands, for those can be seen at a distance, and kept away from; but the field-ice, floating in great quantities, and covering the ocean for miles and miles, in pieces of every size – large, flat, and broken cakes, with here and there an island rising twenty and thirty feet, and as large as the ship's hull – this it is very difficult to steer clear of. A constant look-out was necessary; for any of these pieces, coming with the heave of the sea, were large enough to have knocked a hole in the ship, and that would have been the end of us; for no boat (even if we could have got one out) could have lived in such a sea; and no man could have lived in a boat in such weather. To make our condition still worse, the wind came out due east, just after sundown, and it blew a gale dead ahead, with hail and sleet and a thick fog, so that we could not see half the length of the ship. Our chief reliance, the prevailing westerly gales, was thus cut off; and here we were, nearly seven hundred miles to the westward of the Cape, with a gale dead from the eastward, and the weather so thick that we could not see the ice, with which we were surrounded, until it was directly under our bows. At four pm (it was then quite dark) all hands were called, and sent aloft, in a violent squall of hail and rain, to take in sail. We had now all got on our 'Cape Horn rig' – thick boots, southwesters coming down over our neck and ears, thick trousers and jackets, and some with oil-cloth suits over all. Mittens, too, we wore on deck, but it would not do to go aloft with them, as it was impossible to work with them. A man might fall; for all the hold he could get upon a rope: so we were obliged to work with bare hands, which, as well as our faces, were often cut with the hailstones, which fell thick and large.

Our ship was now all cased with ice, – hull, spars, and standing rigging, and the running rigging so stiff that we could hardly bend it so as to belay it, or, still less, take a knot with it; and the sails frozen. One at a time (for it was a long piece of work and required many hands) we furled the courses, mizzen topsail, and fore-topmast staysail, and close-reefed the fore and main topsails, and hove the ship to under the fore, with the main hauled up by the clew-lines and bunt-lines, and ready to be sheeted home, if we found it necessary to make sail to get to windward of an ice island. A regular lookout was then set, and kept by each watch in turn, until the morning. It was a tedious and anxious night. It blew hard the whole time, and there was an almost constant driving of either rain, hail, or snow. In addition to this, it was 'as thick as muck,' and the ice was all about us. The captain was on deck nearly the whole night, and kept the cook in the galley, with a roaring fire, to make coffee for him, which he took every few hours, and once or twice gave a little to his officers; but not a drop of anything was there for the crew. The captain, who sleeps all the daytime, and comes and goes at night as he chooses, can have his brandy-and-water in the cabin, and his hot coffee at the galley; while Jack, who has to stand through everything, and work in wet and cold, can have nothing to wet his lips or warm his stomach.

Eight hours of the night our watch was on deck, and during the whole of that time we kept a bright lookout: one man on each bow, another in the bunt of the fore yard, the third mate on the scuttle, one man on each quarter, and another always standing by the wheel. The chief mate was everywhere, and commanded the ship when the captain was below. When a large piece of ice was seen in our way, or drifting near us, the word was passed along, and the ship's head turned one way and another; and sometimes the yards squared or braced up. There was little else to do than to look out; and we had the sharpest eyes in the ship on the forecastle. The only variety was the monotonous voice of the lookout forward, – 'Another island!' – 'Ice ahead!' – 'Ice on the lee bow!' – 'Hard up the helm!' – 'Keep her off a little!' – 'Stead-y!'

In the meantime the wet and cold had brought my face into such a state that I could neither eat nor sleep; and though I stood it out all night, yet, when it became light, I was in such a state that all hands told me I must go below, and lie-by for a day or two, or I should be laid up for a long time, and perhaps have the lock-jaw. In the steerage I took off my hat and comforter, and showed my face to the mate, who told me to go below at once, and stay in my berth until the swelling went down, and gave the cook orders to make a poultice for me, and said he would speak to the captain.

I went below and turned in, covering myself over with blankets and jackets, and lay in my berth nearly twenty-four hours, half asleep and half awake, stupid from the dull pain. I heard the watch called, and the men going up and down, and sometimes a noise on deck, and a cry of 'ice', but I gave little attention to anything. At the end of twenty-four hours the pain went down, and I had a long sleep, which brought me back to my proper state; yet my face was so swollen and tender that I was obliged to keep my berth for two or three days longer. During the two days I had been below the weather was much the same that it had been, – head winds and snow and rain; or, if the wind came fair, too foggy, and the ice too thick, to run. At the end of the third day the ice was very thick; a complete fog-bank covered the ship. It blew a tremendous gale from the eastward, with sleet and snow, and there was every promise of a dangerous and fatiguing night. At dark, the captain called all hands aft, and told them that not a man was to leave the deck that night; that the ship was in the greatest danger, any cake of ice might knock a hole in her, or she might run on an island and go to pieces. No one could tell whether she would be a ship the next morning. The lookouts were then set, and every man was put in his station. When I heard what was the state of things, I began to put on my clothes to stand it out with the rest of them, when the mate came below, and, looking at my face, ordered me back to my berth, saying that if we went down, we should all go down together, but if I went on deck I might lay myself up for life. This was the first word I had heard from aft; for the captain had done nothing, nor inquired how I was, since I went below.

In obedience to the mate's orders, I went back to my berth; but a more miserable night I never wish to spend. I never felt the curse of sickness so keenly in my life. If I could only have been on deck with the rest where something was to be done and seen and heard, where there were fellow-beings for companions in duty and danger; but to be cooped up alone in a black hole, in equal danger, but without the power to do, was the hardest trial. Several times, in the course of the night, I got up, determined to go on deck; but the silence which showed that there was nothing doing, and the knowledge that I might make myself seriously ill, for no purpose, kept me back. It was not easy to sleep, lying, as I did, with my head directly against the bows, which might be dashed in by an island of ice, brought down by the very next sea that struck her. This was the only time I had been ill since I left Boston, and it was the worst time it could have happened. I felt almost willing to bear the plagues of Egypt for the rest of the voyage, if I could but be well and strong for that one night. Yet it was a dreadful night for those on deck. A watch of eighteen hours, with wet and cold and constant anxiety, nearly wore them out; and when they came below at nine o'clock for breakfast, they almost dropped to sleep on their chests, and some of them were so stiff that they could with difficulty sit down. Not a drop of anything had been given them during the whole time (though the captain, as on the night that I was on deck, had his coffee every four hours), except that the mate stole a pot-full of coffee for two men to drink behind the galley, while he kept a lookout for the captain. Every man had his station, and was not allowed to leave it; and nothing happened to break the monotony of the night, except once setting the main topsail, to run clear of a large island to leeward, which they were drifting fast upon. Some of the boys got so sleepy and stupefied that they actually fell asleep at their posts; and the young third mate, Mr H—, whose post was the exposed one of standing on the fore scuttle, was so stiff, when he was relieved, that he could not bend his knees to get down. By a constant lookout, and a quick shifting of the helm, as the islands and pieces came in sight, the ship went clear of everything but a few small pieces, though daylight showed the ocean covered for miles. At daybreak it fell a dead calm, and with the sun the fog cleared a little, and a breeze sprung up from the westward, which soon grew into a gale. We had now a fair wind, daylight, and comparatively clear weather; yet, to the surprise of every one, the ship continued hove-to. 'Why does not he run?' 'What is the captain about?' was asked by every one; and from questions it soon grew into complaints and murmurings. When the daylight was so short, it was too bad to lose it, and a fair wind, too, which every one had been praying for. As hour followed hour, and the captain showed no sign of making sail, the crew became impatient, and there was a good deal of talking and consultation together on the forecastle. They had been beaten out with the exposure and hardship, and impatient to get out of it, and this unaccountable delay was more than they could bear in quietness, in their excited and restless state. Some said the captain was frightened, – completely cowed by the dangers and difficulties that surrounded us, and was afraid to make sail; while others said that in his anxiety and suspense he had made a free use of brandy and opium, and was unfit for his duty. The carpenter, who was an intelligent man, and a thorough seaman, and had great influence with the crew, came down into the forecastle, and tried to induce them to go aft and ask the captain why he did not run, or request him, in the name of all hands, to make sail. This appeared to be a very reasonable request, and the crew agreed that if he did not make sail before noon they would go aft. Noon came, and no sail was made. A consultation was held again, and it was proposed to take the ship from the captain and give the command of her to the mate, who had been heard to say that if he could have his way the ship would have been half the distance to the Cape before night, – ice, or no ice. And so irritated and impatient had the crew become, that even this proposition, which was open mutiny, was entertained, and the carpenter went to his berth, leaving it tacitly understood that something serious would be done if things remained as they were many hours longer. When the carpenter left, we talked it all over, and I gave my advice strongly against it. Another of the men, too, who had known something of the kind attempted in another ship by a crew who were dissatisfied with their captain, and which was followed with serious consequences, was opposed to it. S—, who soon came down, joined us, and we determined to have nothing to do with it. By these means the crew were soon induced to give it up for the present, though they said they would not lie where they were much longer without knowing the reason.

The affair remained in this state until four o'clock, when an order came forward for all hands to come aft upon the quarter-deck. In about ten minutes they came forward, and the whole affair had been blown. The carpenter, prematurely, and without any authority from the crew, had sounded the mate as to whether he would take command of the ship, and intimated an intention to displace the captain; and the mate, as in duty bound, had told the whole to the captain, who immediately sent for all hands aft. Instead of violent measures, or, at least, an outbreak of quarter-deck bravado, threats, and abuse, which they had every reason to expect, a sense of common danger and common suffering seemed to have tamed his spirit, and begotten in him something like a humane fellow-feeling; for he received the crew in a manner quiet, and even almost kind. He told them what he had heard, and said that he did not believe that they would try to do any such thing as was intimated; that they had always been good men, – obedient, and knew their duty, and he had no fault to find with them, and asked them what they had to complain of; said that no one could say that he was slow to carry sail (which was true enough), and that, as soon as he thought it was safe and proper, he should make sail. He added a few words about their duty in their present situation, and sent them forward, saying that he should take no further notice of the matter; but, at the same time, told the carpenter to recollect whose power he was in, and that if he heard another word from him he would have cause to remember him to the day of his death.

This language of the captain had a very good effect upon the crew, and they returned quietly to their duty.

For two days more the wind blew from the southward and eastward, and in the short intervals when it was fair, the ice was too thick to run; yet the weather was not so dreadfully bad, and the crew had watch and watch. I still remained in my berth, fast recovering, yet not well enough to go safely on deck. And I should have been perfectly useless; for, from having eaten nothing for nearly a week, except a little rice which I forced into my mouth the last day or two, I was as weak as an infant. To be sick in a forecastle is miserable indeed. It is the worst part of a dog's life, especially in bad weather. The forecastle, shut up tight to keep out the water and cold air; the watch either on deck or asleep in their berths; no one to speak to; the pale light of the single lamp, swinging to and fro from the beam, so dim that one can scarcely see, much less read, by it; the water dropping from the beams and carlines and running down the sides, and the forecastle so wet and dark and cheerless, and so lumbered up with chests and wet clothes, that sitting up is worse than lying in the berth. These are some of the evils. Fortunately, I needed no help from any one, and no medicine; and if I had needed help I don't know where I should have found it. Sailors are willing enough, but it is true, as is often said, – no one ships for nurse on board a vessel. Our merchant ships are always undermanned, and if one man is lost by sickness, they cannot spare another to take care of him. A sailor is always presumed to be well, and if he's sick he's a poor dog. One has to stand his wheel, and another his lookout, and the sooner he gets on deck again the better.

Accordingly, as soon as I could possibly go back to my duty, I put on my thick clothes and boots and southwester, and made my appearance on deck. I had been but a few days below, yet everything looked strangely enough. The ship was cased in ice, – decks, sides, masts, yards, and rigging. Two close-reefed topsails were all the sail she had on, and every sail and rope was frozen so stiff in its place that it seemed as though it would be impossible to start anything. Reduced, too, to her topmasts, she had altogether a most forlorn and crippled appearance. The sun had come up brightly; the snow was swept off the deck and ashes thrown upon them so that we could walk, for they had been as slippery as glass. It was, of course, too cold to carry on any ship's work, and we had only to walk the deck and keep ourselves warm. The wind was still ahead, and the whole ocean, to the eastward, covered with islands and field-ice. At four bells the order was given to square away the yards, and the man who came from the helm said that the captain had kept her off to NNE.

In our first attempt to double the Cape, when we came up to the latitude of it, we were nearly seventeen hundred miles to the westward, but, in running for the Straits of Magellan, we stood so far to the eastward that we made our second attempt at a distance of not more than four or five hundred miles; and we had great hopes, by this means, to run clear of the ice; thinking that the easterly gales, which had prevailed for a long time, would have driven it to the westward. With the wind about two points free, the yards braced in a little, and two close-reefed topsails and a reefed foresail on the ship, we made great way toward the southward; and almost every watch, when we came on deck, the air seemed to grow colder, and the sea to run higher. Still we saw no ice, and had great hopes of going clear of it altogether, when, one afternoon, about three o'clock, while we were taking a *siesta* during our watch below, 'All hands!' was called in a loud and fearful voice. 'Tumble up here, men! – tumble up! – don't stop for your clothes – before we're upon it!' We sprang out of our berths and hurried upon deck. The loud, sharp voice of the captain was heard giving orders, as though for life or death, and we ran aft to the braces not waiting to look ahead, for not a moment was to be lost. The helm was hard up, the after yards shaking, and the ship in the act of wearing. Slowly, with the stiff ropes and iced rigging, we swung the yards round, everything coming hard and with a creaking and rending sound, like pulling up the plank which has been frozen into the ice. The ship wore round fairly, the yards were steadied, and we stood off on the other tack, leaving behind us, directly under our larboard quarter, a large ice island, peering out of the mist, and reaching high above our tops; while astern, and on either side of the island, large tracts of field-ice were dimly seen, heaving and rolling in the sea. We were now safe, and standing to the northward; but, in a few minutes more, had it not been for the sharp lookout of the watch, we should have been fairly upon the ice, and left our ship's old bones adrift in the Southern Ocean. After standing to the northward a few hours, we wore ship, and, the wind having hauled, we stood to the southward and eastward. All night long a bright lookout was kept from every part of the deck; and whenever ice was seen on the one bow or the other the helm was shifted and the yards braced, and, by quick working of the ship, she was kept clear. The accustomed cry of 'Ice ahead!' – 'Ice on the lee bow!' – 'Another island!' in the same tones, and with the same orders following them, seemed to bring us directly back to our old position of the week before. During our watch on deck, which was from twelve to four, the wind came out ahead, with a pelting storm of hail and sleet, and we lay hove-to, under a close-reefed fore topsail, the whole watch. During the next watch it fell calm with a drenching rain until daybreak, when the wind came out to the westward, and the weather cleared up, and showed us the whole ocean, in the course which we should have steered, had it not been for the head wind and calm, completely blocked up with ice. Here, then, our progress was stopped, and we wore ship, and once more stood to the northward and eastward; not for the Straits of Magellan, but to make another attempt to double the Cape, still farther to the eastward; for the captain was determined to get round if perseverance could do it, and the third time, he said, never failed.

With a fair wind, we soon ran clear of the field-ice, and by noon had only the stray islands floating far and near upon the ocean. The sun was out bright, the sea of a deep blue, fringed with the white foam of the waves, which ran high before a strong southwester; our solitary ship tore on through the open water as though glad to be out of her confinement;

and the ice islands lay scattered upon the ocean, of various sizes and shapes, reflecting the bright rays of the sun, and drifting slowly northward before the gale. It was a contrast to much that we had lately seen, and a spectacle not only of beauty, but of life; for it required but little fancy to imagine these islands to be animate masses which had broken loose from the 'thrilling regions of thick-ribbed ice,' and were working their way, by wind and current, some alone, and some in fleets, to milder climes. No pencil has ever yet given anything like the true effect of an iceberg. In a picture, they are huge, uncouth masses, stuck in the sea, while their chief beauty and grandeur – their slow, stately motion, the whirling of the snow about their summits, and the fearful groaning and cracking of their parts – the picture cannot give. This is the large iceberg, – while the small and distant islands, floating on the smooth sea, in the light of a clear day, look like little floating fairy isles of sapphire.

From a northeast course we gradually hauled to the eastward, and after sailing about two hundred miles, which brought us as near to the western coast of Terra del Fuego as was safe, and having lost sight of the ice altogether, – for the third time we put the ship's head to the southward, to try the passage of the Cape. The weather continued clear and cold, with a strong gale from the westward, and we were fast getting up with the latitude of the Cape, with a prospect of soon being round. One fine afternoon, a man who had gone into the fore-top to shift the rolling tackles sung out at the top of his voice, and with evident glee, 'Sail ho!' Neither land nor sail had we seen since leaving San Diego; and any one who has traversed the length of a whole ocean alone can imagine what an excitement such an announcement produced on board. 'Sail ho!' shouted the cook, jumping out of his galley; 'Sail ho!' shouted a man, throwing back the slide of the scuttle, to the watch below, who were soon out of their berths and on deck; and 'Sail ho!' shouted the captain down the companion-way to the passenger in the cabin. Beside the pleasure of seeing a ship and human beings in so desolate a place, it was important for us to speak a vessel, to learn whether there was ice to the eastward, and to ascertain the longitude; for we had no chronometer, and had been drifting about so long that we had nearly lost our reckoning; and opportunities for lunar observations are not frequent or sure in such a place as Cape Horn. For these various reasons the excitement in our little community was running high, and conjectures were made, and everything thought of for which the captain would hail, when the man aloft sung out – 'Another sail, large on the weather bow!' This was a little odd, but so much the better, and did not shake our faith in their being sails. At length the man in the top hailed, and said he believed it was land, after all. 'Land in your eye!' said the mate, who was looking through the telescope; 'they are ice islands, if I can see a hole through a ladder;' and a few moments showed the mate to be right; and all our expectations fled; and instead of what we most wished to see we had what we most dreaded, and what we hoped we had seen the last of. We soon, however, left these astern, having passed within about two miles of them, and at sundown the horizon was clear in all directions.

Having a fine wind, we were soon up with and passed the latitude of the Cape, and, having stood far enough to the southward to give it a wide berth, we began to stand to the eastward, with a good prospect, of being round and steering to the northward, on the other side, in a very few days. But ill luck seemed to have lighted upon us. Not four hours had we been standing on in this course before it fell dead calm, and in half an hour it clouded up, a few straggling blasts, with spits of snow and sleet, came from the eastward, and in an hour more we lay hove-to under a close-reefed main topsail, drifting bodily off to leeward before the fiercest storm that we had yet felt, blowing dead ahead, from the eastward. It seemed as though the genius of the place had been roused at finding that we had nearly slipped through his fingers, and had come down upon us with tenfold fury. The sailors said that every blast, as it shook the shrouds, and whistled through the rigging, said to the old ship, 'No, you don't!' – 'No, you don't!'

For eight days we lay drifting about in this manner. Sometimes – generally towards noon – it fell calm; once or twice a round copper ball showed itself for a few moments in the place where the sun ought to have been, and a puff or two came from the westward, giving some hope that a fair wind had come at last. During the first two days we made sail for these puffs, shaking the reefs out of the topsails and boarding the tacks of the courses; but finding that it only made work for us when the gale set in again, it was soon given up, and we lay-to under our close-reefs. We had less snow and hail than when we were farther to the westward, but we had an abundance of what is worse to a sailor in cold weather – drenching rain. Snow is blinding, and very bad when coming upon a coast, but, for genuine discomfort, give me rain with freezing weather. A snowstorm is exciting, and it does not wet through the clothes (a fact important to a sailor); but a constant rain there is no escaping from. It wets to the skin, and makes all protection vain. We had long ago run through all our dry clothes, and as sailors have no other way of drying them than by the sun, we had nothing to do but to put on those which were the least wet. At the end of each watch, when we came below, we took off our clothes and wrung them out; two taking hold of a pair of trousers, one at each end – and jackets in the same way. Stockings, mittens, and all, were wrung out also, and then hung up to drain and chafe dry against the bulkheads. Then, feeling of all our clothes, we picked out those which were the least wet, and put them on, so as to be ready for a call, and turned-in, covered ourselves up with blankets, and slept until three knocks on the scuttle and the dismal sound of 'All Starbowlines ahoy! Eight bells, there below! Do you hear the news?' drawled out from the deck, and the sulky answer of 'Aye, aye!' from below, sent us up again.

On deck we were all in darkness, a dead calm, with the rain pouring steadily down, or, more generally, a violent gale dead ahead, with rain pelting horizontally, and occasional variations of hail and sleet; decks afloat with water swashing from side to side, and constantly wet feet, for boots could not be wrung out like drawers, and no composition could stand the constant soaking. In fact, wet and cold feet are inevitable in such weather, and are not the least of those items which go to make up the grand total of the discomforts of a winter passage round the Cape. Few words were spoken between the watches as they shifted; the wheel was relieved, the mate took his place on the quarter-deck, the lookouts in the bows; and each man had his narrow space to walk fore and aft in, or rather to swing himself forward and back in, from one belaying-pin to another, for the decks were too slippery with ice and water to allow of much walking. To make a walk, which is absolutely necessary to pass away the time, one of us hit upon the expedient of sanding the decks; and afterwards, whenever the rain was not so violent as to wash it off, the weather-side of the quarter-deck, and a part of the waist and forecastle were sprinkled with the sand which we had on board for holystoning, and thus we made a good promenade, where we walked fore and aft, two and two, hour after hour, in our long, dull, and comfortless watches.

All washing, sewing, and reading was given up, and we did nothing but eat, sleep, and stand our watch, leading what might be called a Cape Horn life. The forecastle was too uncomfortable to sit up in; and whenever we were below, we were in our berths. To prevent the rain and the sea-water which broke over the bows from washing down, we were obliged to keep the scuttle closed, so that the forecastle was nearly air-tight. In this little, wet leaky hole, we were all quartered, in an atmosphere so bad that our lamp, which swung in the middle from the beams, sometimes actually burned blue with a large circle of foul air about it. Still, I was never in better health than after three weeks of this life. I gained a great deal of flesh, and we all ate like horses. At every watch when we came below, before turning in, the bread barge and beef kid were overhauled. Each man drank his quart of hot tea night and morning, and glad enough we were to get it; for no nectar and ambrosia were sweeter to the lazy immortals than was a pot of hot tea, a hard biscuit, and a slice of cold salt beef to us after a watch on deck. To be sure, we were mere animals, and, had this life lasted a year instead of a month, we should have been little better than the ropes in the ship. Not a razor, nor a brush, nor a drop of water, except the rain and the spray, had come near us all the time; for we were on an allowance of fresh water; and who would strip and wash himself in salt water on deck, in the snow and ice, with the thermometer at zero?

After about eight days of constant easterly gales, the wind hauled occasionally a little to the southward, and blew hard, which, as we were well to the southward, allowed us to brace in a little, and stand on under all the sail we could carry. These turns lasted but a short while, and sooner or later it set in again from the old quarter; yet at each time we made something, and were gradually edging along to the eastward. One night, after one of these shifts of the wind, and when all hands had been up a great part of the time, our watch was left on deck, with the mainsail hanging in the buntlines, ready to be set if necessary. It came on to blow worse and worse, with hail and snow beating like so many furies upon the ship, it being as dark and thick as night could make it. The mainsail was blowing and slatting with a noise like thunder, when the captain came on deck and ordered it to be furled. The mate was about to call all hands, when the captain stopped him, and said that the men would be beaten out if they were called up so often; that, as our watch must stay on deck, it might as well be doing that as anything else. Accordingly, we went upon the yard; and never shall I forget that piece of work. Our watch had been so reduced by sickness, and by some having been left in California, that, with one man at the wheel, we had only the third mate and three beside myself to go aloft; so that at most we could only attempt to furl one yard-arm at a time. We manned the weather yard-arm, and set to work to make a furl of it. Our lower masts being short, and our yards very square, the sail had a head of nearly fifty feet, and a short leech, made still shorter by the deep reef which was in it, which brought the clew away out on the quarters of the yard, and made a bunt nearly as square as the mizzen royal yard. Beside this difficulty, the yard over which we lay was cased with ice, the gaskets and rope of the foot and leech of the sail as stiff and hard as a piece of suction hose, and the sail itself about as pliable as though it had been made of sheets of sheathing copper. It blew a perfect hurricane, with alternate blasts of snow, hail, and rain. We had to *fist* the sail with bare hands. No one could trust himself to mittens, for if he slipped he was a gone man. All the boats were hoisted in on deck, and there was nothing to be lowered for him. We had need of every finger God had given us. Several times we got the sail upon the yard, but it blew away again before we could secure it. It required men to lie over the yard to pass each turn of the gaskets, and when they were passed it was almost impossible to knot them so that they would hold. Frequently we were obliged to leave off altogether, and take to beating our hands upon the sail to keep them from freeing. After some time – which seemed for ever – we got the weather side stowed after a fashion, and went over to leeward for another trial. This was still worse, for the body of the sail had been blown over to leeward, and, as the yard was a-cock-bill by the lying over of the vessel, we had to light it all up to windward. When the yard-arms were furled, the bunt was all adrift again, which made more work for us. We got all secure at last, but we had been nearly an hour and a half upon the yard, and it seemed an age. It had just struck five bells when we went up, and eight were struck soon after we came down. This may seem slow work ; but considering the state of everything, and that we had only five men to a sail with just half as many square yards of canvas in it as the mainsail of the *Independence*, sixty-gun ship, which musters seven hundred men at her quarters, it is not wonderful that we were no quicker about it. We were glad enough to get on deck, and still more to go below. The oldest sailor in the watch said, as he went down, 'I shall never forget that main yard; it beats all my going a fishing. Fun is fun, but furling one yard-arm of a course at a time, off Cape Horn, is no better than man-killing.'

During the greater part of the next two days, the wind was pretty steady from the southward. We had evidently made great progress, and had good hope of being soon up with the Cape, if we were not there already. We could put but little confidence in our reckoning, as there had been no opportunities for an observation, and we had drifted too much to allow of our dead reckoning being anywhere near the mark. If it would clear off enough to give a chance for an observation, or if we could make land, we should know where we were; and upon these, and the chances of falling in with a sail from the eastward, we depended almost entirely.

Friday, July 22nd. This day we had a steady gale from the southward, and stood on under close sail, with the yards eased a little by the weather braces, the clouds lifting a little, and showing signs of breaking away. In the afternoon, I was below with Mr H—, the third mate, and two others, filling the bread locker in the steerage from the casks, when a bright gleam of sunshine broke out and shone down the companion-way, and through the skylight lighting up everything below, and sending a warm glow through the hearts of all. It was a sight we had not seen for weeks – an omen, a godsend. Even the roughest and hardest face acknowledged its influence. Just at that moment we heard a loud shout from all parts of the deck, and the mate called out down the companion-way to the captain, who was sitting in the cabin. What he said we could not distinguish, but the captain kicked over his chair, and was on deck at one jump. We could not tell what it was; and, anxious as we were to know, the discipline of the ship would not allow of our leaving our places. Yet, as we were not called, we knew there was no danger. We hurried to get through with our job, when, seeing the steward's black face peering out of the pantry, Mr H— hailed him to know what was the matter. 'Lan'o, to be sure, sir! No you hear 'em sing out, "Lan'o"? De cap'em say 'im Cape Horn!'

This gave us a new start, and we were soon through our work and on deck; and there lay the land, fair upon the larboard beam, and slowly edging away upon the quarter. All hands were busy looking at it – the captain and mates from the quarter-deck, the cook from his galley, and the sailors from the forecastle; and even Mr N—, the passenger, who had kept in his shell for nearly a month, and hardly been seen by anybody, and whom we had almost forgotten was on board, came out like a butterfly, and was hopping round as bright as a bird.

The land was the island of Staten Land, just to the eastward of Cape Horn; and a more desolate-looking spot I never wish to set eyes upon, – bare, broken, and girt with rocks and ice, with here and there, between the rocks and broken hillocks, a little stunted vegetation of shrubs. It was a place well suited to stand at the junction of the two oceans, beyond the reach of human cultivation, and encounter the blasts and snows of a perpetual winter. Yet, dismal as it was, it was a pleasant sight to us; not only as being the first land we had seen, but because it told us that we had passed the Cape, – were in the Atlantic, – and that, with twenty-four hours of this breeze, we might bid defiance to the Southern Ocean. It told us, too, our latitude and longitude, better than any observation; and the captain now knew where we were, as well as if we were off the end of Long Wharf.

In the general joy, Mr N— said he should like to go ashore upon the island and examine a spot which probably no human being had ever set foot upon; but the captain intimated that he would see the island, specimens and all, in – another place, before he would get out a boat or delay the ship one moment for him.

We left the land gradually astern; and at sundown had the Atlantic Ocean clear before us.

*

I think the captain of the *Alert* took an unnecessary risk by treating his crew so harshly. Through being ordered to complete almost impossible tasks in the worst conditions of storm and ice, the strength, efficiency and watchfulness of the hands must have been seriously depleted. Also, judging by Dana's description of the diet, I think that most of the crew must have been suffering from scurvy in some form or other.

It may be claimed that the captain knew the right way to treat a crew of the 1830s, because he succeeded in getting his ship back to Boston, and without having a mutiny. I believe, though, that he had far more than his fair share of luck and that a mutiny, which was attempted, was only just avoided.

Far more is now known about the winds and ice conditions near the Horn than in the early nineteenth century. Today, a captain, sailing down to the Horn from the Line, would pass 600 miles nearer South America on June 26th than the *Alert* did. He would then avoid 250 miles of the *Alert*'s hazardous passage through icebergs and pack ice; though he would still have had to thread his way among them for 300 miles.

Dana's captain was lucky with his navigation when south of the Horn itself. For more than a week he was either drifting about in calms or trying to make headway against the easterly gales. When land was sighted on July 22nd, the captain thought it was Cape Horn, when it was, in fact, Staten Island. Dana said that Staten Island was 'just to the eastward of Cape Horn,' whereas it is a long island between 117 miles and 140 miles from the Horn and lying between NE and NE by E from it. They probably scraped past the Horn the night before without seeing it in fog or a squall; and they had more than their fair share of luck in avoiding it.

Dana's captain would not know of Sumner's great discovery, made in 1837, that an altitude of the sun measured with a sextant was valuable at almost any time of day. It placed the navigator on a line of position which for a long time was called a Sumner Line. A second altitude, taken after a suitable interval, would place the navigator somewhere along a second line of position. The point where those two lines crossed determined the latitude of the observer, even if he had not got the right time; and it fixed his longitude also if he had the right time on board. Formerly, the navigator had relied on shooting the sun when it was north or south to obtain a latitude. This required observing at exactly local noon. It appears that the captain of the *Alert* had no idea of his position when he arrived at Staten Island, thinking that it was Cape Horn, 120 miles to the south-west. Yet he could at least have known his latitude because the text records, 'once or twice a round copper ball showed itself for a few moments in the place where the sun ought to have been.'

I wondered what I would have done in the same place if I had been there single-handed in a yacht without time or radio on board. At that date, the only way of finding the longitude without knowing the correct time was to observe a 'lunar'. I turned up my 1840 edition of Raper's *Navigation*, the volume from which I first started to learn astro-navigation in 1930, and the only text book I have which shows how to work out a lunar. I was horrified at the vast amount of calculation involved. To compute such a thing at sea in a small yacht, without making any mistake, especially if singlehanded, would be most difficult and arduous. Surely there must be an easier way! I pondered the problem and then suddenly thought of a simple solution which I will explain briefly: make a simultaneous observation of the sun and the moon for altitude when the moon is nearly east or west of the ship. From this observation compute a sun–moon fix in the ordinary way, using a guessed-at Greenwich Mean Time. Now compute a second fix from the same observation but using a Greenwich Mean Time which differs from the first one by half an hour or an hour. Now establish the latitude by a meridian altitude of the sun or any other heavenly body as it crosses the meridian. This observation does not require accurate time. Now join the two sun–moon fixes and the point where the line joining them, produced if necessary, cuts the known latitude must be the correct longitude at the time of the observation. Knowing the longitude enables you also to know what the correct Greenwich Mean Time was at the time of the sun–moon fix.

I fear the accuracy of this method, which depends on the rate of movement of the moon in its orbit, would be poor, but it could be a most valuable observation if, for example, one was trying to make a landfall at Cape Horn after a month at sea without having obtained a time check. Dr D. H. Sadler, Superintendent of the Nautical Almanac Office and one of the top men on the theory of navigation, was kind enough to say, 'So far as I can discover, Mr Chichester's actual method of determining positions at sea without reference to GMT is new; and it is certainly elegant.'

The unfortunate thing about this method is that no one thought of it 300 years ago when it would have been a godsend to navigators.

After reading of Drake's, Anson's and Dana's storms, here is the picture of a Cape Horn gale painted in a few words by that great artist, Joseph Conrad, the seaman:

*

Thus there is another gale in my memory, a thing of endless, deep, humming roar, moonlight, and a spoken sentence.

It was off that other Cape which is always deprived of its title as the Cape of Good Hope is robbed of its name. It was off the Horn. For a true expression of dishevelled wildness there is nothing like a gale in the bright moonlight of a high latitude.

The ship, brought-to and bowing to enormous flashing seas, glistened wet from deck to trucks; her one set sail stood out a coal-black shape upon the gloomy blueness of the air. I was a youngster then, and suffering from weariness, cold, and imperfect oilskins which let water in at every seam. I craved human companionship, and, coming off the poop, took my place by the side of the boatswain (a man whom I did not like) in a comparatively dry spot where at worst we had water only up to our knees. Above our heads the explosive booming gusts of wind passed continuously, justifying the sailor's saying, 'It blows great guns'. And just from that need of human companionship being very close to the man, I said, or rather shouted:

'Blows very hard, boatswain.'

His answer was:

'Ay, and if it blows only a little harder things will begin to go. I don't mind as long as everything holds, but when things begin to go it's bad.'

The note of dread in the shouting voice, the practical truth of these words, heard years ago from a man I did not like, have stamped its peculiar character on that gale.

16

Little Ships Double the Horn

THE ACCOUNTS of Drake's, Anson's and Dana's passages round the Horn give a complete picture of the worst that a sailing ship could experience.

What of the little ships? I know of eight attempts which have been made by yachts to round the Horn. Of these, four were crewed-up yachts and four were singlehanders.

The first attempt was in 1911, by *Pandora*, a copy of Joshua Slocum's *Spray*, and built in Australia. Smeeton mentions that she rounded the Horn, was nearly lost in a gale south of the Falkland Islands, and was picked up by a steamer after being completely rolled over. Humphrey Barton in *Atlantic Adventurers* says that she disappeared without trace with her crew but does not say where.

Conor O'Brien in his two-year circumnavigation from Dublin to Dublin in 1923–25 doubled the Horn with no accident or incident. His yacht was 42 feet long overall with a beam of 12 feet and a draught of 6¾ feet. He comments on the Horn in his book *Across Three Oceans*, after an easy passage from New Zealand:

'We had been favoured as perhaps no ship ever was before by the elements.' Of the Horn itself he writes:

Before nightfall everything else was dominated by the steep black cone of Cape Horn itself.

This is not a cape but an island, and derives its name not from its shape, but from the enterprising Dutchman who discovered it. When you see it you have no doubt which is the greatest cape of the world. Its peak is no more than 1,400 feet high, but it has no rivals near, and all that height plunges down almost sheer to the south. One could hardly design a more suitable finish to a great continent.

*

Conor O'Brien's *Saoirse* had four hands aboard but the third and fourth yachts to double the Horn were singlehanders. Hansen's yacht and *Lehg II* of Vito Dumas. Dumas made the passage without any accident except for a broken nose. It was at the end of June 1943 in the dead of winter. He had carefully planned the time because he reckoned that the conditions would be mildest then. His yacht was 31 feet 2 inches long with a beam of 10 feet 9 inches and a depth of 5 feet 7 inches. Dumas was an Argentinian born 26th September 1900. At the age of 23 he swam across the River Plate from Uruguay to the Argentine, a distance of 26¼ miles in

$25\frac{1}{2}$ hours. Dumas writes in his book, *Alone Through the Roaring Forties*:

*

June 24th. Numbers of cormorants came close to inspect the boat; there is nowadays so little navigation in this area that the presence of any ship is a surprise for them. I had still 90 miles to go before striking the longitude of Cape Horn.

That night the north wind had already risen to gale force. I only put my nose outside from time to time to see whether there was anything ahead.

How full of meaning and menace is the sound of those two words: Cape Horn! What a vast and terrible cemetery of seamen lies under this eternally boiling sea! Fear adds its chill to that of the atmosphere, the terror that lurks in a name and the sight of these seas.

Here, everything seems to be attracted and drawn towards the depths, as by some monstrous, supernatural magnet. Had I had a larger surface of wood under my feet, I could have calmed my nerves by pacing the deck, but no; I could not walk my thoughts under control.

That dim light of my compass on this dark Antarctic night made me look with tenderness on these wrought planks, flesh of the beautiful trees of my country, fashioned by human knowledge into a boat. It seemed to me that they were more in their place on land, living under the murmur of warm light breezes; if they had souls, they would reject the present to which I was exposing them. My voyage had been like a stairway which I ascended step by step until I found myself here. Here, hard by Cape Horn. Had it been announced to me as a child, I should not have believed it.

They were ringing in my ears with a note of doom, as if they came from the depths of the sea or the height of heaven, those two words that I could not or would not understand, spoken at Valparaiso before I set out for Cape Horn.

'Wouldn't you like to leave your log here? So that your pains may not be wasted?'

The voice that spoke was trying to be persuasive without sounding ominous. What they wanted to insinuate was quite clear to me: they were not at all confident of my success; they felt that I was lost before I started. But I was full of curiosity about Cape Horn. I wanted to see it, live it, touch it, feel it . . .

Here in my travelling library, close to me, were the records of Cook, of Bougainville, of so many other navigators, books that I had read and reread. I remembered the enthusiasm I felt on hearing the news that Al Hansen had succeeded in rounding Cape Horn from east to west, a feat nowise diminished by his terrible end. Hansen had been powerless to escape the curse that broods between the 50° of the Atlantic and the 50° of the Pacific. I felt his Calvary in my flesh only to think of it. Yet I had taken it upon myself to round the Cape as the only way to make port, refusing to admit any other course. All or nothing. As *Lehg II* neared the grim promontory, through hours made infinitely long by impatience and anxiety, I threw my last card on the table of life.

If luck was against me, it would be easy to say: "It was lunacy to attempt Cape Horn alone, in a 9 tonner – barely that.'

But what if I succeeded?

Imperceptibly, perhaps, the longing of all those who would have liked to make the attempt and were unable to do so, or the hopes of those who have tried without success, crept towards me. Perhaps I had the help of those who perished in this trial; perhaps I was not quite so alone as I thought. Perhaps the seamen of all latitudes were spectators of this struggle against the squalls and the darkness. Perhaps, too, this darkness would go darker yet, that the flickering lantern would cease to glow in front of my eyes, whose lids would close to see nothing any more on earth, now, or ever. This light, of little practical use, was more of an inseparable and invisible companion, standing between me and chaos. Life shone in it, the light of illusion or hope in the possibility – perhaps – of triumph.

It was midnight. According to my speed, Cape Horn should now be abeam. The wind was high and the seas heavy. In the cabin I had to cling to handholds to avoid being thrown against the panels.

Sitting under the light of my little paraffin lamp, I was trying to repair the tell-tale when a shock threw me forward; my face crashed near the deadlight on the other side. The pain was terrible. I was half stunned, but I noticed that I was bleeding violently from the nose.

*

Dumas here describes how he discovered that his nose was broken.

*

For the rest of the night the wind blew furiously from the north; but in the morning it eased off and backed to SW.

I could not observe the slightest scrap of land; only a bank of clouds to the north indicated its presence. I took advantage of the relative calm to bale; and I made a trip to the mirror to see what it had to say. My face was a horrid mess, swollen, distorted and blood-stained. But that was nothing. I was back in the Atlantic.

*

I think Al Hansen, whom Dumas mentions, was undoubtedly the first person to sail round the Horn alone and he went the hard way from east to west; but he did not survive; some wreckage from his yacht was found on the west coast of Patagonia.

The fifth yacht round was also a singlehander, *Les 4 Vents*, 30 feet 8 inches in length, which the Frenchman, Marcel Bardiaux, had built himself and must have built very well. Bardiaux was making a voyage round the world alone which took about 7 years from January 1950 and included 543 landfalls. He must surely be the toughest of tough Frenchmen. In May 1952, he approached the Horn the hard way, from the east, and in the middle of winter when daylight only lasted about 7 hours and the temperature was 14° F. below freezing point. Before reaching the Horn *Les 4 Vents* capsized and turned turtle twice in the Strait of Le Maire. Bardiaux should have entered the Strait at slack water but he was late in arriving and consequently was being rushed through in a strong current flowing against a strong wind. The tidal current here runs up to 9 knots and with a gale or strong wind against it the steep breaking waves must have been terrible. The Admiralty Sailing Directions warn that the tidal race in the Strait is at times very dangerous for steamers.

I will quote from Bardiaux's account where he is sailing along the coast of Tierra del Fuego approaching the Strait of Le Maire between Tierra del Fuego and Staten Island. The way he grounded his boat in a cove in order to obtain a night's sleep shows his outstanding toughness and endurance:

*

On Wednesday, 7th May at nightfall I was close to San Diego Point which is the south-east corner of Tierra del Fuego.

I had already been struggling for an hour against a head current which was getting stronger and at half tide reached 9 knots. It was useless to try to make headway, especially as the wind had risen considerably and was causing enormous waves in the current.

The glass was very low, which threatened a south-westerly squall, and in that event I was likely to be driven far out to sea as was the *Bounty*; after her, many other sailing ships were compelled to go round the world in the opposite direction, by the Cape of Good Hope.

As the size of my boat made her very handy, I took the risk of going into Thetis Bay for shelter.

The anchorage was quite untenable; the currents were violent and the swell threatened to break my chain. I could see a small basin with a rock-strewn channel leading to it, but dared not attempt it in the gathering darkness. The smallest mistake would exact, not damage, but total loss of the boat and probably of myself; for even if I could swim ashore in spite of the cold, it would only put off death by hunger and cold for a few hours.

Having got rather too near this channel, I was caught by a strong current which swept me towards the rocks; I had only just time to heave the anchor with some 15 fathoms of chain to avoid a catastrophe. It was far from long enough, but I dared not increase it for fear of the stern touching. I then spent most of the night getting into a safer place, helped by the eddies of the current; here I put out three anchors and a long warp to a rock. In spite of these precautions I did not sleep and between hot drinks I went on deck to check the moorings.

In the morning a violent hail-storm came drumming on the deck; 2 hours later snow was falling in large flakes. Soon *Les 4 Vents* looked like an iceberg. Utterly exhausted by my 60-hour vigil, I examined the channel at low tide, then, at half-tide, plunged into it after having weighed my three anchors with infinite trouble and cast off the warp from its rock. I deliberately left this operation till the last, preferring to lose a warp, even a new one, rather than an anchor and chain, if the safety of the boat had required this sacrifice.

I shot like an arrow into the cove, where the water was almost calm; the keel touched the bottom lightly once or twice and that was all. There was no spot where I could remain afloat at low tide; I had to go aground, an unsatisfactory operation with my deep keel and such a wind.

When I judged the moment had come, I ran her aground on a bank of sand and mud and when she herself had decided which side to lie on, I made fast two large cork fenders at the level of the bulkheads on that part of the hull which would be in contact with the bottom. I preferred to lay her down like this than to have her blown off her legs by a gust.

So there I was, safe for 10 hours; I would sleep in peace.

With a heavier boat, I would never have attempted such a manoeuvre for the anchors and chains would obviously have been heavier and impossible for one man to weigh. The only solution would have been to stand off and heave to. As the storms in these regions often last for several weeks, this would have meant abandoning my resolve to round Cape Horn from east to west, since the prevailing wind is west.

As for tacking, I was soon to learn that it was impossible in so heavy a swell as occurs here in foul weather.

This was why, before starting, I had set my heart on a

small boat that I could master alone, although less comfortable and even less costly.

This Cape Horn, this goal of my dreams was now less than 100 miles away and in a day or two, perhaps three, according to the weather, I should have rounded it....

The boat woke me ungently by straightening up. At that degree of heel, the hull and not the bunk was nearest to the horizontal and I had arranged the mattress accordingly, telling myself that as she progressed towards an even keel, the slope would awaken me gradually. But I had not realized that the hull would sink deeply into the sand which I thought was hard, forming a suction-cup. As the lift increased this suction suddenly gave way and *Les 4 Vents* leapt to her feet, so to speak, and flung me ungently on the floor.

The barometer was rising slowly and the wind seemed less violent. So, out and away! The rest had set me up again, and I was ready for anything.

Yet a few hours later I thought it was all over. Le Maire Strait was to put me in my place.

I had painfully worked round Cape San Diego, after having to dip my sails in sea-water before leaving in order to unfreeze them, which delayed me a little and upset my calculations; I had planned to pass this awkward spot on the ebb. There is a 9-knot current here which, against the wind, creates enormous breakers. Everything was battened down; the boat could play at submarines without shipping a drop – as far as the cabin was concerned, for a few tons were running over the deck. I should like to have seen a boat with bulwarks under these conditions, such as many had advised me to fit round the deck 'for my own safety'. However strongly fixed, they would not have stood up to this treatment for an hour, whereas my streamlined deck shrugged off the liquid mountains as fast as they came.

The wind which until now had been blowing strongly from the west, suddenly backed to south-west with unparalleled violence. Force 11–12 Beaufort. It was impossible to walk on deck, even hove to, a few minutes later. As it was dead ahead, the only possible course was to heave to, which was quickly done. But I was making so much sternway that I thought of reducing it by putting out a sea-anchor, not wishing to find myself back where I started from. The few seconds I needed to bring it up from the cabin caused the catastrophe. As a flood of water poured down the hatchway which I had merely shut instead of bolting it behind me for such a short time, I was flung over, together with all my equipment, well battened down though it was. Under the pressure of the heavy objects beneath them, the floorboards came adrift from their chocks and a hail of assorted projectiles descended upon me.

Les 4 Vents had turned turtle. Half stunned, I leapt out of the cabin, and had just time to catch hold of the uprights of my canvas shelter and kick the hatch to when over she went again. This time I seemed to be rather long under water and was about to let go, thinking it was all over, when the mast slowly emerged; so did I. My storm trysail was gone, so were the foresails in spite of their strong roping. All that was left of the shelter was the bent wood frame which was bolted through the deck. The shrouds appeared to be intact but the boat had a sinister list. All the equipment and stores plus a few hundredweight of water had been flung on to one beam which explains her slowness in righting herself the second time she turned turtle.

This was not the moment to look for my sea-anchor in the unholy mess below; I replaced it by my long warp which was miraculously still in the cockpit, part of it having got jammed under the binnacle while part had fouled the tiller. I flung it overboard just as it was, after having made fast one end to the anchor chain of which I then ran out some 15 fathoms. The braking effect was at once quite noticeable and the leaps of the ship less dangerous. I was able to leave the helm to pump. I tried to start the engine which operated two bilge-pumps but after such a bath and still half-submerged, it naturally refused to start. For a long time I pumped by hand, wondering whether I had sprung a leak into the bargain. The job finished at last, I looked round at the pitiable state of my cabin.

The bower anchor which was made fast under the table

had succeeded in coming adrift and after smashing the table and a provision chest had made a deep gash in the roof.

There was broken glass everywhere – bottles which had been under the floor-boards, and two fire-extinguishers, one of which had been fixed above the cooker and the other above the engine. The smell was suffocating and I had to go on deck frequently to get some air.

The tide changes every 6 hours and slack water only lasts an hour. It was essential to get as near the coast as possible to get away from the current that was about to turn against me and I even had hopes of making use of an eddy which the configuration of the coastline led me to expect. I therefore took advantage of a slight lull in the wind to hoist a few square yards of canvas (fortunately I had masses of spare sails, else shipwreck had been inevitable), and ride the huge waves obliquely. They were now breaking less dangerously.

The current was now in the same direction as the wind, the seas less high partly because the high cliffs masked it from the wind. But this did not make progress any easier for me; it was very slow. I kept piling on more sail and made the best of the counter-currents along the coast; I would not call these tactics prudent, but I had at all costs to reach Aguirre Bay to tidy up on board and to get a little rest.

Especially I had to dry mattress and blankets, for the temperature made it impossible to do without them.

Night fell long before I reached this bay and I had to fumble for it in pitch darkness. What a joy it was then to put on dry clothes out of a waterproof kit-bag, for my complete immersion had occurred 10 hours before and I had been soaked ever since. The thermometer stood at 18° F.

I spent the night on the bare wood of the bunk and woke up rather stiff. Boiling coffee, then spreading everything wet out on the shrouds – that is, practically all my possessions.

The sun had enough sympathy for my distress to show a pale countenance, but the wind did most of the work. A piece of luck that it was not snowing as it had been the day before.

With my fine confidence somewhat shaken, I left Aguirre Bay at 0300 in total darkness, 30 hours after I had entered it.

It was Sunday, 11th May 1952.

The two nights spent in Aguirre Bay had not rested me as I was without mattress or blankets. Provided all went well, I had to count on two or three more without any rest. My fingers were chapped and split so that I clenched my teeth every time I had to touch a rope. My face and ears were covered with chilblains and one ear seemed to be completely frozen. On a small boat such as this, the cold is more formidable than the sea itself. My right side was terribly painful; it was the beginning of the paralysis of the leg which came later.

I honestly confess that many times, when I saw my sails in ribbons and my poor boat struggling desperately on a raging sea, plunging down terrific precipices, disappearing under monstrous waves that threatened to swallow her, then pointing her bows to the black skies as if to implore the mercy of Him whose will disposes of life and death, yes, many times I said to myself: 'If I get away with it this time, I'll never set foot on a boat again.'

At 0600 [May 12], I should have been about 5 miles off the south-east point of Horn Island. I continued on the same tack until 0900 and should then have been 12 or 13 miles to the south. Estimates of distance under these conditions must be accepted with great reserve. My log showed the miles covered on the surface but, visibility being nil, I had no way of judging what the current might be doing.

My second tack, to the north-west, carried me in fact nearly due north. At 1230, the snow having ceased for a few minutes, I sighted the pyramid of Cape Horn slightly abaft my beam. I knew it was there, otherwise it would have been hard to assert that what I saw was the island and not a cloud darker than the others. What convinced me were the white streaks running down from the summit to the sea.

Under this furious wind, the snow only lies in deep and narrow gullies. There could be no question of taking a photograph under the breakers. In any case, a hailstorm swept over at that moment and the shadowy island disappeared, leaving me wondering whether it was one mile away or five.

As it was now evident that I could not yet round it on the

west without a very good chance of piling up, I made [another] board to the south-west.

My course, by my reckoning, brought me to latitude 56° 20′ at 2300. I did not dare to strike farther south because of ice; I had already passed small floes. As my sails were completely frozen, I had first to boil water in my pressure-cooker. The wind was stronger; I had to take a few turns on the boom and therefore to thaw out the lower part of the mainsail. It might easily have cracked which would have been a catastrophe, since my storm trysail had ended its career in Le Maire Straits. The canvas of the mainsail was new and strong, fortunately so, for it was my only hope.

About 0700 [May 13] I reckoned that Hermite Island was abeam.

At 0900, 13th May, a counterfeit day as pale as yesterday gave me a dim and fleeting sight of land. I knew that it must be False Cape Horn, which is about the same height as the true Cape and which stands on the extreme south-east point of the tattered shores of Hoste Island. It is 32 miles as the gull flies between the False Cape and the true.

In the meantime, *Les 4 Vents* was really and truly the prey of the four winds. The most violent was the north-west which carried me towards the north of Hermite Island. It was high time to get some sail set, in spite of the wind, to work to the north. 'Williwaws' when very violent usually only last for a few hours. But one may get several of them on the same day.

So whatever happened now, Cape Horn was in the bag: I could say: 'Veni, vidi, vici.'

*

As soon as possible after rounding the Horn, Bardiaux doubled back north again to seek shelter and time to recover at Ushaia in the Beagle Channel, after which he continued his voyage through the Magellan Strait.

The sixth and seventh attempts by yachts to round the Horn were made in 1957 by *Tzu Hang* with Brigadier Miles Smeeton, his wife Beryl and John Guzzwell as crew. *Tzu Hang* is a fine ketch of 46 feet overall, 36 feet on the waterline, 11½ feet beam and drawing 7 feet. John Guzzwell has himself completed solo circumnavigation of the world by way of the traditional trade wind path (and is the first Briton to have done so solo). We are lucky to have this account of Smeeton's because he has a style of writing which, with the few words of a true artist, paints the scene and portrays the character of his companions. Here he writes after 36 days at sea and having sailed 3,500 miles from Australia on the way to the Horn:

*

Beryl and John might prefer the grey smoking seas, but I like the sun and movement, this sparkle on the water, the blues and the greens, the dazzle and flash of the spray at the bow, and the small white clouds.

For 3 days the wind stayed fresh in the west, and never had we had such sailing. The stove was kept on all day and it was warm and snug in the cabin, and on deck *Tzu Hang* seemed to be singing a wild saga of her adventure. The big swells built up, showing a greenish blue at their tops against the sky and as they rolled up from behind, *Tzu Hang* leaped forward in a flurry of foam, weaving, swaying and surging, in an ecstasy of movement and sun and spray.

She seemed such a valiant little ship to us; so strong, so competent, so undismayed; so entirely ready to deal with anything that the wind might bring. As we walked around her, feeling the shrouds, checking the shackles, and tallowing the sheets, we felt that there was nothing there now that could let us down. We seemed to know every part of her: her weaknesses and her strength.

Below decks she was the same as ever, a dry boat, and I don't think that I had pumped her out more than once a week since we started, and then a few strokes only. As we sat below, we could hear no complaint from her. Only the noises that we knew so well: the happy noises of a good ship sailing well. However wild it was outside, there was an impression of home and comfort down below. Now that we had to keep the fire going all the time, everything was dry and warm. The kettle on the fire, the cat, the knitting, the rows of books and the made-up bunks gave a feeling of well-being and security not altogether in keeping with the conditions outside.

That was on the 1st February; now, here is Smeeton's record of the happenings on February 14th:

It must have been nearly five in the morning, because it was light again, when the noise of the headsails became so insistent that I decided to take in sail. I pulled on my boots and trousers. Now that I had decided to take some action I felt that it was already late, and was in a fever to get on with it. When I dressed I slid back the hatch, and the wind raised its voice in a screech as I did so. In the last hour there had been an increase in the wind, and the spindrift was lifting, and driving across the face of the sea.

I shut the hatch and went forward to call Beryl. She was awake, and when I went aft to call John, he was awake also. They both came into the doghouse to put on their oilies. As we got dressed there was a feeling that this was something unusual; it was rather like a patrol getting ready to leave, with the enemy in close contact. In a few minutes we were going to be struggling with this gale and this furious-looking sea, but for the time being we were safe and in shelter.

'Got your life-lines?' Beryl asked.

'No, where the hell's my life-line? It was hanging up with the oilies.' Like my reading glasses, it was always missing.

'Here it is,' John said. He was buckling on a thick leather belt over his jacket, to which his knife, shackle spanner, and life-line were attached. His life-line was a thin nylon cord with a snap-hook at the end, and Beryl's, incongruously, was a thick terylene rope, with a breaking strain of well over a ton.

'Got the shackle spanner?' I asked. 'Never mind, here's a wrench. Is the forehatch open?' Someone said that they'd opened it.

'Beryl, take the tiller. John and I'll douse the sails. Come on boys, into battle.' I slid the hatch back again and we climbed up one after the other. We were just on the crest of a wave and could look around over a wide area of stormy greyish-white sea. Because we were on the top of a wave for a moment, the seas did not look too bad, but the wind rose in a high pitched howl, and plucked at the double shoulders of our oilies, making the flaps blow up and down.

The wave passed under *Tzu Hang*. Her bowsprit rose, and she gave a waddle and lift as if to say, 'Be off with you!' Then the sea broke, and we could hear it grumbling away ahead of us, leaving a great wide band of foam behind it.

Beryl slipped into the cockpit and snapped her life-line on to the shrouds. John and I went forward, and as we let go of the handrail on the doghouse, we snapped the hooks of our life-lines on to the rail, and let them run along the wire until we had hold of the shrouds. The wind gave us a push from behind as we moved. I went to the starboard halliard and John to the port, and I looked aft to see if Beryl was ready. Then we unfastened the poles from the mast and let the halliards go, so that the sails came down together, and in a very short time we had them secured. We unhooked them from the stays, bundled them both down the forehatch, and secured the two booms to the rails. As we went back to the cockpit, we were bent against the pitch of the ship and the wind. Beryl unfastened the sheets from the tiller and we coiled them up and threw them below.

'How's she steering?'

'She seems to steer all right. I can steer all right.'

'We'll let the stern line go anyway, it may be some help.'

John and I uncoiled the 3-inch hawser, which was lashed in the stern, and paid it out aft. Then we took in the log-line, in case it should be fouled by the hawser. By the time everything was finished, my watch was nearly due, so I took over the tiller from Beryl, and the others went below. The hatch slammed shut, and I was left to myself. I turned my attention to the sea.

The sea was a wonderful sight. It was as different from an ordinary rough sea, as a winter's landscape is from a summer one, and the thing that impressed me most was that its general aspect was white. This was due to two reasons: firstly because the wide breaking crests left swathes of white all over the sea, and secondly because all over the surface of the great waves themselves, the wind was whipping up lesser waves, and blowing their tops away, so that the whole sea was lined and streaked with this blown spume, and it looked as if all the surface was moving. Here and there, as a wave broke, I could see the flung spray caught and whirled upwards by the wind, which raced up the back of the wave, just like a whirl of wind-driven sand in the desert. I had seen it before, but this moving surface, driving low across a sea all lined and furrowed with white, this was something new to me, and something frightening, and I felt exhilarated with the atmosphere of strife. I have felt this feeling before on a mountain, or in battle, and I should have been warned. It is apt to mean trouble.

For the first time since we entered the Tasman there were no albatrosses to be seen. I wondered where they had gone to, and supposed that however hard the wind blew it could make no difference to them. Perhaps they side-slipped out of a storm area, or perhaps they held their position as best they could until the storm passed gliding into the wind and yet riding with the storm until it left them.

I kept looking aft to make sure that *Tzu Hang* was dead stern on to the waves. First her stern lifted, and it looked as if we were sliding down a long slope into the deep valley between this wave and the one that had passed, perhaps twenty seconds before; then for a moment we were perched on the top of a sea, the wind force rose, and I could see the white desolation around me. Then her bowsprit drove into the sky, and with a lurch and a shrug, she sent another sea on its way. It was difficult to estimate her speed, because we had brought the log in, and the state of the water was very disturbed, but these waves were travelling a great deal faster than she was, and her speed seemed to be just sufficient to give her adequate steerage way, so that I could correct her in time to meet the following wave.

Suddenly there was a roar behind me and a mass of white water foamed over the stern. I was knocked forward out of the cockpit on to the bridge deck, and for a moment I seemed to be sitting in the sea with the mizzen mast sticking out of it upright beside me. I was surprised by the weight of the water, which had burst the canvas windscreen behind me wide open, but I was safely secured by my body-line to the after shroud. I scrambled back into the cockpit and grabbed the tiller again, and pushed it hard over, for *Tzu Hang* had swung so that her quarter was to the sea. She answered slowly but in time, and as the next sea came up, we were stern on to it again. The canvas of the broken windbreak lashed and fluttered in the wind until its torn ends were blown away.

Now the cloud began to break up and the sun to show. I couldn't look at the glass, but I thought that I felt the beginning of a change. It was only the change of some sunlight, but the sunlight seemed to show that we were reaching the bottom of this depression.

John relieved me for breakfast, and when I came up it seemed to be blowing harder than ever.

'How's she steering?' I asked him.

'Not bad,' he said. 'I think she's a bit sluggish, but she ought to do.'

I took over again, and he went below; no one wanted to hang about in this wind. I watched the sixty fathoms of 3-inch hawser streaming behind. It didn't seem to be making a damn of difference, although I suppose that it was helping to keep her stern on to the seas. Sometimes I could see the end being carried forward in a big bight on the top of a wave. We had another sixty fathoms, and I considered fastening it to the other and streaming the two in a loop, but I had done this before, and the loop made no difference, although the extra length did help to slow her down. We had oil on board, but I didn't consider the emergency warranted the use of oil. For four hours now we had been running before this gale, running in the right direction, and we had only had one breaking top on board, and although I had been washed away from the tiller, *Tzu Hang* had shown little tendency to broach to. To stop her and to lie a-hull in this big sea seemed more dangerous than to let her run, as we were doing now. It was a dangerous sea I knew, but I had no doubt that she would carry us safely through, and as one great wave after another rushed past us, I grew more and more confident.

Beryl relieved me at nine o'clock. She looked so gay when she came on deck, for this is the sort of thing that she loves. She was wearing her yellow oilskin trousers and a yellow jumper with a hood, and over all a green oilskin coat. So that she could put on enough pairs of socks, she was wearing a spare pair of John's sea-boots. She was wearing woollen gloves, and she had put a plastic bag over her left hand, which she wouldn't be using for the tiller. She snapped the shackle of her body-line on to the shroud, and sat down beside me, and after a minute or two she took over. I went below to look at the glass and saw that it had moved up a fraction. My camera was in the locker in the doghouse, and I brought it out and took some snaps of the sea. Beryl was concentrating very hard on the steering. She was looking at the compass, and then aft to the following sea, to make sure that she was stern on to it, and then back to the compass again, but until she had the feel of the ship she would trust more to the compass for her course than to the wind and the waves. I took one or two snaps of Beryl, telling her not to look so serious, and to give me a smile. She laughed at me.

'How do you think she's steering?'

'Very well, I think.'

'We could put the other line out. Do you think she needs it? The glass is up a bit.'

'No, I think she's all right.'

'Sure you're all right?'

'Yes, fine, thanks.'

I didn't want to leave her and to shut the hatch on her, and cut her off from us below, but we couldn't leave the hatch open, and there was no point in two of us staying on deck. I took off my oilskins, put the camera back in its plastic bag in the locker, and climbed up into my bunk. The cat joined me and sat on my stomach. She swayed to the roll and purred. I pulled my book out of the shelf and began to read. After a time, I heard John open the hatch again and start talking to Beryl. A little later he went up to do some more filming. As the hatch opened there was a roar from outside, but *Tzu Hang* ran on straight and true, and I felt a surge of affection and pride for the way she was doing. 'She's a good little ship, a good little ship,' I said to her aloud, and patted her planking.

I heard the hatch slam shut again, and John came down. He went aft, still dressed in his oilskins, and sat on the locker by his bunk, changing the film of his camera. Beneath him, and lashed securely to ring-bolts on the locker, was his tool-box, a large wooden chest, about 30 inches by 18 inches by 8 inches, crammed full with heavy tools.

My book was called *Harry Black*, and Harry Black was following up a wounded tiger, but I never found out what happened to Harry Black and the tiger.

When John went below, Beryl continued to steer as before, continually checking her course by the compass, but steering more by the wind and the waves. She was getting used to them now, but the wind still blew as hard as ever. In places the sun broke through the cloud, and from time to time she was in sunshine. A wave passed under *Tzu Hang*, and she slewed slightly. Beryl corrected her easily, and when she was down in the hollow she looked aft to check her alignment. Close behind her a great wall of water was towering above her, so wide that she couldn't see its flanks, so high and so steep that she knew *Tzu Hang* could not ride over it. It didn't seem to be breaking as the other waves had broken, but water was cascading down its front, like a waterfall. She thought, 'I can't do anything, I'm absolutely straight.' This was her last visual picture, so nearly truly her last, and it has remained with her. The next moment she seemed to be falling out of the cockpit, but she remembers nothing but this sensation. Then she found herself floating in the sea, unaware whether she had been under water or not.

She could see no sign of *Tzu Hang*, and she grabbed at her waist for her life-line, but felt only a broken end. She kicked to tread water, thinking, 'Oh, God, they've left me!' and her boots, those good roomy boots of John's, came off as she kicked. Then a wave lifted her, and she turned in the water, and there was *Tzu Hang*, faithful *Tzu Hang*, lying stopped and thirty yards away. She saw that the masts were gone and that *Tzu Hang* was strangely low in the water, but she was still afloat and Beryl started to swim towards the wreckage of the mizzen-mast.

As I read, there was a sudden, sickening sense of disaster, I felt a great lurch and heel, and a thunder of sound filled my ears. I was conscious, in a terrified moment, of being driven into the front and side of my bunk with tremendous force. At the same time there was a tearing cracking sound, as if *Tzu Hang* was being ripped apart, and water burst solidly, raging into the cabin. There was darkness, black darkness, and pressure, and a feeling of being buried in a debris of boards, and I fought wildly to get out, thinking *Tzu Hang* had already gone. Then suddenly I was standing again, waist deep in water, and floorboards and cushions, mattresses and books were sloshing in wild confusion round me.

I knew that some tremendous force had taken us and thrown us like a toy, and had engulfed us in its black maw. I knew that no one on deck could have survived the fury of its strength, and I knew that Beryl was fastened to the shrouds by her life-line, and could not have been thrown clear. I struggled aft, fearing what I expected to see, fearing that I would not see her alive again. As I went I heard an agonized yell from the cat, and thought, 'Poor thing, I cannot help you now.' When I am angry, or stupid and spoilt, or struggling and in danger, or in distress, there is a part of me which seems to disengage from my body, and to survey the scene with a cynical distaste. Now that I was afraid, this other half seemed to see myself struggling through all the floating debris, and to hear a distraught voice crying, 'Oh God, where's Bea, where's Bea?'

As I entered the galley, John's head and shoulders broke water by the galley stove. They may have broken water already, but that was my impression anyway. John himself doesn't know how he got there, but he remembers being thrown forward from where he was sitting and to port, against the engine exhaust and the petrol tank. He remembers struggling against the tremendous force of water in the darkness, and wondering how far *Tzu Hang* had gone down and whether she could ever get up again. As I passed him he got to his feet. He looked sullen and obstinate, as he might look if someone had offended him, but he said nothing. There was no doghouse left. The corner posts had been torn from the bolts in the carlins, and the whole doghouse sheared off flush with the deck. Only a great gaping hole in the deck remained.

As I reached the deck, I saw Beryl. She was thirty yards away on the port quarter on the back of a wave, and for the moment above us, and she was swimming with her head well out of the water. She looked unafraid, and I believe that she was smiling.

'I'm all right, I'm all right,' she shouted.

I understood her although I could not hear the words, which were taken by the wind.

The mizzen-mast was in several pieces, and was floating between her and the ship, still attached to its rigging, and I saw that she would soon have hold of it. When she got there, she pulled herself in on the shrouds, and I got hold of her hand. I saw that her head was bleeding, and I was able to see that the cut was not too serious, but when I tried to pull her on board, although we had little freeboard left, I couldn't do it because of the weight of her sodden clothes and because she seemed to be unable to help with her other arm. I saw John standing amidships. Incredibly he was standing, because, as I could see now, both masts had gone, and the motion was now so quick that I could not keep my feet on the deck. He was standing with his legs wide apart, his knees bent and his hands on his thighs. I called to him to give me a hand. He came up and knelt down beside me, and said, 'This is it, you know, Miles.'

But before he could get hold of Beryl, he saw another wave coming up, and said, 'Look out, this really is it!'

Beryl called, 'Let go, let go!'

But I wasn't going to let go of that hand, now that I had got it, and miraculously *Tzu Hang*, although she seemed to tremble with the effort, rode another big wave. She was dispirited and listless, but she still floated. Next moment John caught Beryl by the arm, and we hauled her on board. She lay on the deck for a moment, and then said, 'Get off my arm, John, I can't get up.'

'But I'm not on your arm,' he replied.

'You're kneeling on my arm, John.'

'Here,' he said, and gave her a lift up. Then we all turned

on our hands and knees, and held on to the edge of the big hole in the deck.

Up to now my one idea had been to get Beryl back on board, with what intent I do not really know, because there was so much water below that I was sure *Tzu Hang* could not float much longer. I had no idea that we could save her, nor, John told me afterwards, had he. In fact, he said, the reason why he had not come at once to get Beryl on board again, was that he thought *Tzu Hang* would go before we did so. After this first action, I went through a blank patch, thinking that it was only a few moments, a few minutes of waiting, thinking despondently that I had let Clio down. Beryl's bright, unquenchable spirit thought of no such thing. 'I know where the buckets are,' she said. 'I'll get them!'

*

This wonderful story continues with their saving the hull from foundering and rigging a jury mast and working a passage to Chile. That unquenchable spirit of Beryl Smeeton comes from we know not where and goes we know not whither. It is granted to only a few in any century. Reading this story, one is filled with wonder and admiration and a kind of exaltation that such women should exist in our time.

John Guzzwell, who was with the Smeetons at the time of their somersault, had interrupted a voyage of his own round the world in order to crew for them. Guzzwell was sailing round the world alone in a small yawl 20½ feet long overall which he had built himself. His voyage does not fit into this book because it was made along the well-beaten trade-wind path, but I must say that his little *Trekka* was the smallest boat ever to circumnavigate the world and Guzzwell was the first Englishman to do so alone. In his book, *Trekka Round the World,* which he wrote about his voyage he includes an account of *Tzu Hang*'s somersault. It is rare to have one good writer to record a unique event, but in this case there were two writers on board and Guzzwell's slightly different viewpoint is most valuable.

*

Early on the morning of 14 February I was on watch from 3 am to 6 am. *Tzu Hang* was running fast under twin-staysails and steering herself, but the wind was increasing, and I heard the top of the staysails fluttering, which they did when it was blowing quite hard. Miles came up to have a look at the weather, and we decided to take in the twins and run along under bare poles for a while. B came on deck and took the tiller while Miles and I went forward to pull the twins down. Each sail was set on its own stay and could be lowered one at a time if need be. We let both come down together then unhanked the sails and bundled them down the forehatch and snapped the twin poles to the lifelines.

By the time we had cleared away on deck the wind had quite a bit of weight to it and was sending us along at about four knots under bare poles. There was still an hour to go on my watch, but Miles was well awake by now, and, as he was on watch next, he decided to take over now instead of waiting until six. I went below and pulled my oilskins off and then climbed into my bunk, which was the quarter berth I had built in alongside the cockpit. It was a dry comfortable bunk and I was soon asleep.

I was awakened by Miles tapping on the side of the cockpit, which was the usual way B called me on watch to take over from her. I was reluctant to leave the warmth of the bunk and wondered if he wanted a hot drink of cocoa or something. I looked out of the hatch and saw that it was light. 'What do you want, Miles?' I asked, rather sleepily, hoping that it would be something easy, so that I could get back into my warm bunk.

'You should see some of these seas now, John. They are really quite impressive, and the biggest I have seen so far. How about filming some with your movie camera?'

I thought of getting back into wet oilskins and going out into the cold and part of me rebelled. 'The light is not very good,' I said, hopefully.

But then Miles was looking aft, and he turned to me and said, 'Look at this one coming along now. You've never seen a sea like that before. Get the camera, you may never have a chance to get a shot like that again.'

When I looked at the scene I saw what he meant. The sea looked different from the weather we'd had the last fifty days. There was a feeling of suppressed power about it, almost as though it were awakening after a long sleep. I saw another sea a quarter of a mile away roll up astern, higher and higher; then *Tzu Hang* started to climb the long slope until the crest passed beneath her and she sank into the trough behind. Miles was right, I had never seen the sea like this before, and I went below to get my camera. I filmed the sea from astern and got a couple of shots of the wind blowing the crests off the big seas.

'I'll shoot more later on, Miles, when B is on watch, the light will be better then, and I'd like to have some shots of her steering.'

The exposed film I put in a plastic bag, and as the tins I had been using were full, I put the bag in Clio's school-locker. I was pleased later that I had done so.

B tumbled out of her bunk at seven o'clock and started making breakfast. I ate mine and then went on deck to take the helm while Miles had his breakfast. He was soon back again at the helm and said to me, 'Before I called you up to film the sea, two quite large seas broke over the stern and washed me right up to the doghouse. You can see how they burst the canvas dodger.'

I thought that he could not have been dead before the sea because during the few minutes I was steering, while Miles had his breakfast, I had been quite impressed at the ease with which the boat steered and rode those enormous seas.

'Goodness, just look at those seas!' exclaimed B when she came on watch at nine o'clock. 'You should be happy now, John, surely. You've been asking for big seas ever since we started for your film. I hope you're satisfied with these.'

'Yes, they ought to look good on the screen, even though the sea always looks flat on film,' I replied.

I went below to get the camera and noticed that Miles was in his bunk reading. Pwe was sitting on his chest purring. I went on deck again and shot more film and finished the roll with a scene of B steering.

'I must just go and put another film in the camera, B,' I said, and slid the hatch back to go below.

I got a roll of film out of the locker and went aft to my bunk to load the camera. I sat on the seat by my bunk and opened the camera. The exposed film I laid on the bunk, then I started to thread the new film into the spool.

Tzu Hang gave a violent lurch to port, and I put my hand out to grab the fuel tank opposite. I had a sudden feeling that something terrible was happening. Then everything was blackness and solid water hit me. I was conscious of a roaring sound and that we were already very deep. 'She's been hit by an enormous sea, and is full of water. She is already sinking, I must get out.' These were the thoughts that flashed through my mind. I knew that I had to go forward then up out of the doghouse hatch and I started to fight my way against the solid water. Suddenly I was looking at a large blue square. 'What on earth is that?' I wondered. Then I heard Miles's anguished voice. 'Where's B? Where's B? Oh, God, where's B?' He stumbled past me crying out, 'Where's B?' and I watched him climb into the blue square. I realized that I was lying on my back in the galley and looking at the sky through the opening in the deck where the doghouse had been.

I scrambled out on to the deck and saw B in the water about thirty yards away. It is a picture I will never forget. She was wearing a bright yellow oilskin, the sea was almost white with spume and overhead the sky was a hard blue. B's face was covered with blood and for a crazy moment I thought, 'Oh, what a shot for colour film.'

B raised her hand and shouted, 'I'm all right, I'm all right.' While she started to swim towards us I looked about me and saw that both masts were in the water and all smashed into short lengths as though they had exploded apart. The doghouse had been wiped off at deck level and I noticed that both dinghies had gone. The side skylights were both smashed and the lids had gone too. I looked up and saw another monster of a sea approaching and I thought, 'What a bloody shame! No one will ever know what happened to us.'

'Hang on,' I shouted, and *Tzu Hang* lifted sluggishly to meet the crest, she had a slow hopeless feel about her and I watched more water pour down the great hole in the deck.

Miles called to me to give a hand at getting B aboard. I looked at the ruin everywhere and thought, 'I might as well jump in alongside her.'

B had something the matter with her arm, for when we hauled her aboard she thought I was kneeling on it.

'Well, this is it, Miles,' I said, knowing that we had come to the end of the trail.

He nodded. 'Yes, it looks like it, John.'

'Hang on!' I cried, as another big sea came along. *Tzu Hang* again made a tremendous effort, but she lifted, and I felt a spark of hope. 'We've got a chance,' I cried. And just then B said, 'I know where the buckets are.'

The two of us climbed down into the waist-deep water that was splashing backwards and forwards in what a few seconds before had been our comfortable little home. My main thought was to prevent more water getting below and that meant we had to cover the doghouse opening with sails or something. I climbed into the forecabin and started pulling the twin staysails aft, they would help.

For bearers to cover the opening I took the rods from Miles's bunk and the door off his hanging locker. My tools were still intact and the box was jammed on top of the galley sink. By some extraordinary luck the galvanised nails were still in the paint-locker though everything else had gone. It was difficult working on deck for there was nothing to hold on to, everything had been wiped bare except part of the aft end of the doghouse, the winches and the mainsheet horse. Miles gave me a hand to cover up the doghouse opening and we spread the Terylene genoa over the bearers I had nailed across, but soon I was able to carry on alone and he went to help B with the Herculean task of bailing out a few thousand gallons of water from *Tzu Hang*'s bilges.

I let go all the rigging-screws except the forestays in the hope that the wreckage of the masts and sails would act as a sea-anchor and hold us head to sea, for a few seconds she came around into the wind but then she broke free and fell back with the wind on her beam.

I transferred the warp trailing aft to the bow, and secured

the jib to it in the hope that it would act as a sea-anchor, but there was not enough drag to it and we continued to lie with the seas on our beam. Just inside the forehatch there were two gallons of fish oil together with the canvas bags it was supposed to be used with. I thought I'd never have a better opportunity to try oil on breaking seas, so I punctured both cans and emptied the lot over the side, there was not time to fill the bags. I felt that even a few minutes' respite would help. I also emptied four gallons of engine oil over the side. There was no sign of either on the water and it did not have the slightest effect.

The one thought that gave me hope was that I knew the barometer had started to rise again just before the smash, which indicated that the centre of the depression had passed. If we could keep *Tzu Hang* afloat for a few hours we stood a reasonable chance of getting out of this mess.

Miles and B were bailing out of one of the side skylights. I covered the other with the red storm-jib, lashing it down as best I could. I could hear B's steady call 'Right,' as she handed another bucket of water up to Miles who emptied it over the side.

I got a bucket and bailed out of the forecabin skylight, my feet were spread wide on each bunk as I bailed. At first I could easily reach the water bending down with the bucket, but as we slowly made progress I found that I had to climb down to fill the bucket then step up on to the bunks to empty it out on deck.

By dark we had got most of the water out of *Tzu Hang*. But what a pitiful condition she was in! The bilge was full of wreckage, hundreds of cans of food, most of them with no labels, clothing, broken glass, jars, books, coal and eggs, parts of the stove and miles of B's coloured wool that had somehow tied everything together in a most infuriating way. B had been wearing a pair of my sea-boots when she went overboard and had kicked them off while in the water. For hours she had stumbled about in the wreckage below with only thick socks on her feet, that night she noticed that one foot was badly strained.

Miles and I were still vague as to what had happened but

B was able to give us a fairly good idea. She said that she had been steering *Tzu Hang* down wind and had met each of the big following seas stern on, but when she looked over her shoulder again she had a brief glimpse of an enormous wall of water bearing down on *Tzu Hang*. Water appeared to be running down the face of it and she could see no white crests. She could not see how *Tzu Hang* could possibly rise to it but knew that she was dead stern on, there was a feeling of being pressed down into the cockpit then she was in the water and thinking that she had been left behind. She looked around and then saw *Tzu Hang* very low in the water and dismasted.

*

Guzzwell in his book gives his theory of what caused the accident.

*

The state of the sea when *Tzu Hang* pitchpoled was very similar to what would be encountered with a long swell passing over a shoal area, very steep seas, some of which toppled over and broke like surf on a beach.

Quite recently I wrote to the Hydrographic Department in London seeking information on the depth of water in this part of the ocean, the reply I received is of sufficient interest to repeat an extract here.

'Admiralty Chart No 789 shows only one line of soundings crossing the meridian of 98° W longitude in about 50° 42′ south latitude. This line of soundings was taken by the United States ship *Enterprise* in 1883–86. The soundings nearest to your position are 2,383 fathoms and 2,291 fathoms. The only other soundings in this vicinity shown on the chart are 2,565 fathoms about 290 miles to the NE and 2,555 fathoms about 310 miles to the south.'

The closest soundings of 2,291 fathoms are in fact about 40 miles from the scene of *Tzu Hang*'s somersault.

In recent years, ships equipped with echo-sounders have discovered many 'seamounts' in the North Pacific, shoals like mountain peaks which rise rapidly from the bed of the ocean to within a few hundred feet of the surface of the sea. These discoveries have been made largely by accident by shipping crossing the North Pacific on the great circle course from the West Coast of the United States to the Far East Ports.

I see no reason to doubt that there are similar undiscovered seamounts in the South Pacific which have remained undetected solely because so little shipping uses the old sailing-ship route from Australia to Cape Horn.

If soundings which were taken in 1883 are to be taken seriously what of other soundings that were also taken during the last century?

Take the case of the Maria Augustina Bank, the position of which *Trekka* passed 120 miles northward of during the run from Thursday Island to Cocos. The Admiralty Pilot Book tells the history of this in these words.

'In 1856 the Captain of the Spanish frigate *Maria Augustina,* when cruising about 540 miles east-by-south of the Cocos Islands, perceived a change in the colour of the water, and soundings taken immediately showed depths of 11, 9, 7, 5, and 13 fathoms, sand and mud; at the same time a black object on which the sea broke was observed about half a mile northward of the vessel. After sailing a further 7½ miles on a course of 211° soundings of 6, 8, and 10 fathoms were obtained.

'From good observations taken at the time, and later verified at Java Head, the southern entrance point of the western end of Sunda Strait the position of the rock was established at latitude 14° 05′ S and longitude 105° 56′ E. Discoloured water had been previously reported at approximately the same position, by the master of the *Helen Stuart* in 1845, who stated that he ran over a milk-white patch for about 50 miles in an east and west direction, no soundings, however, were taken.

'The existence of the above bank is considered doubtful.'

What do you make of that one? The closest sounding to the bank other than those mentioned above is 2,825 fathoms, 120 miles to the northward.

Perhaps someday when the oceans of the world have been accurately sounded we may be able to piece together some of the riddles of the sea, of the ships like *Tzu Hang* who survived a catastrophe and of the many who didn't and left their bones rotting on the bed of the ocean, or perhaps some uncharted shoal.

*

After making a 1,500-mile passage to Talcahuano near Concepcion in Chile they spent 9 months repairing the yacht, remasting and rerigging her and then on December 9th they set off once more to round the Horn. This time the crew were Miles and Beryl Smeeton. John Guzzwell was not with them. On December 25th, Christmas Day, they were about in latitude 48° 30′ S and about 350 miles west of Chile. Miles Smeeton wrote as follows:

We went below and *Tzu Hang* ran on into the night under her little storm-jib, heading south with the wind and sea on her quarter, and it was still safe to leave her unattended. We didn't think that we would be able to let her run for long, as the glass was down to 29.2 inches when we turned in.

Through the dark restless hours she reeled on, while the mugs on their hooks, the stoves in their gimbals, and the shadows from the cabin lamp, swung in unison to the quick lurches. There was little sleep for either of us, and we were glad when with daylight the rising note of the wind, the almost incessant noise of spray on the deck, and the deeper sound of the seas, told us that it was time to stop. We got on deck to find that the spindrift was lifting and that wide crests were breaking all round. *Tzu Hang* had done well to keep on going through the night. Beryl took the helm while I pulled down the jib and put it away. Then I joined her in the cockpit. As a wave passed we put the helm down, and she swung slowly. The next wave caught us beam on, but without breaking and nothing came on board, and then she swung slowly up towards the wind, but fell away again into the trough, and began to drift sideways to the wind and sea. We lashed the helm down so that if she fell away and began to sail again, it would bring her up. The water boiled up from underneath her keel as she drifted and made little swirls and eddies along the weather side of the ship, but it made little difference to the water to windward and in a very few yards the smooth trail of her sideways drift had disappeared. As I went below I looked at the glass and saw that it was 28.8 inches. When I tapped it, it moved downwards again.

By ten o'clock the gale was at its height, and the glass was down to 28.6. There it stayed. The sea had taken on its whitish look again, all streaked and furrowed with foam, the low raddled sky was grey, and the wide white tops came roaring up on the spume ridden wind. 'Don't let the *tigrés* get you,' they said to us when we left Talcahuano, and here they were after us in earnest, flinging their raging crests far ahead of them, and striving for a kill.

We either lay on our bunks and read or watched the seas through the doghouse windows. Sometimes we could see a shaggy monster raise his head above the others, and sometimes a wave would seem to break all down its front, a rolling cascading mass of white foam, pouring down the whole surface of the wave like an avalanche down a mountainside. There was no point in speculating what would happen to us if one of them hit us, in fact the whole business of watching the seas seemed to us unprofitable. The most terrifying toppling masses of water as often as not passed us without even a slap, but the wind would bellow as we rose on a wave, and *Tzu Hang* would heel away from it. Then we would hear the wave grumbling and growling away, spreading an ever-widening swath of foam behind, and as we sank into the hollow the noise in the rigging fell.

'What do you think?' I said to Beryl. 'Do you think that we should try and put the sea-anchor out?'

'I don't know,' she said, 'I think that it's a bit late. She seems to be doing all right, doesn't she?'

'The glass seems to have stopped falling now, and she's done all right so far, and we don't really know how the sea-anchor is going to work, so we'll leave her as she is.'

I did not think of using oil, and although we had some spare engine oil we had no oil bags. I decided not to use the sea-anchor because I believed that with all the sea-room we needed we would do best lying a-hull. I knew that there was danger, but I thought that the sea-anchor would only succeed in holding the bow half up to the sea, offering an ineffectual resistance, which would be worse than drifting away. Moreover, although we had had the opportunity, we hadn't yet tried out the sea-anchor, and now it looked as if it would be dangerous work getting it out. We were doing what we had done successfully in other gales, but never in such bad conditions as these.

'Do you think that we're imagining that it's worse than it really is?' Beryl asked.

'I don't know about imagining. I know it's quite bad enough and I'll be damn glad when it's over.'

'So shall I,' she said with feeling.

We lay down on our bunks again, Beryl in the forecabin and I in the main, and both on the port side, the side of the greatest heel, but we kept our boots and oilskin trousers on. Sometimes, when *Tzu Hang* heeled very quickly and steeply, or when we heard a deep rumbling roar approaching, we clutched the side of our bunks tense and anxious, and held our breath, and when it was over we looked at each other with a rueful grin. The cat went from one to the other to be petted, pricking her ears and crouching at the more alarming sounds, but on the whole less anxious than we were.

At four o'clock I thought that I'd make some tea. It was summer and for ten hours now it had been blowing a full gale, so I thought that the change must come soon, now that the glass had steadied. When the glass began to rise the wind would still blow for a few hours, but this must be the worst of it now. Almost as I thought this, *Tzu Hang* heeled steeply over, heeled over desperately into a raging blackness, and everything within me seemed to rebel against this fate. All my mind was saying, 'Oh no, not again! Not again!'

Again the water burst violently into the ship, and again I found myself struggling under water in total darkness, and hit on the head, battered and torn in a kind of mob violence, and wondering when *Tzu Hang* would struggle up. I could not tell what was happening to me, but I knew all the time what was happening to the ship. I felt her heavy and deep as the keel came over, and felt her wrench herself from the spars deep below her. I heard the noise of their breaking, and saw the light again from the port skylight, as it spun over my head. I found myself struggling to my feet knee-deep in water, and saw Beryl doing the same in the forecabin. I scrambled aft. The doghouse was still there, badly stove-in on the lee side, and the hatch was gone. When I looked out, I saw that the mainmast had gone at the deck, and the mizzen at the lower cross-trees. The broken spars were lying on the weather side of the ship.

'It's all the same again,' I said to Beryl, who was just behind me, and as I said it a sluice of water poured into the doghouse. I climbed up on deck to look at the ruin, and heard Beryl say, 'I'll get the jib.'

*

On the first occasion *Tzu Hang* had been somersaulted stern over stem; this time she had been rolled over sideways. Once again the Smeetons succeeded in making repairs and rigging jury masts and reaching port 1,100 miles away at Valparaiso to the north-east.

The eighth rounding of the Horn in a yacht was on 7th January 1965 by Nance, an Australian. Not only was his a singlehand effort but also the biggest achievement for the following reasons: his yacht, *Cardinal Vertue,* was the smallest of them all, it sailed at a record speed, 6,500 miles from Auckland to Buenos Aires in 53 days, an average of 122½ miles per day. This was the second longest solo passage ever made after Vito Dumas' 7,400 miles from Cape Town to Wellington, New Zealand. I think Nance had an unsuitable yacht for the Southern Ocean and was fortunate that he did not run into a real Cape Horn snorter; it would have been difficult for *Cardinal Vertue* with her high doghouse to survive a rough capsize off the Horn. *Cardinal Vertue* had already had the top part of her mast snap off in the Indian Ocean and later, near Australia, had had the bows seriously damaged by a big sea on one occasion, and had been capsized on another.

I cannot leave the subject of Cape Horn without mention of the greatest singlehander of all, Captain Joshua Slocum, the first man to sail round the world alone. Although he was not following the clipper way but passed west about and also did not round the Horn but made a passage through the Magellan Strait, he had a great adventure after passing through the Magellan Strait when, like Sir Francis Drake, he was caught by a storm and driven from Cape Pillar towards Cape Horn in the open ocean.

*

On 3rd March, 1896, the *Spray* neared Cape Pillar rapidly, and, nothing loath, plunged into the Pacific Ocean at once, taking her first bath of it in the gathering storm. There was no turning back even had I wished to do so, for the land was now shut out by the darkness of night. The wind freshened, and I took in a third reef. The sea was confused and treacherous. In such a time as this the old fisherman prayed, 'Remember, Lord, my ship is so small and thy sea is so wide!' I saw now only the gleaming crests of waves. They showed white teeth while the sloop balanced over them. 'Everything for an offing,' I cried, and to this end I carried on all the sail she would bear. She ran all night with a free sheet, but on the morning of March 4th the wind shifted to southwest, then back suddenly to northwest, and blew with terrific force. The *Spray*, stripped of her sails, then bore off under bare poles. No ship in the world could have stood up against so violent a gale. Knowing that this storm might continue for many days, and that it would be impossible to work back to the westward along the coast outside of Tierra del Fuego, there seemed nothing to do but to keep on and go east about, after all. Anyhow, for my present safety the only course lay in keeping her before the wind. And so she drove southeast, as though about to round the Horn, while the waves rose and fell and bellowed their never-ending story of the sea; but the Hand that held these held also the *Spray*. She was running now with a reefed forestay-sail, the sheets flat amidships. I paid out two long ropes to steady her course and to break combing seas astern, and I lashed the helm amidship. In this trim she ran before it, shipping never a sea. Even while the storm raged at its worst, my ship was wholesome and noble. My mind as to her seaworthiness was put to ease for aye.

When all had been done that I could do for the safety of the vessel, I got to the fore-scuttle, between seas, and prepared a pot of coffee over a wood fire, and made a good Irish stew. Then, as before and afterward on the *Spray*, I insisted on warm meals. In the tide-race off Cape Pillar, however, where the sea was marvellously high, uneven, and crooked, my appetite was slim, and for a time I postponed cooking. (Confidentially, I was seasick!)

The first day of the storm gave the *Spray* her actual test in the worst sea that Cape Horn or its wild regions could afford, and in no part of the world could a rougher sea be found than at this particular point, namely, off Cape Pillar, the grim sentinel of the Horn.

Further offshore, while the sea was majestic, there was less apprehension of danger. There the *Spray* rode, now like a bird on the crest of a wave, and now like a waif deep down in the hollow between seas; and so she drove on. Whole days passed, counted as other days, but with always a thrill – yes, of delight.

On the fourth day of the gale, rapidly nearing the pitch of Cape Horn, I inspected my chart and pricked off the course and distance to Port Stanley, in the Falkland Islands, where I might find my way and refit, when I saw through a rift in the clouds a high mountain, about seven leagues away on the port beam. The fierce edge of the gale by this time had blown off, and I had already bent a square-sail on the boom in place of the mainsail, which was torn to rags. I hauled in the trailing ropes, hoisted this awkward sail reefed, the forestaysail being already set, and under this sail brought her at once on the wind heading for the land, which appeared as an island in the sea. So it turned out to be, though not the one I had supposed.

I was exultant over the prospect of once more entering the Strait of Magellan and beating through again into the Pacific, for it was more than rough on the outside coast of Tierra del Fuego. It was indeed a mountainous sea. When the sloop was in the fiercest squalls, with only the reefed forestaysail set, even that small sail shook her from keelson to truck when it shivered by the leech. Had I harboured the shadow of a doubt for her safety, it would have been that she might spring a leak in the garboard at the heel of the mast; but she never called me once to the pump. Under pressure of the smallest sail I could set she made for the land like a race-horse, and steering her over the crest of the waves so that she might not trip was nice work. I stood at the helm now and made the most of it.

Night closed in before the sloop reached the land, leaving her feeling the way in pitchy darkness. I saw breakers ahead before long. At this I wore ship and stood offshore, but was immediately startled by the tremendous roaring of breakers again ahead and on the lee bow. This puzzled me for there should have been no broken water where I supposed myself to be. I kept off a good bit, then wore round, but finding broken water also there, threw her head again offshore. In this way, among dangers, I spent the rest of the night. Hail and sleet in the fierce squalls cut my flesh till the blood trickled over my face; but what of that? It was daylight, and the sloop was in the midst of the Milky Way of the sea, which is northwest of Cape Horn, and it was the white breakers of a huge sea over sunken rocks which had threatened to engulf her through the night. It was Fury Island I had sighted and steered for, and what a panorama was before me now and all around! It was not the time to complain of a broken skin. What could I do but fill away among the breakers and find a channel between them, now that it was day? Since she had escaped the rocks through the night, surely she would find her way by daylight. This was the greatest sea adventure of my life. God knows how my vessel escaped.

The sloop at last reached inside of small islands that sheltered her in smooth water. Then I climbed the mast to survey the wild scene astern. The great naturalist Darwin looked over this seascape from the deck of the *Beagle*, and wrote in his journal, 'Any landsman seeing the Milky Way would have nightmare for a week.' He might have added, 'or seamen as well.'

*

Cape Horn engenders fascination and dread in a small boat sailor. It is certainly one of the greatest challenges left. For years I told myself that anyone who tried to sail round the Horn in a small yacht must be crazy; and the record of attempts sounds gloomy. However, every time a passage is made or fails, then something more is learned. And anyone studying these accounts might begin to cheer up, because, after all, only Hansen failed to survive, although most of the yachts seem to me unsuitable for the job.

I have my own ideas on how a small boat should be designed for storm conditions, how it should be handled and what would be most suitable tactics in the stark, elemental situations that have been described, but, as they are only theories, which have not been put to the test, I will keep quiet about them.

It is not always rough off Cape Horn. In 1854 the *Ocean Chief* was becalmed for three days off the Horn.

17

Survival

THERE HAVE been some wonderful stories of survival after disasters, such as stranding, fire and collision with ships or ice, which have ended in awe-inspiring heartening achievements.

One of these took place near the clipper way in 1914. Sir Ernest Shackleton had set out to cross Antarctica but his ship, the *Endurance*, was crushed in the ice and sunk. Shackleton and all his men lived on the ice for months until, in the end, they were able to reach Elephant Island, 61° S, 54° 45′ W, about 570 miles south-east of Cape Horn. Elephant Island was uninhabited, covered with ice and without any food except what could be caught or killed. There was no chance of rescue unless someone could reach a radio station and organize a rescue expedition. Shackleton tells how he set out with a chosen crew of five men in an ordinary ship's boat to seek help from South Georgia which was 800 miles away to the north-east and about 100 miles north of Cape Horn in latitude. This voyage across what is probably the stormiest area of the world and certainly the region of the roughest, largest and coldest seas, was made at the beginning of the southern winter.

Shackleton wrote in his book, *South*:

*

The decision made [to seek help from South Georgia] I walked through the blizzard with Worsley and Wild to examine the *James Caird*. The 20-foot boat had never looked big; she appeared to have shrunk in some mysterious way when I viewed her in the light of our new undertaking. She was an ordinary ship's whaler, fairly strong, but showing signs of the strains she had endured since the crushing of the *Endurance*. Where she was holed in leaving the pack was, fortunately, above the water-line and easily patched. Standing beside her, we glanced at the fringe of the storm-swept, tumultuous sea that formed our path. Clearly our voyage would be a big adventure. I called the carpenter and asked him if he could do anything to make the boat more sea-worthy. He first enquired if he was to go with me, and seemed quite pleased when I said, 'Yes'. He was over fifty years of age and not altogether fit, but he had a good knowledge of sailing boats and was very quick. McCarthy said that he could contrive some sort of covering for the *James Caird* if he might use the lids of the cases and the four sledge-runners. He proposed to complete the covering with some of our canvas, and he set about making his plans at once . . .

The weather was fine on April 23, and we hurried forward our preparations. It was on this day I decided finally that the crew for the *James Caird* should consist of Worsley, Crean, McNeish, McCarthy, Vincent, and myself. A storm came on about noon, with driving snow and heavy squalls. Occasionally the air would clear for a few minutes, and we could see a line of pack-ice, five miles out, driving across from west to east. This sight increased my anxiety to get away quickly. Winter was advancing, and soon the pack might close completely round the island and stay our departure for days or even for weeks. I did not think that ice would remain around Elephant Island continuously during the winter, since the strong winds and fast currents would keep it in motion. We had noticed ice and bergs going past at the rate of four or five knots. A certain amount of ice was held up about the end of our spit, but the sea was clear where the boat would have to be launched.

Worsley, Wild, and I climbed to the summit of the seaward rocks and examined the ice from a better vantage-point than the beach offered. The belt of pack outside appeared to be sufficiently broken for our purposes, and I decided that, unless the conditions forbade it, we would make a start in the *James Caird* on the following morning. Obviously the pack might close at any time. This decision made, I spent the rest of the day looking over the boat, gear, and stores, and discussing plans with Worsley and Wild.

Our last night on the solid ground of Elephant Island was cold and uncomfortable. We turned out at dawn and had breakfast. Then we launched the *Stancomb Wills* and loaded her with stores, gear, and ballast, which would be transferred to the *James Caird* when the heavier boat had been launched. The ballast consisted of bags made from blankets and filled with sand, making a total weight of about 1,000 lbs. In addition we had gathered a number of boulders and about 250 lbs of ice, which would supplement our two casks of water.

The stores taken in the *James Caird*, which would last six men for one month, were as follows:

30 boxes of matches.
6½ gallons paraffin.
1 tin methylated spirit.
10 boxes of flamers.
1 box of blue lights.
2 Primus stoves with spare parts and prickers.
1 Nansen aluminium cooker.
6 sleeping bags.
A few spare socks.
Few candles and some blubber-oil in an oil bag.

Food:

3 cases sledging rations.
2 cases nut food.
2 cases biscuits.
1 case lump sugar.
30 packets of Trumilk.
1 tin of Bovril cubes.
1 tin of Cerebos salt.
36 gallons of water.
250 lbs. of ice.

Instruments:

Sextant.
Binoculars.
Prismatic compass.
Sea-anchor.
Charts.
Aneroid.

The swell was slight when the *Stancomb Wills* was launched and the boat got under way without any difficulty; but half an hour later, when we were pulling down the *James Caird*, the swell increased suddenly. Apparently the movement of the ice outside had made an opening and allowed the sea to run in without being blanketed by the line of pack. The swell made things difficult. Many of us got wet to the waist while dragging the boat out – a serious matter in that climate. When the *James Caird* was afloat in the surf she nearly capsized among the rocks before we could get her clear, and Vincent and the carpenter, who were on the deck, were thrown into the water. This was really bad luck, for the two men would have small chance of drying their clothes after we had got under way. Hurley, who had the eye of the professional photographer for 'incidents', secured a picture of the upset, and I firmly believe that he would have liked the two unfortunate men to remain in the water until he could get a 'snap' at close quarters; but we hauled them out immediately, regardless of his feelings.

The *James Caird* was soon clear of the breakers. We used all the available ropes as a long painter to prevent her drifting away to the north-east, and then the *Stancomb Wills* came alongside, transferred her load, and went back to the shore for more. As she was being beached this time the sea took her stern and half filled her with water. She had to be turned over and emptied before the return journey could be made. Every member of the crew of the *Stancomb Wills* was wet to the skin. The watercasks were towed behind the *Stancomb Wills* on this second journey, and the swell, which was increasing rapidly, drove the boat on to the rocks, where one of the casks was slightly stove in. This accident proved later to be a serious one, since some sea-water had entered the cask and the contents were now brackish.

By midday the *James Caird* was ready for the voyage. Vincent and the carpenter had secured some dry clothes by exchange with members of the shore party (I heard afterwards that it was a full fortnight before the soaked garments were finally dried), and the boat's crew was standing by waiting for the order to cast off. A moderate westerly breeze was blowing. I went ashore in the *Stancomb Wills* and had a last word with Wild, who was remaining in full command, with directions as to his course of action in the event of our failure to bring relief, but I practically left the whole situation and scope of action and decision to his own judgment, secure in the knowledge that he would act wisely. I told him that I trusted the party to him and said good-bye to the men. Then we pushed off for the last time, and within a few minutes I was aboard the *James Caird*. The crew of the *Stancomb Wills* shook hands with us as the boats bumped together and offered us the last good wishes. Then, setting our jib, we cut the painter and moved away to the north-east. The men who were staying behind made a pathetic little group on the beach, with the grim heights of the island behind them and the sea seething at their feet, but they waved to us and gave three hearty cheers. There was hope in their hearts and they trusted us to bring the help that they needed.

I had all sails set, and the *James Caird* quickly dipped the beach and its line of dark figures. The westerly wind took us rapidly to the line of pack, and as we entered it I stood up with my arm round the mast, directing and steering, so as to avoid the great lumps of ice that were flung about in the heave of the sea. The pack thickened and we were forced to turn almost due east, running before the wind towards a gap I had seen in the morning from the high ground. I could not see the gap now, but we had come out on its bearing and I was prepared to find that it had been influenced by the easterly drift. At four o'clock in the afternoon we found the channel, much narrower than it had seemed in the morning but still navigable. Dropping sail, we rowed through without touching the ice anywhere, and by 5.30 pm we were clear of the pack with open water before us. We passed one more piece of ice in the darkness an hour later, but the pack lay behind, and with a fair wind swelling the sails we steered our little craft through the night, our hopes centred on our distant goal. The swell was very heavy now, and when the time came for our first evening meal we found great difficulty in keeping the Primus lamp alight and preventing the hoosh splashing out of the pot. Three men were needed to attend to the cooking, one man holding the lamp and two men guarding the aluminium cooking-pot, which had to be lifted clear of the Primus whenever the movement of the boat threatened to cause a disaster. Then the lamp had to be protected from water, for sprays were coming over the bows and our flimsy decking was by no means water-tight. All these operations were conducted in the confined space under the decking, where the men lay or knelt and adjusted themselves as best they could to the angles of our cases and ballast. It was uncomfortable, but we found consolation in the reflection that without the decking we could not have used the cooker at all.

The tale of the next sixteen days is one of supreme strife amid heaving waters. The sub-Antarctic Ocean lived up to its evil winter reputation. I decided to run north for at least two days while the wind held and so get into warmer weather before turning to the east and laying a course for South Georgia. We took two-hourly spells at the tiller. The men who were not on watch crawled into the sodden sleeping bags and tried to forget their troubles for a period; but there was no comfort in the boat. The bags and cases seemed to be alive in the unfailing knack of presenting their most uncomfortable angles to our rest-seeking bodies. A man might imagine for a moment that he had found a position of ease, but always discovered quickly that some unyielding point was impinging on muscle or bone. The first night aboard the boat was one of acute discomfort for us all, and we were heartily glad when the dawn came and we could set about the preparation of a hot breakfast.

This record of the voyage to South Georgia is based upon scanty notes made day by day. The notes dealt usually with the bare facts of distances, positions, and weather, but our memories retained the incidents of the passing days in a period never to be forgotten. By running north for the first two days I hoped to get warmer weather and also to avoid lines of pack that might be extending beyond the main body. We needed all the advantage that we could obtain from the higher latitude for sailing on the great circle, but we had to be cautious regarding possible ice-streams. Cramped in our narrow quarters and continually wet by the spray, we suffered severely from cold throughout the journey. We fought the seas and the winds and at the same time had a daily struggle to keep ourselves alive. At times we were in dire peril. Generally we were upheld by the knowledge that we were making progress towards the land where we would be, but there were days and nights when we lay to, drifting across the storm-whitened seas and watching with eyes interested rather than apprehensive the uprearing masses of water, flung to and fro by Nature in the pride of her strength. Deep seemed the valleys when we lay between the reeling seas. High were the hills when we perched momentarily on the tops of giant combers. Nearly always there were gales. So small was our boat and so great were the seas that often our sail flapped idly in the calm between the crests of two waves. Then we would climb the next slope and catch the full fury of the gale where the wool-like whiteness of the breaking water surged around us. We had our moments of laughter – rare, it is true, but hearty enough. Even when cracked lips and swollen mouths checked the outward and visible signs of amusement we could see a joke of the primitive kind. Man's sense of humour is always most easily stirred by the petty misfortunes of his neighbours, and I shall never forget Worsley's efforts on one occasion to place the hot aluminium stand on top of the Primus stove after it had fallen off in an extra heavy roll. With his frost-bitten fingers he picked it up, dropped it, picked it up again, and toyed with it gingerly as though it were some fragile article of lady's wear. We laughed, or rather gurgled with laughter.

The wind came up strong and worked into a gale from the north-west on the third day out. We stood away to the east. The increasing seas discovered the weaknesses of our decking. The continuous blows shifted the box-lids and sledge-runners so that the canvas sagged down and accumulated water. Then icy trickles, distinct from the driving sprays, poured fore and aft into the boat. The nails that the carpenter had extracted from cases at Elephant Island and used to fasten down the battens were too short to make firm the decking. We did what we could to secure it, but our means were very limited, and the water continued to enter the boat at a dozen points. Much baling was necessary, and nothing that we could do prevented our gear from becoming sodden. The searching runnels from the canvas were really more unpleasant than the sudden definite douches of the sprays. Lying under the thwarts during watches below, we tried vainly to avoid them. There were no dry places in the boat, and at last we simply covered our heads with our Burberrys and endured the all-pervading water. The baling was work for the watch. Real rest we had none. The perpetual motion of the boat made repose impossible; we were cold, sore, and anxious. We moved on hands and knees in the semi-darkness of the day under the decking. The darkness was complete by 6 pm, and not until 7 am of the following day could we see one another under the thwarts. We had a few scraps of candle, and they were preserved carefully in order that we might have light at meal-times. There was one fairly dry spot in the boat, under the solid original decking at the bows, and we managed to protect some of our biscuits from the salt water; but I do not think any of us got the taste of salt out of our mouths during the voyage.

The difficulty of movement in the boat would have had its humorous side if it had not involved us in so many aches and pains. We had to crawl under the thwarts in order to move along the boat, and our knees suffered considerably. When a watch turned out it was necessary for me to direct each man by name when and where to move, since if all hands had crawled about at the same time the result would have been dire confusion and many bruises. Then there was the trim of the boat to be considered. The order of the watch was four hours on and four hours off, three men to the watch. One man had the tiller-ropes, the second man attended to the sail, and the third baled for all he was worth. Sometimes when the water in the boat had been reduced to reasonable proportions, our pump could be used. This pump, which Hurley had made from the Flinder's bar case of our ship's standard compass, was quite effective, though its capacity was not large. The man who was attending the sail could pump into the big outer cooker, which was lifted and emptied overboard when filled. We had a device by which the water could go direct from the pump into the sea through a hole in the gunwale, but this hole had to be blocked at an early stage of the voyage, since we found that it admitted water when the boat rolled.

While a new watch was shivering in the wind and spray, the men who had been relieved groped hurriedly among the soaked sleeping-bags and tried to steal a little of the warmth created by the last occupants; but it was not always possible for us to find even this comfort when we went off watch. The boulders that we had taken aboard for ballast had to be shifted continually in order to trim the boat and give access to the pump, which became choked with hairs from the moulting sleeping-bags and finneskoe. The four reindeer-skin sleeping-bags shed their hair freely owing to the continuous wetting, and soon became quite bald in appearance. The moving of the boulders was weary and painful work. We came to know every one of the stones by sight and touch, and I have vivid memories of their angular peculiarities even today. They might have been of considerable interest as geological specimens to a scientific man under happier conditions. As ballast they were useful. As weights to be moved about in cramped quarters they were simply appalling. They spared no portion of our poor bodies. Another of our troubles, worth mention here, was the chafing of our legs by our wet clothes, which had not been changed now for seven months. The insides of our thighs were rubbed raw, and the one tube of Hazeline cream in our medicine-chest did not go far in alleviating our pain, which was increased by the bite of the salt water. We thought at the time that we never slept. The fact was that we would doze off uncomfortably, to be aroused quickly by some new ache or another call to effort. My own share of the general unpleasantness was accentuated by a finely developed bout of sciatica. I had become possessor of this originally on the floe several months earlier.

Our meals were regular in spite of the gales. Attention to this point was essential, since the conditions of the voyage made increasing calls upon our vitality. Breakfast, at 8 am, consisted of a pannikin of hot hoosh made from Bovril sledging ration, two biscuits, and some lumps of sugar. Lunch came at 1 pm, and comprised Bovril sledging ration, eaten raw, and a pannikin of hot milk for each man. Tea, at 5 pm, had the same menu. Then during the night we had a hot drink, generally of milk. The meals were the bright beacons in those cold and stormy days. The glow of warmth and comfort produced by the food and drink made optimists of us all. We had two tins of Virol, which we were keeping for an emergency; but, finding ourselves in need of an oil-lamp to eke out our supply of candles, we emptied one of the tins in the manner that most appealed to us, and fitted it with a wick made by shredding a bit of canvas. When this lamp was filled with oil it gave a certain amount of light, though it was easily blown out, and was of great assistance to us at night. We were fairly well off as regarded fuel, since we had 6½ gallons of paraffin.

A severe south-westerly gale on the fourth day out forced us to heave to. I would have liked to have run before the wind, but the sea was very high and the *James Caird* was in danger of broaching to and swamping. The delay was vexatious, since up to that time we had been making sixty or seventy miles a day, good going with our limited sail area.

We hove to under double-reefed mainsail and our little jigger, and waited for the gale to blow itself out. During that afternoon we saw bits of wreckage, the remains probably of some unfortunate vessel that had failed to weather the strong gales south of Cape Horn. The weather conditions did not improve, and on the fifth day out the gale was so fierce that we were compelled to take in the double-reefed mainsail and hoist our small jib instead. We put out a sea-anchor to keep the *James Caird*'s head up to the sea. This anchor consisted of a triangular canvas bag fastened to the end of the painter and allowed to stream out from the bows. The boat was high enough to catch the wind, and, as she drifted to leeward, the drag of the anchor kept her head to windward. Thus our boat took most of the seas more or less end on. Even then the crests of the waves often would curl right over us and we shipped a great deal of water, which necessitated unceasing baling and pumping. Looking out abeam, we would see a hollow like a tunnel formed as the crest of a big wave toppled over on to the swelling body of water. A thousand times it appeared as though the *James Caird* must be engulfed; but the boat lived. The south-westerly gale had its birthplace above the Antarctic Continent, and its freezing breath lowered the temperature far toward zero. The sprays froze upon the boat and gave bows, sides, and decking a heavy coat of mail. This accumulation of ice reduced the buoyancy of the boat, and to that extent was an added peril; but it possessed a notable advantage from one point of view. The water ceased to drop and trickle from the canvas, and the spray came in solely at the well in the after part of the boat. We could not allow the load of ice to grow beyond a certain point, and in turns we crawled about the decking forward, chipping and picking at it with the available tools.

When daylight came on the morning of the sixth day out we saw and felt that the *James Caird* had lost her resiliency. She was not rising to the oncoming seas. The weight of the ice that had formed in her and upon her during the night was having its effect, and she was becoming more like a log than a boat. The situation called for immediate action. We first broke away the spare oars, which were encased in ice and frozen to the sides of the boat, and threw them overboard. We retained two oars for use when we got inshore. Two of the fur sleeping-bags went over the side; they were thoroughly wet, weighing probably 40 lbs each, and they had frozen stiff during the night. Three men constituted the watch below, and when a man went down it was better to turn into the wet bag just vacated by another man than to thaw out a frozen bag with the heat of his unfortunate body. We now had four bags, three in use and one for emergency use in case a member of the party should break down permanently. The reduction of weight relieved the boat to some extent, and vigorous chipping and scraping did more. We had to be very careful not to put axe or knife through the frozen canvas of the decking as we crawled over it, but gradually we got rid of a lot of ice. The *James Caird* lifted to the endless waves as though she lived again.

About 11 am the boat suddenly fell off into the trough of the sea. The painter had parted and the sea-anchor had gone. This was serious. The *James Caird* went away to leeward, and we had no chance at all of recovering the anchor and our valuable rope, which had been our only means of keeping the boat's head up to the seas without the risk of hoisting sail in a gale. Now we had to set the sail and trust to its holding. While the *James Caird* rolled heavily in the trough, we beat the frozen canvas until the bulk of the ice had cracked off it and then hoisted it. The frozen gear worked protestingly, but after a struggle our little craft came up to the wind again, and we breathed more freely. Skin frost-bites were troubling us, and we had developed large blisters on our fingers and hands. I shall always carry the scar of one of these frost-bites on my left hand, which became badly inflamed after the skin had burst and the cold had bitten deeply.

We held the boat up to the gale during that day, enduring as best we could discomforts that amounted to pain. The boat tossed interminably on the big waves under grey, threatening skies. Our thoughts did not embrace much more than the necessities of the hour. Every surge of the sea was an enemy to be watched and circumvented. We ate our scanty meals, treated our frost-bites, and hoped for the improved conditions that the morrow might bring. Night fell early, and in the lagging hours of darkness we were cheered by a change for the better in the weather. The wind dropped, the snow-squalls became less frequent, and the sea moderated. When the morning of the seventh day dawned there was not much wind. We shook the reef out of the sail and laid our course once more for South Georgia. The sun came out bright and clear, and presently Worsley got a snap for longitude. We hoped that the sky would remain clear until noon, so that we could get the latitude. We had been six days out without an observation, and our dead reckoning naturally was uncertain. The boat must have presented a strange appearance that morning. All hands basked in the sun. We hung our sleeping-bags to the mast and spread our socks and other gear all over the deck. Some of the ice had melted off the *James Caird* in the early morning after the gale began to slacken, and dry patches were appearing in the decking. Porpoises came blowing round the boat, and Cape pigeons wheeled and swooped within a few feet of us. These little black-and-white birds have an air of friendliness that is not possessed by the great circling albatross. They had looked grey against the swaying sea during the storm as they darted about over our heads and uttered their plaintive cries. The albatrosses, of the black or sooty variety, had watched with hard, bright eyes, and seemed to have a quite impersonal interest in our struggle to keep afloat amid the battering seas. In addition to the Cape pigeons an occasional stormy petrel flashed overhead. Then there was a small bird, unknown to me, that appeared always to be in a fussy, bustling state, quite out of keeping with the surroundings. It irritated me. It had practically no tail, and it flitted about vaguely as though in search of the lost member. I used to find myself wishing it would find its tail and have done with the silly fluttering.

We revelled in the warmth of the sun that day. Life was not so bad, after all. We felt we were well on our way. Our gear was drying, and we could have a hot meal in comparative comfort. The swell was still heavy, but it was not breaking and the boat rode easily. At noon Worsley balanced himself on the gunwale and clung with one hand to the stay of the mainmast while he got a snap of the sun. The result was more than encouraging. We had done over 380 miles and were getting on for half-way to South Georgia. It looked as though we were going to get through.

The wind freshened to a good stiff breeze during the afternoon, and the *James Caird* made satisfactory progress. I had not realized until the sunlight came how small our boat really was. There was some influence in the light and warmth, some hint of happier days, that made us revive memories of other voyages, when we had stout decks beneath our feet, unlimited food at our command, and pleasant cabins for our ease. Now we clung to a battered little boat, 'alone, alone – all, all alone; alone on a wide, wide sea.' So low in the water were we that each succeeding swell cut off our view of the sky-line. We were a tiny speck in the vast vista of the sea – the ocean that is open to all and merciful to none, that threatens even when it seems to yield, and that is pitiless always to weakness. For a moment the consciousness of the forces arrayed against us would be almost overwhelming. Then hope and confidence would rise again as our boat rose to a wave and tossed aside the crest in a sparkling shower like the play of prismatic colours at the foot of a waterfall. My double-barrelled gun and some cartridges had been stowed aboard the boat as an emergency precaution against a shortage of food, but we were not disposed to destroy our little neighbours, the Cape pigeons, even for the sake of fresh meat. We might have shot an albatross, but the wandering king of the ocean aroused in us something of the feeling that inspired, too late, the Ancient Mariner. So the gun remained among the stores and sleeping-bags in the narrow quarters beneath our leaking deck, and the birds followed us unmolested.

The eighth, ninth, and tenth days of the voyage had few features worthy of special note. The wind blew hard during those days, and the strain of navigating the boat was unceasing; but always we made some advance towards our goal. No bergs showed on our horizon, and we knew that we were clear of the ice-fields. Each day brought its little round of troubles, but also compensation in the form of food and growing hope. We felt that we were going to succeed. The odds against us had been great, but we were winning through. We still suffered severely from the cold, for, though the temperature was rising, our vitality was declining owing to shortage of food, exposure, and the necessity of maintaining our cramped positions day and night. I found that it was now absolutely necessary to prepare hot milk for all hands during the night, in order to sustain life till dawn. This meant lighting the Primus lamp in the darkness and involved an increased drain on our small store of matches. It was the rule that one match must serve when the Primus was being lit. We had no lamp for the compass and during the early days of the voyage we would strike a match when the steersman wanted to see the course at night; but later the necessity for strict economy impressed itself upon us, and the practice of striking matches at night was stopped. We had one water-tight tin of matches. I had stowed away in a pocket, in readiness for a sunny day, a lens from one of the telescopes, but this was of no use during the voyage. The sun seldom shone upon us. The glass of the compass got broken one night, and we contrived to mend it with adhesive tape from the medicine-chest. One of the memories that comes to me from those days is of Crean singing at the tiller. He always sang while he was steering, and nobody ever discovered what the song was. It was devoid of tune and as monotonous as the chanting of a Buddhist monk at his prayers; yet somehow it was cheerful. In moments of inspiration Crean would attempt 'The Wearing of the Green'.

On the tenth night Worsley could not straighten his body after his spell at the tiller. He was thoroughly cramped, and we had to drag him beneath the decking and massage him before he could unbend himself and get into a sleeping-bag. A hard north-westerly gale came up on the eleventh day (May 5) and shifted to the south-west in the late afternoon. The sky was overcast and occasional snow-squalls added to the discomfort produced by a tremendous cross-sea – the worst, I thought, that we had experienced. At midnight I was at the tiller and suddenly noticed a line of clear sky between the south and south-west. I called to the other men that the sky was clearing, and then a moment later I realised that what I had seen was not a rift in the clouds but the white crest of an enormous wave. During twenty-six years' experience of the ocean in all its moods I had not encountered a wave so gigantic. It was a mighty upheaval of the ocean, a thing quite apart from the big white-capped seas that had been our tireless enemies for many days. I shouted, 'For God's sake, hold on! It's got us.' Then came a moment of suspense that seemed drawn out into hours. White surged the foam of the breaking sea around us. We felt our boat lifted and flung forward like a cork in breaking surf. We were in a seething chaos of tortured water; but somehow the boat lived through it, half full of water, sagging to the dead weight and shuddering under the blow. We baled with the energy of men fighting for life, flinging the water over the sides with every receptacle that came to our hands, and after ten minutes of uncertainty we felt the boat renew her life beneath us. She floated again and ceased to lurch drunkenly as though dazed by the attack of the sea. Earnestly we hoped that never again would we encounter such a wave.

The conditions in the boat, uncomfortable before, had been made worse by the deluge of water. All our gear was thoroughly wet again. Our cooking stove had been floating about in the bottom of the boat, and portions of our last hoosh seemed to have permeated everything. Not until 3 am, when we were all chilled almost to the limit of endurance, did we manage to get the stove alight and make ourselves hot drinks. The carpenter was suffering particularly, but he showed grit and spirit. Vincent had for the past week ceased to be an active member of the crew, and I could not easily account for his collapse. Physically he was one of the strongest men in the boat. He was a young man, he had served on North Sea trawlers, and he should have been able to bear hardships better than McCarthy, who, not so strong, was always happy.

The weather was better on the following day (May 6), and we got a glimpse of the sun. Worsley's observation showed that we were not more than a hundred miles from the northwest corner of South Georgia. Two more days with a favourable wind and we would sight the promised land. I hoped that there would be no delay, for our supply of water was running very low. The hot drink at night was essential, but I decided that the daily allowance of water must be cut down to half a pint per man. The lumps of ice we had taken aboard had gone long ago. We were dependent upon the water we had brought from Elephant Island, and our thirst was increased by the fact that we were now using the brackish water in the breaker that had been slightly stove in in the surf when the boat was being loaded. Some sea-water had entered at that time.

Thirst took possession of us. I dared not permit the allowance of water to be increased since an unfavourable wind might drive us away from the island and lengthen our voyage by many days. Lack of water is always the most severe privation that men can be condemned to endure, and we found, as during our earlier boat voyage, that the salt water in our clothing and the salt spray that lashed our faces made our thirst grow quickly to a burning pain. I had to be very firm in refusing to allow any one to anticipate the morrow's allowance, which I was sometimes begged to do. We did the necessary work dully and hoped for the land. I had altered the course to the east so as to make sure of our striking the island, which would have been impossible to regain if we had run past the northern end. The course was laid on our scrap of chart for a point some thirty miles down the coast. That day and the following day passed for us in a sort of nightmare. Our mouths were dry and our tongues were swollen. The wind was still strong and the heavy sea forced us to navigate carefully, but any thought of our peril from the waves was buried beneath the consciousness of our raging thirst. The bright moments were those when we each received our one mug of hot milk during the long, bitter watches of the night. Things were bad for us in those days, but the end was coming. The morning of May 8 broke thick and stormy, with squalls from the north-west. We searched the waters ahead for a sign of land, and though we could see nothing more than had met our eyes for many days, we were cheered by a sense that the goal was near at hand. About ten o'clock that morning we passed a little bit of kelp, a glad signal of the proximity of land. An hour later we saw two shags sitting on a big mass of kelp, and knew then that we must be within ten or fifteen miles of the shore. These birds are as sure an indication of the proximity of land as a lighthouse is, for they never venture far to sea. We gazed ahead with increasing eagerness, and at 12.30 pm, through a rift in the clouds, McCarthy caught a glimpse of the black cliffs of South Georgia, just fourteen days after our departure from Elephant Island. It was a glad moment. Thirst-ridden, chilled, and weak as we were, happiness irradiated us. The job was nearly done.

We stood in towards the shore to look for a landing-place, and presently we could see the green tussock-grass on the ledges above the surf-beaten rocks. Ahead of us and to the south, blind rollers showed the presence of uncharted reefs along the coast. Here and there the hungry rocks were close to the surface, and over them the great waves broke, swirling viciously and spouting thirty and forty feet into the air. The rocky coast appeared to descend sheer to the sea. Our need of water and rest was well-nigh desperate, but to have attempted a landing at that time would have been suicidal. Night was drawing near, and the weather indications were not favourable. There was nothing for it but to haul off till the following morning, so we stood away on the starboard tack until we had made what appeared to be a safe offing. Then we hove to in the high westerly swell. The hours passed slowly as we waited the dawn, which would herald, we fondly hoped, the last stage of our journey. Our thirst was a torment and we could scarcely touch our food; the cold seemed to strike right through our weakened bodies. At 5 am the wind shifted to the north-west and quickly increased to one of the worst hurricanes any of us had ever experienced. A great cross-sea was running, and the wind simply shrieked as it tore the tops off the waves and converted the whole seascape into a haze of driving spray. Down into valleys, up to tossing heights, straining until her seams opened, swung our little boat, brave still but labouring heavily. We knew that the wind and set of the sea was driving us ashore, but we could do nothing. The dawn showed us a storm-torn ocean, and the morning passed without bringing us a sight of the land; but at 1 pm, through a rift in the flying mists, we got a glimpse of the huge crags of the island and realized that our position had become desperate. We were on a dead lee shore, and we could gauge our approach to the unseen cliffs by the roar of the breakers against the sheer walls of rock. I ordered the double-reefed mainsail to be set in the hope that we might claw off, and this attempt increased the strain upon the boat. The *Caird* was bumping heavily, and the water was pouring in everywhere. Our thirst was forgotten in the realization of our imminent danger, as we baled unceasingly, and adjusted our weights from time to time; occasional glimpses showed that the shore was nearer. I knew that Annewkow Island lay to the south of us, but our small and badly marked chart showed uncertain reefs in the passage between the island and the mainland, and I dared not trust it, though as a last resort we could try to lie under the lee of the island. The afternoon wore away as we edged down the coast, with the thunder of the breakers in our ears. The approach of evening found us still some distance from Annewkow Island, and, dimly in the twilight, we could see a snow-capped mountain looming above us. The chance of surviving the night, with the driving gale and the implacable sea forcing us on to the lee shore, seemed small. I think most of us had a feeling that the end was very near. Just after 6 pm, in the dark, as the boat was in the yeasty backwash from the seas flung from this iron-bound coast, then, just when things looked their worst, they changed for the best. I have marvelled often at the thin line that divides success from failure and the sudden turn that leads from apparently certain disaster to comparative safety. The wind suddenly shifted, and we were free once more to make an offing. Almost as soon as the gale eased, the pin that locked the mast to the thwart fell out. It must have been on the point of doing this throughout the hurricane, and if it had gone nothing could have saved us; the mast would have snapped like a carrot. Our backstays had carried away once before when iced up and were not too strongly fastened now. We were thankful indeed for the mercy that had held that pin in its place throughout the hurricane.

We stood off shore again, tired almost to the point of apathy. Our water had long been finished. The last was about a pint of hairy liquid which we strained through a bit of gauze from the medicine-chest. The pangs of thirst attacked us with redoubled intensity, and I felt that we must make a landing on the following day at almost any hazard. The night wore on. We were very tired. We longed for day. When at last the dawn came on the morning of May 10 there was practically no wind, but a high cross-sea was running. We made slow progress towards the shore. About 8 am the wind backed to the north-west and threatened another blow. We had sighted in the meantime a big indentation which I thought must be King Haakon Bay, and I decided that we must land there. We set the bows of the boat towards the bay and ran before the freshening gale. Soon we had angry reefs on either side. Great glaciers came down to the sea and offered no landing-place. The sea spouted on the reefs and thundered against the shore. About noon we sighted a line of jagged reef, like blackened teeth, that seemed to bar the entrance to the bay. Inside, comparatively smooth water stretched eight or nine miles to the head of the bay. A gap in the reef appeared, and we made for it. But the fates had another rebuff for us. The wind shifted and blew from the east right out of the bay. We could see the way through the reef, but we could not approach it directly. That afternoon we bore up, tacking five times in the strong wind. The last tack enabled us to get through, and at last we were in the wide mouth of the bay. Dusk was approaching. A small cove, with a boulder-strewn beach guarded by a reef, made a break in the cliffs on the south side of the bay, and we turned in that direction. I stood in the bows directing the steering as we ran through the kelp and made the passage of the reef. The entrance was so narrow that we had to take in the oars, and the swell was piling itself right over the reef into the cove; but in a minute or two we were inside, and in the gathering darkness the *James Caird* ran in on a swell and touched the beach. I sprang ashore with the short painter and held on when the boat went out with the backward surge. When the *James Caird* came in again three of the men got ashore, and they held the painter while I climbed some rocks with another line. A slip on the wet rocks twenty feet up nearly closed my part of the story just at the moment when we were achieving safety. A jagged piece of rock held me and at the same time bruised me sorely. However, I made fast the line, and in a few minutes we were all safe on the beach, with the boat floating in the surging water just off the shore. We heard a gurgling sound that was sweet music in our ears, and, peering around, found a stream of fresh water almost at our feet. A moment later we were down on our knees drinking the pure ice-cold water in long draughts that put new life into us. It was a splendid moment.

*

Due to this great feat of Shackleton and his boat's crew, not one man of the *Endurance* lost his life. When Shackleton reached South Georgia he still had another ordeal to face, though he did not know it – the gargantuan task of crossing the 10,000-foot range of ice-covered rock and glaciers to reach the whaling station on the other side of the Island. After that a ship made four attempts to reach Elephant Island before it succeeded and was able to rescue all the men there.

18

The South Atlantic

AFTER ROUNDING the Horn the clipper crews used to feel that they were in home waters although in fact they still had 8,000 miles to sail to reach the English Channel. They felt safe and secure and they looked forward to a pampered existence for the rest of the voyage. Their feelings were not always justified. For instance, if they swept up the middle of the South Atlantic east of the Falkland Islands they were in the area of possible icebergs for 2,000 miles.

The ice conditions in the Southern Ocean vary from year to year. Most passages were made without a sight of ice. Two of the worst years were 1892 and 1893. Many ships then saw icebergs they reckoned to be over 1,000 feet in height.

Captain E. H. Andrew of the *Cromdale* described his

experience to the secretary of the London Ship Masters Society as follows:

*

We left Sydney on 1st March and having run our easting down on the parallel of 49°-50° S rounded the Horn on 30th March without having seen ice, the average temperature of the water being 43° during the whole run across.

At midnight on 1st April at 56° S, 58° 32′ W, the temperature fell to 37½°, this being the lowest for the voyage, but no ice was seen though there was a suspicious glare to the southward.

At 4.00 am on 6th April in 46° S, 36° W, a large berg was reported right ahead, just giving us time to clear it. At 4.30 with the first signs of daybreak, several could be distinctly seen to windward, the wind being north-west and the ship steering NE about 9 knots. At daylight, 5.20 am, the whole horizon to windward was a complete mass of bergs of enormous size, with an unbroken wall at the back; there were also many to leeway.

I now called all hands, and after reducing speed to 7 knots, sent the hands to their stations and stood on. At 7.00 am there was a wall extending from a point on the lee bow to about 4 points on the lee quarter, and at 7.30 both walls joined ahead. I sent the chief mate aloft with a pair of glasses to find a passage out but he reported from the top gallant yard that the ice was unbroken ahead. Finding myself embayed and closely beset with innumerable bergs of all shapes, I decided to tack and try and get out the way I had come into the bay.

The cliffs were now truly grand, rising up 300 feet on either side of us and as square and true at the edge as if just out of the joiner's shop, with the sea breaking right over the southern cliff and whirling away in a cloud of spray.

Tacked ship at 7.30, finding the utmost difficulty in keeping clear of the huge pieces strewn so thickly in the water and having on several occasions to scrape her along one to keep clear of the next.

We stood on this way until 11.00 am, when to my horror, the wind started to veer with every squall till I drew quite close to the southern barrier, having the extreme point a little on my lee bow. I felt sure we must go ashore without a chance of saving ourselves. Just about 11.30 the wind shifted to SW with a strong squall, so we squared away to the NW and came past the same bergs as we had seen at daybreak, the largest being about 1,000 feet high, anvil shaped. At 2.00 pm we got on the NW side of the northern arm of the horseshoe-shaped mass. It then reached from 4 points on my lee bow to as far as could be seen astern in one unbroken line.

*

The following year, 1893, Captain Woodget wrote an account in his journal of the *Cutty Sark*'s encounter with ice:

*

Wednesday, 8th February. – Latitude 50° 08′ S, longtitude 46° 41′ W, course N 50° E, distance (run) 150 miles. Gentle SW breeze and fine. 6.00 am, foggy; 6.30 fog lifted and we found ourselves surrounded by icebergs; 8.00 am, foggy again; ice ahead, in fact there was ice all round. As soon as we cleared one berg another would be reported. You could hear the sea roaring on them and through them, the ice cracking sometimes like thunder, at other times like cannon, and often like a sharp rifle report, and yet could not see them.

At 1.00 pm the top of an iceberg was seen which one could hardly believe was ice, it looked like a streak of dark cloud. Then we could see the ice a few feet down, but we could not see the bottom. It was up at an angle of 45°, we were only about 1,000 feet off, so it would be 1,000 feet high, it had a circular top but we could not see the ends.

A few minutes later another was under the bows, we only cleared it by a few feet. It was about 100 feet high and flat topped, just as we were passing the corner there was a sharp report that made you jump, as if it was breaking in two.

When we had cleared the big one, I saw its north end and took bearings, after sailing 8 miles I took other bearings and found that the east side was 19 miles long; and we could not see the end of the side we sailed along. We sailed about 6 miles alongside of it, water now quite smooth. Before the noon the water was quite lumpy from all ways.

*

Much of the ice risk could be avoided by keeping from 40 to 140 miles off the coast of Patagonia. Here a sailing ship would be on the edge of the area of possible icebergs all the way up the coast till level with Buenos Aires. The big ships preferred to keep in mid-Atlantic where the advantages of stronger winds and steadier winds outweighed the ice risk, but I think that yachts and certainly singlehanders would be better off passing through Le Maire Strait between Staten Island and Tierra del Fuego, and then heading northwards to keep near the South American coast until the latitude of Buenos Aires is reached. However, if by doing so they escaped the ice risk, or at least decreased it, they would need to keep a sharp look-out for a pampero, a violent squall caused by a wind descending from the Andes and then passing over the heated flat plain of the Argentine. The pampero is formidable because it can suddenly appear with almost no warning in a fine cloudless sky. Vito Dumas describes how *Lehg II* was struck by one before he set off on his voyage round the world:

*

I was surprised by a pampero squall blowing at between 60 and 70 knots . . . It was in the evening. I was making myself some chocolate and hoped to spend as pleasant a night as possible. The wind outside was so violent that a sail had been blown to ribbons and the raging seas were something to shudder at. I was hove to close to the wind. Suddenly there was a terrific crash. I followed the motion of the boat and found myself sitting on the ceiling of the cabin. This was it. For several seconds of eternity the masts were pointing to the depths and the keel skywards. The chocolate was flowing over the ceiling. I was sealed in, in the total darkness, and assumed that I was sinking. I was partly stunned and there was nothing that I could do. The end of everything. I felt hot blood running on my hand. There was no way out of the darkness and confusion, and *Lehg II*, keel in the air, would soon fill and sink.

It was a coffin more than a prison. Then came resignation and I relaxed. I cannot say whether my mood was one of acceptance, thankfulness even, or a kind of reverence for death, so often defied. I left everything to fate. To struggle was quite useless; I seemed to be returning to infancy. Then *Lehg II* slowly rolled over; and keeping pace with the movement of the boat hope came back.

*

Joseph Conrad also relates an experience of a pampero:

*

That one was a gale that came upon the ship swiftly, like a pampero, which last is a very sudden wind indeed. Before we knew very well what was coming all the sails we had set had burst; the furled ones were blowing loose, ropes flying, sea hissing – it hissed tremendously – wind howling, and the ship lying on her side, so that half of the crew were swimming and the other half clawing desperately at whatever came to hand, according to the side of the deck each man had been caught on by the catastrophe, either to leeward or to windward. The shouting I need not mention – it was the merest drop in an ocean of noise – and yet the character of the gale seems contained in the recollection of one small, not particularly impressive, sallow man without a cap and with a very still face. Captain Jones – let us call him Jones – had been caught unawares. Two orders he had given at the first sign of an utterly unforeseen onset; after that the magnitude of his mistake seemed to have overwhelmed him. We were doing what was needed and feasible. The ship behaved well. Of course, it was some time before we could pause in our fierce and laborious exertions; but all through the work, the excitement, the uproar, and some dismay, we were aware of this silent little man at the break of the poop, perfectly motionless, soundless, and often hidden from us by the drift of sprays.

When we officers clambered at last upon the poop, he seemed to come out of that numbed composure, and shouted to us down wind: 'Try the pumps'. Afterwards he disappeared. As to the ship, I need not say that, although she was presently swallowed up in one of the blackest nights I can remember, she did not disappear.

*

Joshua Slocum had an adventure with a big wave well off the coast of Patagonia:

*

Hoping that she [*Spray*] might go clear of the destructive tide races, the dread of big craft or little along this coast, I gave all the capes a berth of about 50 miles, for these dangers extend many miles from the land. But where the sloop avoided one danger she encountered another. For, one day, well off the Patagonian coast, while the sloop was reaching under short sail, a tremendous wave, the culmination, it seemed, of many waves, rolled down upon her in a storm, roaring as it came. I had only a moment to get all sail down and myself up on the peak halyards, out of danger when I saw the mighty crest towering masthead-high above me, The mountain of water submerged my vessel. She shook in every timber and reeled under the weight of the sea, but rose quickly out of it, and rose grandly over the rollers that followed. It may have been a minute that from my hold in the rigging I could see no part of the *Spray*'s hull. Perhaps it was even less time than that, but it seemed a long while, for under great excitement one lives fast, and in a few seconds one may think a good deal of one's past life. Not only did the past, with electric speed, flash before me, but I had time while in my hazardous position for resolutions for the future that would take a long time to fulfil. The first one was, I remember, that if the *Spray* came through this danger I would dedicate my best energies to building a larger ship on her lines, which I hope yet to do. Other promises, less easily kept, I should have made under protest. However, the incident, which filled me with fear, was only one more test of the *Spray*'s worthiness.

*

As soon as the ships reached the latitude of Rio de Janeiro they were due to pass into the zone of the choicest sailing in the world. Ernesto Uriburu re-creates the atmosphere of this halcyon sailing in his book, *Seagoing Gaucho*. I love his book; he treats sailing in the way it should be treated as an amusing, happy sport. Most seafaring authors, like myself, keep on stressing the fatigues and serious adventures without letting readers share the wonderful joys and delights of a voyage. The yacht *Gaucho* is on passage from Rio to Dakar in West Africa not far from the Cape Verde Islands. Although it is only a short distance of 3,000 miles it is mostly along the route of the homeward bound clippers.

*

Gradually, however, the winds freshen, and on our tenth day out we awake to find ourselves in the south-east Trades. Like a horse with the scent of home in its nostrils, *Gaucho* quickens her gait. Up go a balloon and a mizzen staysail, and the miles reel off our stern – 150 to 170 a day. We relax. We are really on our way.

I turn my attention to the culinary department. I am not only captain but, for most of our voyage, cook. This is a good system, because the other Gauchos, who could complain about the food, don't; whereas I, who would complain, cannot.

Without refrigeration, we depend on dried and canned goods. Corned beef, jerked beef turn up pretty often on the menu, with potatoes, garlic and onions to keep them company. Those who like fresh fish can collect them on deck; each morning we pick up a batch of flying fish which crashed during the night. As a matter of fact, *Cypselurus heterurus* is quite tasty. Vasquez and Bobby devise a method of filleting and frying it in butter which brings it well up to the standard of *truite meunière*.

Schools of porpoises sport around us at all hours; Lobo and Vasquez do not harpoon them but ride horseback on the bowsprit and shove hardtack into the porpoises' 'nostrils' to make them cough. The rest of our fishing is done in tins, with a beautifully designed, edge-flattening can opener.

For dessert we munch on nuts or candy or dried fruits. For breakfast I usually dish up cocoa or coffee, with hot hardtack and jam. For almost any meal, potatoes, thriftily boiled in their jackets in sea water, or a mulligan whose contents are never the same twice. I tolerate no grousing; whenever mutiny seems imminent, I read to the crew the menu of a banquet offered by King Leopold of Belgium to England's Edward

VII. They cannot stand it. Before I have finished detailing the third or fourth course, they feel full.

Those who crave iced drinks are sternly reminded by Bobby that 'All ice-cold drinks reach body temperature between the lips and throat. So why bother? Ice is not only unhealthy, it's unnecessary.' But Lobo merely shakes his head at this and mutters: 'Just wait till we hit Dakar and I'll show you how I'll take care of my health. I'll have fifteen helpings of ice cream in one sitting, and then I'll begin over again.'

I would not put it past Lobo, either. He has rather odd eating habits. He will stuff himself for a week, then nibble like a humming-bird for the next. Or he will switch from a diet of nothing but potatoes smothered with olive oil to one of honey and marmalade. As for Bobby and Vasquez, they will occasionally break training and snitch a can of red salmon or a couple of feet of strong Spanish sausage before I get up in the morning.

We do other things beside eat, and perhaps that has more to do with our losing an average of seventeen pounds apiece on the crossing than does my cooking; at least I hope so. Each member of the crew spends six hours a day at the tiller, in two-hour relays. We scrub down the decks. We polish up the brass. We paint eternally. We mend sail. Looking at our pictures, the ones taken just before we put out of Buenos Aires, we pat our relatively flat stomachs and feel very trim and tough.

Right away we adopt certain rules to keep from slitting each other's throats. We don't play cards, and we don't tell weather-beaten jokes. None of us, as it happens, smokes, so there is no tenseness from tobacco running low or getting stale. We don't touch liquor at sea. And we don't make too insufferable remarks about each other's beards. The result is that we growl, but never bite.

Bobby and Lobo get along fine. They argue all the time, but without depth; they are merely stubborn. When they discuss something, their first word is 'No!' – which serves to get things off to a formal start and defines everybody's position. But, once started, they feel no necessity to stick to one side of the argument; they often wind up by exchanging viewpoints, and going on from there. Sometimes, too, they become so lost in their own maze of sophistry that they are very unsure who's doing what and to whom. All they know is that they are against it. . . .

The only thing that calls a halt to the Lobo–Bobby debate is talk about sailing and ships. Here they are on common ground. From furious contention they will drift off onto famous rigs and infamous races. 'I remember,' Bobby will say with a yawn at last, 'it was 1924, at Cowes —'

'— The year you had Camper and Nicholson build you that 8-metre job,' Lobo will chime in.

'Always wondered why they used such heavy planking in that boat . . .'

'Wondered, too.'

Vasquez will turn in his bunk and bellow: 'May the little boys stop talking like sailors!'

Sometimes that shuts them up. Sometimes not.

Little by little, we get used to the sea. At first the sight of the big waves is awesome, or maybe I really mean frightening – especially at night, when we feel them coming out of the darkness and suddenly see their towering white crests ready to roll right down on us. Yet, each time, miraculously, the ship rides up and over, and after a while we begin to take survival a bit more for granted.

Always, however, the elements are battering home their rather rude lesson: that man (especially me) is insignificant. The wind whistles like a madman on an organ, it howls into your ear that you are a speck in the heavens' immensity. The sea, slapping at the gunwhales, adds a sardonic footnote: there's plenty of room below.

Nature out here on the South Atlantic reveals its true qualities only in contrast, only as they clash against each other – the wind with the sea, the sun with the clouds. Waves blow themselves to particles against the bow, and the sun hangs rainbows in the created mist. A seagull comes into its whiteness against the dark of the sky. Where there is no contrast, the sailor looks for it. The wind falls, the sea flattens into a desert and the lonesome helmsman scans the horizon for a sail, a feather of black smoke, the profile of an island.

Often at night in my cabin I hear the *Gaucho*'s sails flap; I look at my compass. We are off-course. Going topside, I find Lobo or Vasquez dreaming at the tiller. But I do not blame them. The long hours on watch turn the mind in upon itself, upon the wide panorama of past life, the mixed chronology of mistakes and triumphs, the private theatre with unending repertory, in which we are both audience and actors. Yet there is an external reality to which we must wake: 15 degrees, the rhumb line to Dakar....

I grow fond of the South Atlantic. It behaves so very nicely. The wind holds steady, the temperature is moderate, the days fair. Squalls come seldom, and when they do we undress and bathe under the mainsail. If the rain pelts down long enough, we wash our clothes, congratulating ourselves on the fresh water we're saving.

We don't use many clothes, anyway. Bobby, for instance, always wears the same outfit – a shirt and a pair of shorts. In his locker he has enough new suits, fancy ties and loud shirts to start a haberdashery. But at sea he just wears a thing till it's dirty, washes it and puts it on again. I follow much the same routine. Clothes are a bother. Even on shore I have never owned a pair of garters, a vest, suspenders, an undershirt, a watch or a ring. Why should I? Just something more to buy, to repair, to lose.

The days roll on – twenty-eight of them before we see another boat. Whales and sharks and sea birds have kept us company, but no signs of men. Then one night I see a light on the horizon. A star, I think. But another light appears, and another. It is a ship, a fishing schooner. It crosses our bow, not far off, one green position light staring at us, her black hull leaving behind the rumour of engines, stitching the waves like a sewing-machine. In my cabin, later, I write a poem about it – a good poem in Spanish; in English not so hot.

Another day should bring us a landfall. Razors and clippers come out; the unflattering vegetation is harvested from chin and cheek. Off the menu go garlic and onion. After all, we have certain responsibilities to our public.

Dusk descends. Three minutes after Vasquez's predicted time, a pinpoint of light appears in the east. Five seconds, flash; five seconds, flash – the Dakar beam! Ahead, as we sail through a phosphorescent sea, the distant light winks at us like a lady of the evening. Hundreds of porpoises form a guard of honour; their glowing wakes weave a luminous garland around us. In the calm water the stars are mirrored in a second sky. Lining the rail, the five Gauchos thankfully salute Cape Miguel.

19

Ships' Pets

THESE GAY Argentinians enjoyed their cruise from start to finish. They were such a happy crew that they had no need of any pets aboard. I suppose cats are the favourites on a small boat. Other animals do not always make good shipmates.

Slocum records how, on his voyage north through the Atlantics during his circumnavigation he called at St Helena and was given a goat by an American there, who 'urged that the animal, besides being useful, would be as companionable as a dog.'

*

I soon found that my sailing companion, this sort of dog with hooves, had to be tied up entirely. The mistake I made was that I did not chain him to the mast instead of tying him with grass ropes less securely, and this I learned to my cost. Except for the first day, before the beast got his sea-legs on, I had no peace of mind. After that, actuated by a spirit born, maybe, of his pasturage, this incarnation of evil threatened to devour everything from flying-jib to stern-davits. He was the worst pirate I met on the whole voyage. He began depredations by eating my chart of the West Indies, in the cabin, one day, while I was about my work for'ard, thinking that the critter was securely tied on deck by the pumps. Alas! there was not a rope in the sloop proof against that goat's awful teeth!

It was clear from the very first that I was having no luck with animals on board. There was the tree-crab from the

Keeling Islands. No sooner had it got a claw through its prison-box than my sea-jacket, hanging within reach, was torn to ribbons. Encouraged by this success, it smashed the box open and escaped into my cabin, tearing up things generally, and finally threatening my life in the dark. I had hoped to bring the creature home alive, but this did not prove feasible. Next the goat devoured my straw hat, and so when I arrived in port I had nothing to wear ashore on my head. This last unkind stroke decided his fate. On the 27th of April the *Spray* arrived at Ascension, which is garrisoned by a man-of-war crew, and the boatswain of the island came on board. As he stepped out of his boat the mutinous goat climbed into it, and defied boatswain and crew. I hired them to land the wretch at once, which they were only too willing to do, and there he fell into the hands of a most excellent Scotsman, with the chances that he would never get away. I was destined to sail once more into the depths of solitude, but these experiences had no bad effect upon me; on the contrary, a spirit of charity and even benevolence grew stronger in my nature through the meditations of these supreme hours on the sea.

In the loneliness of the dreary country about Cape Horn I found myself in no mood to make one life less in the world, except in self-defence, and, as I sailed, this trait of the hermit character grew till the mention of killing food-animals was revolting to me.

As to pet animals, there was no room for a noble large dog on the *Spray* on so long a voyage, and a small cur was for many years associated in my mind with hydrophobia. I witnessed once the death of a sterling young German from that dreadful disease. I have seen the whole crew of a ship scamper up the rigging to avoid a dog racing about the decks in a fit. It would never do, I thought, for the crew of the *Spray* to take a canine risk, and with these just prejudices indelibly stamped on my mind, I have, I am afraid, answered impatiently too often the query, 'Didn't you have a dog?' with, 'I and the dog wouldn't have been very long in the same boat, in any sense.' A cat would have been a harmless animal, I dare say, but there was nothing for puss to do on board, and she is an unsociable animal at best. True, a rat got into my vessel at the Keeling Cocos Islands, and another at Rodriguez, along with a centipede stowed away in the hold; but one of them I drove out of the ship, and the other I caught. This is how it was: for the first one with infinite pains I made a trap, looking to its capture and destruction; but the wily rodent, not to be deluded, took the hint and got ashore the day the thing was completed.

It is, according to tradition, a most reassuring sign to find rats coming to a ship, and I had a mind to abide the knowing one of Rodriguez; but a breach of discipline decided the matter against him. While I slept one night, my ship sailing on, he undertook to walk over me, beginning at the crown of my head, concerning which I am always sensitive. Before his impertinence had got him even to my nose I cried 'Rat!' had him by the tail, and threw him out of the companionway into the sea.

As for the centipede, I was not aware of its presence till the wretched insect, all feet and venom, beginning, like the rat, at my head, wakened me by a sharp bite on the scalp. This also was more than I could tolerate. After a few applications of kerosene, the poisonous bite, painful at first, gave me no further inconvenience.

From this on for a time no living thing disturbed my solitude; no insect even was present in my vessel, except the spider and his wife, from Boston, now with a family of young spiders.

*

I only once had a pet – if I could call it that – when sailing the Atlantic alone in 1962. Off the South of Ireland a pigeon came aboard *Gipsy Moth III*. At first he was an exciting companion in my solitude. Here is the saga of his 18-day voyage across the Atlantic; I have culled it from *The Lonely Sea and the Sky*:

*

3 June. A handsome homing pigeon with bold black bars slashed across its folded wings sheltering in the lee of a sail on the foredeck. Pidgy, as he was soon to be called, was shy and not to be caught. He was intensely curious, and as soon

as we had met he followed me about the ship, watching closely everything I did, his head cocked slightly to one side, one bright round eye attentive. Each time I went below he perched on the companionway. I soon discovered that his personal habits were shocking; he was nearer to discovering the secret of a perpetual motion than any scientist ever will be – I had to follow him round the deck with a mop and bucket. . . . It was not long before I decided that Pidgy had a most stupid streak in his character; he kept on pecking frantically at a saucer, long after he had finished everything in it, and refused to look at another one with a new supply of food which I put in the box, although I showed it to him several times.

4 June. *Gipsy Moth* was running well, but it was a rolling twisting ride in the Atlantic. It made me feel queasy, and I was not the only one; Pidgy looked terrible, all fluffed up with his head tucked under his wing, and bleary eyed when he looked up at me. I feared that he was going to die. I had heard that birds are unable to be seasick, and are therefore worse off than humans. Next morning, however, he was still alive. He looked miserable and twice his size, a huge puffed out ball, with his head nearly sunk in his shoulders . . .

Pidgy was squatting on the corner of the cockpit seat and took no notice when I stepped right alongside him. He must have been feeling awful. I too felt sick, and had some hot water and sugar, my latest seasickness cure . . .

5 June. But at least he could do something that I couldn't; he was standing on one leg on the cockpit seat, and swaying to the roll of the ship without looking. It was real Atlantic weather; grey mist, turbulent sea, moaning wind. . . .

6 June. I made him a hut under the seat with a transparent plastic covering, and gave him a dish of Macvita and bread, with a bowl of fresh water, both of which he went for. Later he seemed better. . . .

9 June. Big news! In the middle of the night Pidge gave tongue – *roucou*! *roucou*! Perhaps he was feeling better, or was it only a dream in the dark? No, in the daylight he suddenly began imitating an eagle! Standing head up, chest out, he spread his wings like the eagle of the old German flag and

flapped them bravely, hopping on his toes. In the morning I made a tent for him with two thicknesses of old canvas which I stretched from the cockpit coaming to the edge of the seat. I provided him with a plastic bag for a ground sheet....

With Pidgy's tent at the forward end of the cockpit seat, I could not see him from below. I missed his beady eyes so, after cleaning up after him in the cockpit, I made a new tent at the other end of the seat where he would stand in the entrance and, no doubt, laugh secretly at me as I cleaned up his mess....

11 June. Pidgy looked disgusted; what a life for a bird. Streams of water were sluicing into the cockpit, the air was wet and windy. During the night he had moved from his new camp and stood on the seat beside the companionway, but I had to move him back for fear I should tread on him. He tried other spots, but he was in the way wherever he went, poor devil. I debated taking him into the cabin and putting up with his indescribable mess, but then I thought, 'Surely a bird is used to the open air', and contented myself with making his tent as snug as possible. I gave him a box full of muesli which was his favourite food (except for the raisins which he threw out). A big sea gave his den a fair washout, and swamped the rest of the muesli. I gave him another plateful in the tent, but he just sat outside waiting till that too had got soaked. That night I was woken frequently by crashes and once wondered if something had broken or come adrift but all was well. *Gipsy Moth* was sailing at 6 knots through rough water. During the night Pidge seemed quite happy, squatting inside his wigwam facing the entrance. He chattered his beak silently at me when I spoke to him.

How often has a delightful friendship ashore between two beings turned sour in a small boat! Trivial things can start up a frenzy of resentment, dislike or even hatred:

In the morning for some reason I laughed at Pidge. To my surprise he was sensitive about it, and much disliked it. He stamped to and fro, chattered his beak and gave me dirty looks....

13 June. Great sailing! A rough breaking sea, with *Gipsy Moth* crashing through fast and strongly as if she loved it. Great sailing, for not for Pidge; I saw the look of disgust on his face when he caught a sea (I think he must have been a crabby old bachelor). Sometimes he seemed to give me a malicious look. Later when I went on deck I found that the log had stopped, and at first was puzzled why. Indirectly Pidge was responsible. I had given up stowing the coiled ends of the ropes in the lockers under the cockpit seats because Pidge fouled them up so horribly. I had left them coiled on the deck beside the cockpit coaming. The seas breaking on the deck had washed them overboard, where they had tangled with the log line. Ropes trailing in the water are used to slow up a yacht, so that this schemozzle must have cost us speed. On top of that I spent hours untangling the log line with its thousands of tight twists. A lot of clear white sparkling sea was coming aboard as I did so; it was blowing a gale though the sun was shining. I could not be sure how long the log had been out of action.

15 June. Pidge! Pidge! Pidge! He ruled my life then. Every morning I had to feed and water him as soon as I emerged, before I trimmed the sails and got the ship back on to her proper heading. I couldn't bear his forlorn beady look. Then I would notice the various messes on the cockpit seat, etc., which I'd tread in while handling the ropes, so I had to go round and clear all of them up before getting to work on the ship. During the night, even if I darted out in an emergency, I had to shine my torch round and locate Pidge before stepping into the cockpit for fear of treading on him. That morning when I fed him, and gave his tabernacle another covering, he let me stroke him, so I reckoned that he must be pretty fed up. He looked like a sick jackdaw.

I was beginning to build up a love-hate feeling. I was racing against time and as usual driving myself at the limit of my strength to work the ship so as to get the greatest speed out of it. I resented the constant worry of protecting the pigeon from harm and constantly clearing up the effects of his revolting personal habits. But the more he irritated me the more unhappy I became about his weakening health and the more responsible I felt for his welfare.

16 June. Pidge seemed to like bread chopped small better than anything else now. I had tried him with both cheese and sugar, but he turned them down. He had two red bands on his tough, scaly legs, and I passed his number to London. It turned out that he was a French aristocrat coming from a long distance racing family and that he was racing from the Channel Islands to Preston, Lancashire, when he came down on *Gipsy Moth*. Perhaps the very old blood in his veins made his manners so peculiar! He never finished more than two-thirds of any dishful I gave him, and rejected any piece which was a fraction bigger than his maximum. I never understood this; if a pigeon can swallow a whole acorn, why can he not eat a piece of bread a fifth of the size? . . .

18 June. When I came aft from the jib picnic, Pidge was missing. My heart dropped; I thought that he must have been washed overboard. In the end I found him back in his locker under the cockpit seat, very forlorn, wet and bedraggled. I gave him one of Stalker's oat cakes; nothing but the best for him on such an occasion. He seemed to love it. . . .

19 June. Poor Pidge. The cockpit was half full of water, and I could see his skin as if his bedraggled feathers did not exist. He looked so miserable that I took him below and tried to settle him in a large biscuit tin. Unfortunately I had nothing really suitable. He would not stay in the tin, so I took him back to his cubbyhole. I supposed that a pigeon was used to roosting out in anything, but it was bitingly cold.

On the Grand Banks, after he had crossed the Atlantic, he fluttered into the sea when circling the boat, which it was his habit to do most days:

21 June. At first he flapped the water to try to take off, then turned round and started flapping frantically to catch up the ship. It was heartrending to see his panic as the stern moved steadily away. I sprang to the cockpit, grabbed the tiller and brought the yacht round.

I aimed to arrive at the spot nearly dead into wind, so that the yacht would be moving slowly. I could not reduce sail, or do anything which would make me take my eye off the pigeon. I knew from experience that I should never see him again if I once lost sight of him – one tiny grey pigeon in the middle of the Atlantic. I had to come up to him, so that he would be within a foot of the side of the ship, otherwise I should not be able to reach him. . . . Pidgy was right there, and I clutched at him with my hand. But when I pushed my arm down suddenly, as I had to do in a hurry, he must have thought I was going to strike him, for he flapped madly away from me as I touched him, and I missed my hold. I felt terrible, that he should take me for an enemy. I ran back to the tiller and slowly, as it seemed, came round again. I had to stay by the tiller till the last moment, and then make a rush and a grab. Once I slipped, but I had no time to clip on my safety-harness. The next three passes I made at him he eluded me. . . . I think I made fourteen circuits and passes at Pidge. After failing with my hand, I tried with a bucket tied to a boathook. I had him in the bucket about four times, but unfortunately as I lifted the bucket out of the water the overflow from it washed the pigeon out. The last time he was washed out he was swamped by the water and lay inert, with only a little of his back at the surface of the water. Next time I came round I picked him out easily with my hand as he lay inert.

I felt cut up as I held his soaking body; I felt responsible for him, and somehow his mean crabbed nature and his dreadful habits made me feel worse . . . It was the breakdown in communication between a human being and an animal which was so distressing. If only he could have trusted me, could have understood that I was trying to help him, and not hurt him, he would have still been alive.

I gave him a sea burial in my best biscuit tin with holes punched in it so that it would sink. I watched it till I could see it no longer as *Gipsy Moth* sailed away.

The fact that I had risked my life trying to save the pigeon – because a yacht with a self-steering windvane in operation will not stop if the owner falls overboard – did not lessen the misery I felt at the pigeon's death. I had failed in my responsibility for him.

The sort of pet needed on the ocean is one with acute hearing which will give warning of an unseen ship approaching. Bullen in *The Cachalot* must have wished that the ship they met in the North Atlantic had had such a pet:

*

We had reached the northern verge of the tropics in a very short time, owing to the favourable cant in the usual direction of the north-east trades before noted, and had been met with north-westerly winds and thick, dirty weather, which was somewhat unusual in so low a latitude. Our look-outs redoubled their vigilance, one being posted on each bow always at night, and relieved every hour, as we were so well manned. We were now on the port tack, of course, heading about north-east-by-north, and right in the track of outbound vessels from both the United Kingdom and the States. One morning, about three am – that fateful time in the middle watch when more collisions occur than at any other – suddenly out of the darkness a huge ship seemed to leap right at us. She must have come up in a squall, of which there were many about, at the rate of some twelve knots an hour, having a fair wind, and every rag of sail set. Not a gleam of light was visible anywhere on board her, and, to judge from all appearances, the only man awake on board was the helmsman.

We, being 'on the wind, close-hauled,' were bound by the 'rule of the road at sea' to keep our course when meeting a ship running free.[1] The penalty for doing *anything* under such circumstances is a severe one. First of all, you do not *know* that the other ship's crew are asleep or negligent, even though they carry no lights; for, by a truly infernal parsimony, many vessels actually do not carry oil enough to keep their lamps burning all the voyage, and must therefore economize in this unspeakably dangerous fashion. And it may be

1. *Note.* The Rule of the Road in 1966 is that the ship on the starboard tack has right-of-way whether beating, reaching or running. Sail has right-of-way over steam off-shore.

that just as you alter your course, daring no longer to hold on, and, as you have every reason to believe, be run down, the other man alters his. Then a few breathless moments ensue, an awful crash, and the two vessels tear each other to pieces, spilling the life that they contain over the hungry sea. Even if you escape, *you* are to blame for not keeping your course, unless it can be proved that you were not seen by the running ship.

Well, we kept our course until, I verily believe, another plunge would have cut us sheer in two halves. At the last moment our helm was put hard down, bringing our vessel right up into the wind at the same moment as the helmsman on board the other vessel caught sight of us, and instinctively put his helm down too. The two vessels swung side by side amidst a thunderous roar of flapping canvas, crackling of fallen spars, and rending of wood as the shrouds tore away the bulwarks. All our davits were ripped from the starboard side, and most of our bulwarks too; but strangely enough, we lost no spars nor any important gear. There seemed to be a good deal of damage done on board the stranger, where, in addition, all hands were at their wits' end. Well they might be, aroused from so criminal a sleep as theirs. Fortunately, the third mate had a powerful bull's-eye lantern, which in his watch on deck he always kept lighted. Turning it on the stern of the delinquent vessel as she slowly forged clear of us, we easily read her name, which, for shame's sake as well as for prudential reasons, I withhold. She was a London ship, and a pretty fine time of it I had for the next day or two, listening to the jeers and sarcasms on the quality of British seamanship.

20

Luck and Navigation

SOME SHIPS become famous or infamous for their luck. I claim, however, that most of the losses through shipwreck or stranding were wholly due to bad navigation and not to bad luck. The captain did not know that the land or rocks were there; he had fixed his position elsewhere. But, I am convinced that a good navigator, however skilful he may be, needs good luck at times. And I am quite sure that many ships headed for disaster due to bad navigation have been saved simply through good luck.

For instance, there was the *Sobraon*, which was thought to be unlucky under her first captain. At the end of her maiden voyage she was running up the English Channel, so the captain thought, after several days of thick weather. Sailing downwind at twelve knots with her two acres (87,000 square feet) of sail set, she would have been unable to fetch up into wind in time if she had suddenly come upon land or rocks with a visibility or only three or four hundred yards. Fortunately the captain was lucky enough to come upon a fishing boat and ask for his position. He was told he was not in the English Channel at all but in the Bristol Channel.

On the *Sobraon*'s next voyage, she had a new captain, J. A. Elmslie, who remained so for 24 years. At the end of this time the *Sobraon* was considered one of the finest passenger ships ever launched; and she had gained a reputation of being a lucky ship. After the amazing escape from running onto the Scillies on her maiden voyage, her good record was attributed to her good luck – but was it really due to the good navigation and leadership of her captain? For one thing she never lost any of her crew overboard. Once an apprentice fell overboard but a boat was launched and found him calmly swimming with his heavy boots slung round his neck. He had unlaced these, taken them off and slung them round his neck so as not to lose them. He was a remarkably cool hand considering that a man overboard from a sailing ship was rarely recovered because, for one thing, it took so long to put a square rigger about, with its large number of big sails set.

Twice she survived fire at sea. She did lose two of her crew killed through falling from aloft, but those accidents seemed to be accepted as normal hazards of the occupation.

In 1888, 22 years after she was first launched, she again escaped disaster when running up the Channel. She had had a sight of Land's End and then sailed on in fog for 24 hours. Suddenly the fog lifted and there was Chesil Beach between

Portland Bill and the mainland dead ahead, less than a mile off. This certainly was good luck but it was a luck which saved her from the effects of bad navigation.

In the case of the *Lanoma* the navigation was not bad; she was not more than twelve miles out after running blind for, I guess, 500 miles; and some good luck could have saved her: she was coming up the Channel in March 1888 'in thick, blowing south-westerly weather, under a very experienced commander, Captain G. Whittingham. The captain had had no observation for several days, so an extra smart lookout was being kept. Just before midnight it must have cleared a bit for the land suddenly loomed up close to on the starboard bow, the helm was at once put down and the ship brought to the wind, and Captain Whittingham tried to stay her. Unfortunately she missed stays, and fell off again, there was no time to wear her, and she stranded broadside on to Chesil Beach inside the Bill of Portland.' Perhaps his navigation should have been better to give Portland Bill a safe offing; perhaps too if the seamanship had been better she would not have missed her tack. Or could it be attributed solely to bad luck? Some ships seems to develop a personality or character. Joseph Conrad wrote from his own experience:

*

I think I have known ships who really seemed to have had eyes, or else I cannot understand on what ground a certain 1,000-ton barque of my acquaintance on one particular occasion refused to answer her helm, thereby saving a frightful smash to two ships and to a very good man's reputation. I knew her intimately for two years, and in no other instance either before or since have I known her to do that thing.

*

One of the most lethal errors in navigation along the great clipper route occurred in 1707 long before clippers were built. Admiral Sir Clowdisley Shovel was in command of a fleet returning from the Straits of Gibraltar to the English Channel. Of 20 ships in the fleet 4 were wrecked on the rocks of the Scilly Isles. From the first 3 ships to strike, only the Admiral and one other man got ashore alive. The Admiral was promptly murdered by the local women who cut off his finger to get at his ring, so the story goes. Another ship which struck the rocks got off but sank later with only 23 survivors.

Commander W. E. May of the National Maritime Museum has thoroughly investigated the navigation of the fleet, checking through 44 log books from the surviving ships. He found that observations of the sun for latitude were taken on 11 days. The *average* spread of the latitudes so obtained each day was no less than 25½ miles. During the 22 days of the voyage the dead reckoning latitudes obtained by working up the ship's position from the previous day spread on the average over no less than 73 miles each day.

There was even greater variation in the longitudes reckoned by the navigators because, to start with, the longitudes of the Scilly Isles given in the manuals they used were themselves in error by up to 2° 16′ (about 90 miles). It is no surprise that the fleet should run among the rocks round the Bishop in thick weather.

21

The Great Clipper Race

NOTHING BRINGS out the competitive instinct more than sailing. Does there exist a captain who has not raced in some way or other – if not boat against boat, then against his own previous time or against a rival's time. The clipper captains were world famous for their racing urge. It was not often that they sighted a rival or, if they did, kept her in view for long during a race half-way round the world; but it did happen occasionally and perhaps the most famous occasion was when five clippers raced home from China and three of them, the *Taeping*, the *Ariel* and the *Serica* arrived in the Downs with the *Taeping* leading by ten minutes from the *Ariel* and the *Serica* only four hours astern after a 99 days' race. This was in 1866, and the centenary of this great clipper race is being celebrated the year this book is published.

Every yachtsman knows the intense excitement of a good race, but it has not often been captured in print. That superb artist, John Masefield, can quicken your heartbeats with race fever if you read his lovely book, *The Bird of Dawning. The Cock*, as *The Bird of Dawning* was called, is manned by a boatload of seamen who have survived after their own ship has been run down by a steamer and has foundered. After 8 days in an open boat these survivors have come upon *The Bird of Dawning* deserted on the high seas. They are sailing her back to England when they sight some rival clippers and 'Cruiser' Trewsbury, who is in command, starts a thrilling race against them up-Channel.

I can quite understand the mate's anxiety about running blind into the Channel with full sail set when they have had no position fix (from sun observations, etc.) for several days. Perhaps he remembered the *Sobraon* and the *Lanoma*.

However, I can also understand Cruiser's reply to the mate, 'Take anything in!' he said. 'I was just thinking if we couldn't set a royal.'

The same situation still occurs. In the 1959 Fastnet Race the leading yachts were running fast for a lee shore in a near gale with bad visibility. This was outside Plymouth where the race was to end. I quote from my book, *The Lonely Sea and the Sky*: 'My great friend, Michael Richey, was navigating the Swedish yacht *Anitra*. They had come along earlier, but with the visibility worse. Mike said to the owner, "If my navigation is correct, we shall make Plymouth breakwater (the finishing line) and win the race, but if it isn't, we shall pile up on the rocks outside. It's your yacht, you decide." Sven Hanson, the owner, said, "Carry on." And *Anitra* won the Fastnet Race of 1959.'

Masefield's story is fiction, but gives the true feeling of a great race:

*

On the second day, the wester, which had been blowing steadily, increased in strength and blew a full true gale, with abundant rain keeping down the sea. They ran before this, day after day, in exultation, striding over an expanse of two thousand miles across. Presently, it became blind going, so that they went by log and a guess; yet still the wind increased, till Mr Fairford looked grave and old Kemble shook his head. Mr Fairford coming up to Cruiser as the night closed in suggested that if anything were coming in, it would be handled more easily in daylight. Cruiser had not been below for more than twenty minutes at a time for a week. He had slept, if at all, in a hammock slung under the weather mizen pin-rail; the exultation of the wind and the going had entered into him; he shook the rain from his face and grinned back at Fairford.

'Take anything in,' he said. 'I was just thinking if we couldn't set a royal.'

Fairford was too old a sailor to say anything; he looked at the royal mast, and looked to windward, and looked at Cruiser.

Fairford said nothing more about shortening sail. He made one more suggestion: 'I suppose you wouldn't care for a cast of the lead, sir, about midnight tonight? We should be about on Soundings, wouldn't we?'

'We're all right,' Cruiser said. 'Why, Mister, you couldn't have the heart to stop her, could you?'

'It's a good slant, sir,' Fairford said. 'But blind going's bad going, if you ask me.'

'She's all right, Mister.'

'Very good, Captain Trewsbury.' Fairford walked to the break of the poop. Efans, the sea-lawyer, was talking to Stratton. 'These poys, look you, they wass not prudent men: they take the sticks clean out of her, as sure as Cot's my uncle.'

All night long she drove before the thrust of the wester, in a succession of staggering and surging leaps that sent the crests of the waves flying white before her. At midnight she was running twelve, at two, thirteen, and at the changing of the watch fourteen knots. Though she had ever steered easily, she was now more than one man's task: the lee wheel was manned, and kept busy.

At five in the morning Cruiser turned out after an hour of uneasy sleep in his hammock to find the ship roaring on up Channel in the breaking darkness, a high grey Channel sea running under a wild heaven, and the teeth of the waves gleaming out from the grey. He lurched to the mate, who was forward, putting an extra tackle on the fore-tack. When the tack was home, he asked:

'Have you picked up any light, Mister?'

'No, sir, all blind as you see.'

'Well, we must be there or thereabouts.'

'Yes, sir. It's been a good slant.'

'Get a hand aloft when it lightens a bit; he may be able to see the land.'

'Very good, Captain Trewsbury.' The mate hesitated for a moment, then said:

'If you please, sir, we're doing more than fourteen, and we haven't had a sight for four days. We're well into the Channel: and thick as it is we may be on top of anything before we see it.'

'No: keep her going,' Cruiser said. 'Our luck's in. We'll not throw it away.'

'Very good, Captain Trewsbury.'

The ship was running on, with the same desperate haste, an hour later when Trewsbury returned. It was now in the wilderness of an angry morning, with a low, hurrying heaven and leaping sea, that showed green under the grey, and rose and slipped away with a roar. The ship was careering with an aching straining crying from every inch of her, aloft and below. Her shrouds strained and whined and sang, the wind boomed in her sail, the sheet blocks beat, the chain of their pendants whacked the masts. All the mighty weight of ship and cargo heaved itself aloft, and surged and descended and swayed, smashing the seas white, boring into and up and out of the hills and the hollows of the water, and singing as she did it, and making all hands, as they toiled, to sing.

'Run, you bright bird,' Trewsbury said, 'that's what you were born to.'

There was no chance of a sight with that low heaven: the man aloft could see nothing: all hands were on deck getting the anchors over. There came a sudden cry from them of 'Steamer, dead ahead.'

She must have seen them on the instant, and ported on the instant, enough to clear. Cruiser saw her as it were climbing slowly and perilously to port for twenty seconds: then as he leaped for the signals flags to ask, 'Where are we?' she was surging past close alongside, a little grey coastal tramp, with a high bridge over her central structure, butting hard into it with a stay foresail dark with wet to steady her, and her muzzle white to the eyes. As she had just fired, a stream of black smoke blew away and down from her, with sudden sparks in it, as Cruiser thought. Cruiser saw two figures in yellow oilskins staring at them from behind the dodger. He knew well with what admiration and delight those sailors stared. Then the little coaster's stern hove up in a smother, as her head dipped to it, and she was past and away, with one man behind the dodger waving a hand. The reek of her smoke struck Cruiser's nostrils; then she was gone from them, her name unknown.

The mate was at Cruiser's side.

'That shows you how we're in the fairway, sir,' he said. 'We may be on top of something at any minute. We've only a minute to clear anything, in this.'

'I know it.'

'Yes, sir.'

'Did you ever hear of a China clipper throwing away a fair wind in soundings?'

'No, sir.'

'Did you ever hear of a China clipper being sunk in the Channel when running?'

'No, Captain Trewsbury, and I don't want to be the first.'

'Well, I do want to be the first, Mister, and I mean to be it, the first to London Docks, if you understand. And to get there, I have to use whatever chance throws in my way. It's going to break, presently.'

There came a hail from the main cross-trees, where the look-out had a speaking trumpet. 'Ship on starboard bow.' They turned to look at her, and Cruiser who was ready now ran up the signal flags of, 'What is my position?'

As the flags blew out clear the ship hove up alongside. She was a big full-rigged ship, painted black, and very loftily rigged with skysail yards on all three masts. She was now under her fore and main lower topsails and fore topmast staysail, beating her way down Channel. She was streaming with glittering water. At each 'scend the sea ran white along her rail, which bowed to it and lipped it in. Then, out of the pause, the bowed fabric seemed to dive forward, though with difficulty. Cruiser saw the watch gathered on the poop, all staring; even the man at the wheel was staring. The ship beat past them on a lurching leap, her maindeck full and spouting, no one answering the signal, not even acknowledging it.

'There's discourtesy,' the mate said. 'She wouldn't even dip her colours.'

'She never saw our signal,' Cruiser said. 'She's an outward-bounder, with everything on top and nothing to hand. Besides she was watching us.'

'We must be well worth the watching, sir,' the mate said, moving away. To himself, as he moved, he added, 'and I hope all who meet us will watch out for us.'

It grew lighter in the sky, but no lighter to landward, they were running in a blind and moving seascape not a thousand yards across, all cloud and water, both mad. The ship strode into it, and streaked her way across it, smashing on to the greyness a track of a paleness and a greenness of many million bubbles, over which the petrels scuttered.

Where they were Cruiser did not know, and did not much care. The exultation that was so movingly in the ship was in himself. They were getting up Channel with a marvellous slant, and who could tell that they were not leading the fleet. It would clear up presently, and they would see where they were, or pass something that would tell them.

'Forward there,' he called. 'Up there two of you, and get a good burton on the foreyard. Lively now, I'm going to give her a stunsail.'

'Burton on the foreyard: ay, ay, sir.'

He turned to the helmsmen. Coates, who had the weather spokes, was enjoying it; he loved to see a ship driven; but Bauer at the lee wheel was scared.

'How is she, Coates?' he asked.

'She's begun to be a bit kittenish,' Coates said, 'but nothing to hurt, sir.'

'You're keeping a good course. You can steer, Coates.'

'Yes, sir. And she can kick, I tell you.'

'Keep your eyes forward, Bauer,' Cruiser said. 'There's nothing for you to look at behind you.'

There was, though. There was a toppling, toppling running array of heaping water ever slipping over at the top.

'If you let her broach to, Bauer,' he said, 'you'll be the first man drowned and the last man God will forgive and that's what you'll get by it.'

Bauer smiled a sickly smile, and licked his dry lips and said: 'Yes, sir.'

'All ready the burton, forward?'

'All ready, sir.'

'Bowse it well taught.' He went forward to see to the setting of the sail.

As the courses of the *Bird of Dawning* were very deep as well as square, the lower studding sail was a great sail, needing much care in the setting, in such a wind as was blowing. The boom was run forward and guyed. All hands mustered to the job. They well knew that if it were not done smartly, the sail would go. A wild sea spread from under their feet into the hurrying cloud; but those there felt, from the push of the rain that came down upon them, that the greyness was about to go. The rain that had streamed from all things relented suddenly and died into a pattering.

'Let her go,' Cruiser called. The tackles skirled as the men went away with them; he paid out the tripping line as they ran. The boom dipped under as it went and the great sail darkened with the wet half up it. As the stops came adrift, the sail lifted and strove to flog itself clear, but the checks of the gear came on to it and stayed it. One instant before it had been a bulge of canvas, flapping at folds where the wind could catch it, now it was a straining curve of sail, held by check and countercheck, leaning like a wing to the ship over all that hurry of leaping sea. She put down her foot, and the foot of the sail stooped into it, as a gull stoops upon the wing. She rose, with the water dripping from the scoop, and again plunged and arose shaking.

'That's got her where she lives,' Clutterbucke said. 'That's made her lift her feet.'

'Just as well she's got that burton on her yardarm.'

The effect on the ship was instantaneous. She had been leaping, now she seemed to lift from sea to sea, and tread down their crests into subjection.

'I think she'll stand a topmast stunsail,' Cruiser said to himself.

He went aft to watch the steering, which was grown the livelier for the sail. From the poop, he had a new impression of the power of her drive: she was swooping and swerving, like a thing alive; in fact she was a thing alive: she had ceased to be wood and iron, laden with cases: she was something of the spirit of the wind, and of the kindled wit of man, that laughed as she flew.

Suddenly, as he stood by the wheel, watching her head, and letting his eyes run aloft to the curves of the leaches under strain, the greyness in the heaven parted as though the sheets had given, with the effect of a sail suddenly let go and clued up. The cloud tattered itself loose to windward and rived itself apart, and blue sky showed and spread. Instantly, a blueness and a brightness came upon the water. To leeward before them the storm passed away like a scroll. There, to port, far away, was the Chesil Beach, with the Needles beyond it, and the far and faint line of England stretching astern to the Start. The sun appeared and beauty came with him, so that all the tumbling and leaping brightness rejoiced.

One of the first things revealed was a fine clipper ship two miles ahead, lying almost the same course. On the starboard quarter, perhaps two miles away, another lofty ship came racing up Channel, and far astern a third showed. This third was perhaps not one of the China fleet.

'We've turned into the straight,' Cruiser said. 'There seem to be three left in it.'

'Yes, sir,' Fairford said, 'unless the race is already won.'

'We'll learn soon enough if it's already won,' Cruiser said. 'Get a tackle on the yard-arm there,' he called. 'All hands set studding sails.' The mate and the men marvelled, but they leaped to the order. They were now as keen as Cruiser to bring their ship home. Not a man thought that perhaps the race had been already won by someone; to them the race was now beginning.

Cruiser was on the fo'c's'le head with the telescope trying to make out the ship ahead. Under the tapering clouds of sail he could see a dark green hull, with an old-fashioned transom look about her stern. She could be no other than the *Caer Ocvran*. She had been running with prudence, not knowing where she was; now that the sky had cleared she was making sail.

'All ready, the foretopmast stunsail, sir,' Mr Fairford reported, adding under his breath, 'If you think she'll stand them, sir.'

'No time for prudence now,' Cruiser said, 'hoist away there – lively now.'

One at a time the mighty wings of studding sail swayed aloft and shook themselves out of their bundles with a roaring into service. Cruiser saw the topsail yard lift and the booms buckle as the strain came upon them; but the gear held. A whiteness boiled along the *Bird*'s side and flew in a sheet over the waist as she felt the new power given to her. Cruiser watched for a minute, standing well forward, eyeing the straining booms. 'They'll hold,' he thought, 'as long as the wind keeps steady and the helmsmen behave.' He crossed the fo'c's'le and eyed the ship ahead. She had set her lower studding sail, and no doubt was setting more as fast as the men could move, but the *Bird of Dawning* seemed sailing two feet to her one.

He watched for half a moment; Fairford and others were at his side, staring.

'Ah, she's holding us,' Fairford said suddenly. 'Yes, she's holding us. There go her topmast studding sails: beautifully done too. She's got forty hands at stations. It's something to have a full crew.'

'We've got twelve,' Cruiser said. 'Twelve good men upset the Roman Empire. Get the topgallant stunsails on her.'

The men ran to it: he slipped aft with the telescope, partly to con the ship, partly to see what the ship astern might be. He steadied the glass against a mizzen shroud and stared at the ship astern. She was on the starboard quarter, and plainly much nearer than she had been. She was not more than a mile and a half away. Not much of her showed except a tower of leaning sail, winged out with studding sails, a jib-boom poising and bowing, and a roll of white water under her bows. He broke off from his staring to rate Bauer at the lee wheel. 'Never mind what's astern of you,' he called. 'Watch your steering or you'll have the masts out of her and we'll skin you alive.'

He looked again at the ship astern. Someone forward had said that she was the *Min and Win*. He was satisfied that she was not the *Min and Win*, but a much bigger and newer ship, the *Fu-Kien*, commanded by a reckless dare-devil known as Bloody Bill China. 'Well, what Bill can carry we can drag,' he said, so he leaped down into the waist, to the job of getting more sail on to a ship that already had plenty.

'Doctor, there,' he called to Perrott, 'and you, Chedglow, get breakfast along on deck. Chedglow, get tongues and sardines and what you like out of the stores: the best there is. Hands must breakfast as they can, on deck, three at a time.' He watched the setting of the new sail and its effect upon the ship. She was holding her own now, perhaps gaining a very little on the *Caer Ocvran*, and hardly losing to the *Fu-Kien*.

'She's gaining on us, though,' Cruiser muttered. He could see now plainly, her anchors over the bows dripping brightness whenever she rose from the sea. 'Well, I'll try what the skysail will do. Up there, one of you, and loose the skysail.'

They loosed it and hoisted it, and had the sight of the pole bending like a whip of whalebone to the strain. Bill replied by loosing his main skysail, which blew away in the setting. They raced on now, hardly changing position. All hands in all three ships had all that they could do: getting a pull here, a pull there, a better set on this and a better trim to the other. Even Stratton, sullen as he was, seemed interested in the race, even Efans forgot his rights in the thought of how much better Captain Duntisbourne would have handled her. They raced in the laughing morning, while the coast slipped by them, all the landmarks long looked for. . . .

As he had expected, the change of the lifting of the gale brought with it a lessening of the wind and a shifting of it to two points to the northward. All three ships now had set every sail that they could carry, to the royal studding sails and trust-to-gods. Cruiser had guyed out a boom below the jibboom and had set a spritsail: Bloody Bill China had bonnets on his courses and contrivances that he called puffballs in the roaches of his topsails. What the *Caer Ocvran* was doing they could not clearly see: she was almost dead ahead of them. The three ships were drawing nearer to each other, the *Caer Ocvran* coming back, the *Fu-Kien* coming on. If the race had not been already won by some ship in ahead of them, it was the finest finish seen since the China prize was raced for.

An outward-bound ship came ratching past with the sprays like clouds of smoke at her bows. Her mate and various boys were on her fo'c's'le at work: they all knocked off to see those racers, no such sight had been seen in the Channel as those three driven clippers making the utmost of the day. Cruiser signalled to her an urgent signal, and asked, spelling the hoists, 'Has any China ship arrived yet?' He could see the ship's captain with a couple of boys busy at the signal halliards, acknowledging each hoist. The answer, when they made it, was the affirmative pennant without any ship's number to show the winning ship.

'So we're beaten to it, then, sir,' Fairford said. 'I wonder if the *Natuna* got it.'

Cruiser stared after the now receding ship, now being spoken by Bloody Bill, to whom she gave nothing but her own number, the *Inkerman* of London, and a dipped ensign.

'I don't believe she understood,' Cruiser said, 'and I'm not going to take that as gospel. We'll race these two ships at least.'

Still, something of the zest was gone from the contest when he thought that after all another ship might have docked even a couple of days before, and now lay discharging, with a gilt cock at her masthead. Then as the day drew on, the tide slackened and the wind dropped and shifted still more to the north: it gave them a beam sea and much anxiety for their gear, which held, but only just held.

At one that afternoon, as they passed Beachy all three

ships began to feel the turn of the tide, the flying kites had to come in lest they should pitch the spars away. Then in little short spells of twenty minutes the wind would lull and the kites would be set again; and in this kind of sailing Bloody Bill China had an advantage: as Cruiser could see, he had the boys aloft in the tops all the time ready to race up to loose the light sail or take them in. He was creeping up a little and a little, and was now only about a mile astern, having gained certainly a mile and a half in five hours. In another five hours the *Fu-Kien* would be half a mile ahead, having the pick of the tugs at the South Foreland. The *Caer Ocvran* was at a slight disadvantage, being not quite so happy in fresh or clearing weather as in light airs. However, her captain was fighting for every inch she lost. Cruiser with his small crew had only the miracle of the ship in his favour. He felt more and more keenly every instant that the ship was the best ship in the race. In other voyages she may not have been so: in this race all had conspired together, her builder and some happy combination in her trim, to make her supreme, but now she was short of hands, unable to do her best.

A darkness gathered into the heaven astern of them as the secondary moved up. The hours of the afternoon dragged by as the ships strained up Channel, all drawing nearer, all watched by thousands ashore, who now guessed that those moving beauties were the clippers of the China fleet.

Just off the Fairlight a little steamer, going with coals for Fowey, edged close in to the *Bird of Dawning*, so as to have a good look at her. Cruiser hailed her through the trumpet.

'Ahoy, there, the *Chaffinch*, what China ship won the Race?'

'No ship,' the *Chaffinch*'s skipper shouted back. 'You are the Race. Go in and win.'

'Thank you,' Cruiser shouted. 'Is that straight?'

'Yes. Get to it. Knock the bastards silly.'

This was greeted with a cheer from all hands: they had a chance still.

There came a sudden hurrying, greyness astern: it sent before it a hissing noise which put Cruiser's heart into his boots. He shouted out, 'Let go your royal halliards. Stand by topgallant braces,' and had let fly the main royal halliards as a rain squall swept over them and blotted out ships, sea and land in a deluge that filled the scupper. Out of the deluge there came wind in a gust that tore the flying royals into tatters. Something more than the royals went, the topgallant stunsails went at tack and halliards, blew out in the rain like dirty flags, flogged once, twice and away, with whips of their gear lashing round anything they touched. The masts bent, the yards curved at the arms under the pull of the sheets, and the ship leaped forward as though suddenly lashed.

The men ran to the gear: nothing more was lost: the split sails were cleared and new ones bent but not set. The rain made a darkness about them for twenty minutes, during which Cruiser had two men on the fo'c's'le looking out.

As the squall cleared off, the sun drawing to the west shone out and made a rainbow upon its darkness. Under the arch of colours they saw the *Caer Ocvran* not two hundred yards from them on the starboard bow. She seemed to be stuck there in tossing waters that whitened about her in a great bubble.

Through the glass Cruiser could plainly see her captain, pacing his weather poop, glancing quickly aloft and at the *Bird of Dawning*. 'Ah, yes, sir,' Fairford said, as he watched, 'you can glance and you can curse the helmsman, but the *Bird of Dawning*'s got you beat to the wide.'

'That's Captain Winstone,' Cruiser said. 'He was the mate of the *Bidassoa* when I was in her. Look at that now: did you ever see a ship so wet?'

'She's famous for it, sir; the *Caer*. A fine ship, too.'

Presently they were abreast of her, and forging ahead upon her, so that they could see her in her glory. She had a straight sheer and a transom stern, having been built upon the lines of the famous French frigate, *L'Aigle*. In a light air no ship of her time could touch her, and she could run with the swiftest. She had a name through the seven seas for being wet: her decks now were running bright: for she was a caution in a head sea. They were watching and tending her now, getting some of her after-sail off her to keep her from burying her bow. Cruiser dipped his colours to her as he passed, but would not hail his old captain. As he drew clear, he saw her famous figurehead of Queen Gwenivere bowing down into the smother, then rising and pausing, then plunging down till the fo'c's'le-rail was lipping green.

'Look at that,' Cruiser said. 'Did you ever see a ship pitch like that?'

As he spoke, she took a deeper 'scend than usual, and rose with a snapped stunsail boom lifting on a loose wing.

The *Fu-Kien* drew clear of the *Caer Ocvran* on her lee-side: she was now a quarter of a mile away and gaining perhaps twenty yards a minute. Dungeness lay ahead, distant perhaps eight miles, and somewhere about Dungeness there would be pilots and perhaps tugs. There or thereabouts the race would be decided, another hour would see it out. Cruiser's men had been hard at it all day, and were showing signs of wear. They drank strong tea, syrupy with sugar and laced with brandy, as they got their hawsers ready forward and eyed the distant winning post.

All the issue from the gate of the Channel were about them: all the ships of a tide or two before from London and Antwerp, all the fishermen of Kent and Sussex. Every seaman who came past had no eyes for anything but those two superb clippers disputing for pride of place.

When the squall had passed by both had set every rag that could be brought to draw: they were now straining under clouds of canvas with a strong beam wind, and a head tide. Tarlton, who had been in the *Fu-Kien*, was not encouraging. 'Just the wind she likes most,' he said, 'she's a glutton for it. And she laps up a head sea like a rum milk-punch.' All the marvellous evening shone out mile after mile as they raced: the French coast plain as far as Calais, England white to windward, with occasional windows flashing like jewels, and a darkness of passing storm beyond. Occasional violent gusts kept men in both ships at the upper halliards; and still the *Fu-Kien* gained.

Cruiser was watching her now; she was not more than a hundred yards astern and to leeward, her decks full of men, and spare sails, all made up for bending, on each hatch, and the ship herself a picture of perfection, all bright for port, the paintwork and tarring finished; the hull black, with a white sheer-straik to set off her sheer, the yards black, man-of-war fashion, but with white yard-arms, and her masts all scraped clean with glass, of shining yellow pine. All her brass was bright, and the scroll below her bowsprit had been freshly gilt. She was driving on easily with great laughing leaps. Cruiser could see, in the bearing of the men in her, their certainty that they were winning. Both ships were hauling their wind now to turn the bend. Both could see now, coming out from Dungeness, the pilot cutter, standing towards them, not two miles away, and beyond, making for them what seemed to be tugs, but might be small coasters.

'Too bad, sir,' old Fairford said. 'We'd have done it if we'd had a bit more luck.'

Cruiser was feeling broken-hearted at being passed on the post, but he could not take this view of it. 'No, no,' he said. 'We've had such luck as no sailors ever had before. Think of what has come to us.' All the same, he had to move away. When he was on the lee-poop staring at the *Fu-Kien*, old Fairford could not see how bitterly he felt.

As they hauled their wind, the *Fu-Kien* forged ahead upon them, standing close in upon them, intending to weather upon them and drive across their bows. Bloody Bill China was there on his poop, an unmistakable big figure with a hard tall grey hat jammed sideways on his head and a long pistol in his right hand. 'That's Bloody Bill, sir,' Tarlton said to Mr Fairford. 'Bloody Bill China, sir, the Captain. You'll see him send a bottle of brandy out to the yard-arm in a moment.'

Sure enough a lad with a line went up the mizen-rigging and out to the crojick yard with it, rove it through a jewel block at the yard-arm, and brought it down on deck. A bottle of brandy was hauled out to the yard-arm upon it and dangled there. 'That's Bloody Bill's way, sir,' Tarlton said. 'If ever he weathers on a ship he shoots a bottle of brandy at the yard-arm and then splits another on all hands.'

Twenty faces stared at the *Bird of Dawning* from the *Fu-Kien*'s side. Those men of the sea, negroes, Malays and Europeans, grinned and cheered as their ship slid past.

Bloody Bill China, who was certainly half drunk, shouted

something to his steward, who was standing near the break of the poop beside a grog-kid. The steward put a corkscrew into the cork of a bottle which he held. Bloody Bill strode to the ship's rail, and yelled at Cruiser, whom he took to be Captain Miserden, 'Give my love to the Prophet Habakkuk.'

Voices from the *Fu-Kien*'s waist, eager for the promised grog, and full of joy in their victory shouted 'Habakkuk, Yah Yah, Habakkuk,' and instantly the *Fu-Kien*'s mainmast was ahead of the *Bird of Dawning*'s mizen, and at once the *Fu-Kien*'s crew manned the rail and cheered and beat the fire signal on both her bells. Bloody Bill China brandished his pistol above his head, brought it down, and fired it as he fell: the bottle at the yard-arm was shattered – the brandy spilled. Instantly the steward drew his cork and Bloody Bill China shouted, 'Grog-oh! The *Fu-Kien* wins the China Race.'

She tore past the *Bird of Dawning*. She cleared her by a cable, then by three hundred yards. 'Look out, sir,' Tarlton cried to Cruiser. 'He'll cross your bows as sure as God made Sunday.'

And instantly Bloody Bill China did; he luffed up out of bravado, so as to get windward of the *Bird of Dawning*.

He was going to cross her bows, just to show her. As he luffed, one of the violent gusts beat down upon both ships. Cruiser saw it coming and let go in time, but it caught the *Fu-Kien* fairly, and whipped her topgallant masts clean off in succession as one might count one, two, three. The great weight of gear swung to and fro on each mast, the foreupper topsail went at the weather clue, the main-upper topsail halliards parted and the yard coming down brought the lower topsail with it, bending the truss and cockbilling the yard. The helmsman let her go off, she fell off, thumping and thrashing while gear came flying down from the ruin. With a crash, the wreck of the foretopgallant mast, with its three yards, and stunsail booms and weight of sail and half a mile of rigging, collapsed about the forehatch.

It all had happened in a moment. Cruiser had been warned and had just time to heave the helm up. The *Bird of Dawning* always steered like a bird: she answered to a touch; she answered to it now, but the *Fu-Kien* was right athwart her hawse not three hundred yards away, falling off and coming down on her, with all the wreck on her mainmast visibly shaking the whole mast. One active daredevil soul was already racing with an axe to the splintered mast-head, to hack through the shrouds.

Cruiser saw her come round almost on her heel, straight at the *Bird of Dawning*. For about half a minute it seemed certain that the two would go into each other and sink each other. The mizen royal yard slid out of its bands and smote the *Fu-Kien*'s deck end-on like a harpoon. The terrified helmsman hove the helm hard down; the ship, having still way on her, swung back into the wind; with a running, ripping, walloping crash, her main topgallant wreck came down into her waist, going through the bunt of the mainsail as it went.

The *Bird of Dawning* went past her and missed her by thirty yards. As they passed, Bloody Bill China leaped on to the top of the wheelbox, hurled his hard hat at Cruiser, and while it was still in the air, settling to the sea, put three bullets through it with his pistol: he then hurled his pistol after it and leaped down cursing on to the main-deck to clear the wreck.

Cruiser left him to clear it; there, ranging down upon him, was the pilot cutter. In another minute that graceful boat rounded to with her pilot, who caught the tackle flung, and in an instant was swung high and brought upon the *Bird of Dawning*'s deck.

The Pilot was a short man of enormous breadth, with a gentle manner. He seemed puzzled at the smallness of the crew and at the unusual untidiness of the deck, the planks not scrubbed nor oiled, the paint not freshened. He came up the weather ladder to Cruiser and shook him by the hand.

'I'm proud to welcome you, Captain,' he said. 'You're the first China clipper to take a pilot this year.'

Alan Villiers

THE WAR WITH CAPE HORN 75p

The stirring story of the great square-rigged ships and the toughest regular voyaging man has ever made as part of his workaday life.

Here are mystery and drama – ghost ships and lost ships, memorable captains and shivering apprentices battling mutiny, hardship and death – told against the beat and lash of wind and wave.

'With Conrad and Masefield he can distil the very essence of life at sea in these tall ships' – YORKSHIRE POST